PHILIP'S

STREET

Cardiff

Barry, Penarth, Rumney

www.philips-maps.co.uk

First published in 2007 by

Philip's, a division of
Octopus Publishing Group Ltd
www.octopusbooks.co.uk
2-4 Heron Quays, London E14 4JP
An Hachette Livre UK Company

First edition 2007
First impression 2007

ISBN-10   0-540-09197-9
ISBN-13   978-0-540-09197-3

© Philip's 2007

This product includes mapping data licensed
from Ordnance Survey®, with the
permission of the Controller of Her Majesty's
Stationery Office.© Crown copyright 2007.
All rights reserved.
Licence number 100011710

Photographic acknowledgements:
VIII and IX by James Hughes

Printed by Toppan, China

Contents

II **Key to map symbols**

III **Key to map pages**

IV **Route planning**

VIII **Illustrated guide to visitor attractions**

2 **Street maps** at 4½ inches to 1 mile

62 **Street maps of central Cardiff** at 7 inches to 1 mile

64 **Index**

86 **List of numbered locations**

Key to map symbols

Roads

(12)	**Motorway** with junction number
A34	**Primary route** – dual, single carriageway
A40	**A road** – dual, single carriageway
B1289	**B road** – dual, single carriageway
	Through-route – dual, single carriageway
	Minor road – dual, single carriageway
	Rural track, private road or narrow road in urban area
	Path, bridleway, byway open to all traffic, road used as a public path
	Road under construction
	Pedestrianised area
	Gate or obstruction to traffic restrictions may not apply at all times or to all vehicles
P P&R	**Parking, Park and Ride**

Railways

	Railway
	Miniature railway
	Metro station, private railway station

Emergency services

◆ ◆	**Ambulance station, coastguard station**
◆ ◆	**Fire station, police station**
H ✚	**Hospital, Accident and Emergency entrance to hospital**

General features

+ PO	**Place of worship, Post Office**
i	**Information centre** (open all year)
◣ 🛒	**Bus or coach station, shopping centre**
	Important buildings, schools, colleges, universities and hospitals
	Woods, built-up area
Tumulus FORT	**Non-Roman antiquity, Roman antiquity**

Leisure facilities

	Camping site, caravan site
	Golf course, picnic site

Boundaries

• • • • • • •	**Postcode boundaries**
—— · ——	**County and unitary authority boundaries**

Water features

River Ouse	**Tidal water, water name**
	Non-tidal water – lake, river, canal or stream
⟨ ╎	**Lock, weir**

Enlarged mapping only

	Railway or bus station building
	Place of interest
	Parkland

Scales

Blue pages: 4½ inches to 1 mile 1:14 080

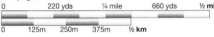

0	220 yds	¼ mile	660 yds	½ mi
0	125m	250m 375m	½ km	

Red pages: 7 inches to 1 mile 1:9051

0	110 yds	220 yds 330 yds	¼ mile
0	125m	250m	375m ½ km

Adjoining page indicators The colour of the arrow and the band indicates the scale of the adjoining page (see above)

Abbreviations

Acad	Academy	Mkt	Market
Allot Gdns	Allotments	Meml	Memorial
Cemy	Cemetery	Mon	Monument
C Ctr	Civic Centre	Mus	Museum
CH	Club House	Obsy	Observatory
Coll	College	Pal	Royal Palace
Crem	Crematorium	PH	Public House
Ent	Enterprise	Recn Gd	Recreation Ground
Ex H	Exhibition Hall	Resr	Reservoir
Ind Est	Industrial Estate	Ret Pk	Retail Park
IRB Sta	Inshore Rescue Boat Station	Sch	School
		Sh Ctr	Shopping Centre
Inst	Institute	TH	Town Hall/House
Ct	Law Court	Trad Est	Trading Estate
L Ctr	Leisure Centre	Univ	University
LC	Level Crossing	Wks	Works
Liby	Library	YH	Youth Hostel

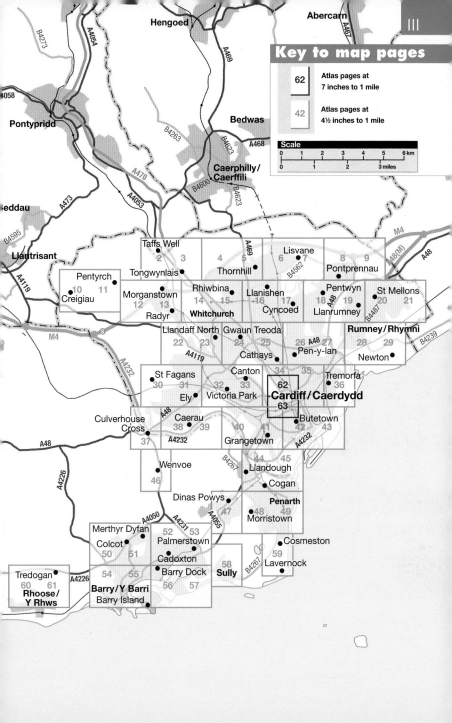

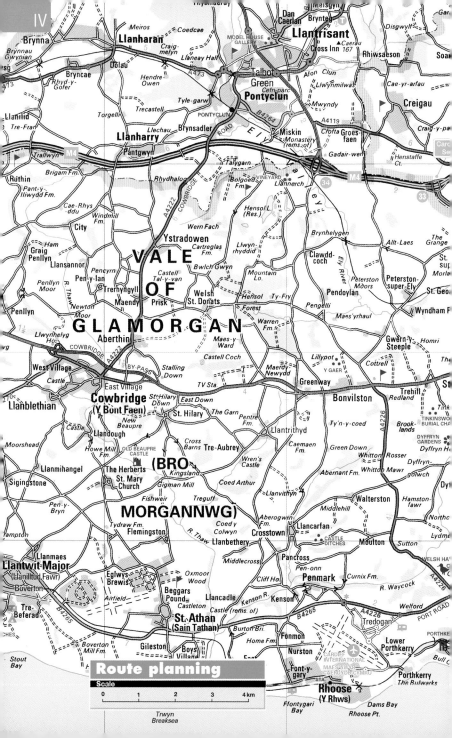

Route planning

Scale

0   1   2   3   4 km

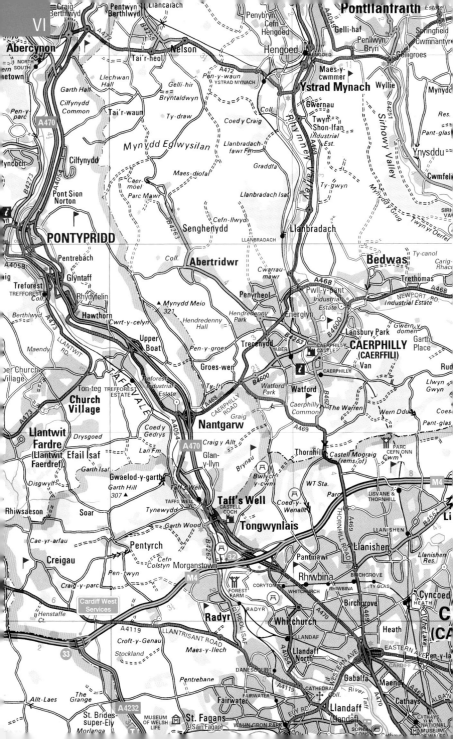

Visitor attractions

Museums and Galleries

National Museum Cardiff / Amgueddfa Ganadiathol Cymru *Cathays Park, Cardiff* A wide-ranging collection including archaeology, palaeontology (including dinosaur fossils) Impressionist paintings, works by Welsh artists and Earth sciences. 🖳 www.museumwales.ac.uk ☎ 029 2039 7951 62 B4

St Fagans National History Museum / Sain Ffagan Amgueddfa Werin Cymru *St Fagans, Cardiff* Open-air museum celebrating the culture and history of the Welsh people over the last 2000 years. The beautiful gardens of the Elizabethan manor house known as St Fagans Castle are also open to the public.
🖳 www.museumwales.ac.uk
☎ 029 2057 3500 30 A3

Techniquest *Stuart Street, Cardiff Bay* A science discovery centre with more than 160 interactive exhibits, Science Theatre, Planetarium and Discovery Room. 029 2047 5475 🖳 www.techniquest.org 42 A1

Turner House Gallery *Plymouth Road, Penarth* Temporary exhibitions of works from the National Museums and Galleries of Wales. ☎ 01223 708870 🖳 www.ffotogallery.org/turnerhouse/index.htm 49 B3

Welch Regiment Military Museum at Cardiff Castle *Castle Street, Cardiff* Museum honouring the accomplishments and services of Welsh regimental forces since 1719. 🖳 www.rrw.org.uk ☎ 029 2022 9367 62 B3

Historic Sites

Cardiff Castle *Castle Street, Cardiff* The site of three successive Roman forts and an 11th-century castle which was much extended in the middle ages. This was then turned into a Victorian mansion, in the form of a Victorian Gothic fantasy castle. The site of many of the city's annual events such as medieval banquets and concerts. ☎ 029 2087 8100 🖳 www.cardiff.gov.uk 62 B3

Castell Coch *Tongwynlais* A late nineteenth-century 'fairytale' castle, built on medieval remains, by William Burges for the third marquess of Bute, with lavish interior decoration and Victorian Gothic furnishings.
🖳 www.cadw.wales.gov.uk
☎ 029 2081 0101 3 A2

Cosmeston Medieval Village *Lavernock Road, Cosmeston, Penarth* A reconstructed medieval village located in Cosmeston Lakes Country Park with gardens, rare breeds animals and museum. Tours, costumed villagers and special events throughout the year. 🖳 www.valeofglamorgan.gov.uk ☎ 029 2070 1678 59 A2

The Wales Millennium Centre

Places of Worship

Cardiff Metropolitan Cathedral of St David *Charles Street, Cardiff* St David's was built as Cardiff's principal Catholic church in 1887, and it became a cathedral and seat of the Roman Catholic Archbishop of Cardiff in 1916. ☎ 029 2023 0427 63 C2

Llandaff Cathedral / Eglwys Gadeiriol Llandaf *Cathedral Close, Llandaff, Cardiff* The Cathedral Church of Saints Peter and Paul, Dyfrig, Teilo and Euddogwy is on one of the oldest Christian sites in Britain. In the sixth century St Dyfrig founded a community close to the ford where the Roman road crossed the river Taff. A Celtic cross from about this time stands near the door of the Chapter House. The medieval buildings include the Chapter House, Lady Chapel and Bell Tower. The west front has some of the best medieval art in Wales. 24 A1

Other Sights

The National Assembly for Wales / Cynulliad Cenedlaethol Cymru *Pierhead Street, Cardiff Bay* The Senedd building has areas open to the public and public galleries are open when the Assembly is in session. 🖳 www.assemblywales.org ☎ 0845 010 5500 42 C2

Green Spaces

Bute Park *North Road, Cardiff* An extensive area of mature parkland, Bute Park is a very popular green area in the heart of the city. Includes Cardiff Castle, Blackfriars, the Gorsedd Stones, the Animal Wall and an Arboretum. Bats, kingfishers, woodpeckers and egrets can be seen by the River Taff. Many of the city's cultural, sporting and annual events are held here. ☎ 029 2068 4000 🖳 www.cardiff.gov.uk 62 A3

Cosmeston Lakes Country Park *Lavernock Road, Cosmeston, Penarth* More than 90 hectares of lakes, woodlands and meadows, with a boardwalk through the reedbeds. ☎ 029 2070 1678 🖳 www.valeofglamorgan.gov.uk 59 A3

Forest Farm Country Park / Parc Cefn Gwlad Fferm y Fforest *Forest Farm Road, Whitchurch* A nature reserve which straddles the last remaining stretch of the old Cardiff Merthyr canal. Beech and oak woodland, ponds, scrapes and wetland, bird hides for viewing wildfowl, kingfishers and herons. 14 A2

Heath Park *King George V Drive West, Cardiff* A 37-ha park with pitches, woodlands, ponds and recreational facilities. Great crested newts in the pond and woodlands full of wildlife. Tennis courts, sports pitches, 'pitch and putt' golf and playground. Model railway on open days.
☎ 029 2068 4000
🖳 www.cardiff.gov.uk 25 B4

Howardian Local Nature Reserve *Hammond Way, Cardiff* The pond, reedbed and scrape provide habitats for rarities such as kingfisher and snipe, as well as sedge warblers, herons and reptiles. There is also a variety of woodlands. 🖳www.cardiff.gov.uk ☎029 2068 4000 27 A2

Porthkerry Country Park *Park Road, Barry* 220 acres of woods and meadowland in a sheltered valley leading to a pebble beach and spectacular cliffs. Nature trails, play area, picnic sites, café, barbecue area and mini golf courses. ☎01446 733589 🖳www.valeofglamorgan.gov.uk 54 A2

Roath Park *Lake Road, Cardiff* Cardiff's most popular park, with a Victorian atmosphere, historic and horticultural interest, with a variety of environments. Fishing and rowing on the lake, floral displays, conservatory and sporting and recreational facilities. ☎029 2068 4000 🖳www.cardiff.gov.uk 26 A3

Activities

Red Dragon Centre *Hemingway Road, Cardiff* Leisure and entertainment complex, including restaurants, bowling alley, casino and cinema. ☎029 2025 6261 🖳www.thereddragoncentre.co.uk 42 B2

Barry Island Pleasure Park *Barry Island* More than 50 rides and attractions for all ages. Seasonal and variable opening times. Telephone in advance for details. 🖳www.pleasureparkonline.co.uk ☎01446 732844 55 B1

Cardiff Arms Park *Westgate Street, Cardiff* Home of Cardiff RFC. ☎029 20 30 2000 🖳www.cardiffrfc.com 63 A2

Cardiff Bay Visitor Centre *Harbour Drive, Inner Harbour, Cardiff* Known locally as 'The Tube', the centre provides displays, a number of exhibitions, video information on the Bay and houses a large-scale model of the area. Highlights include the World War II exhibition and the views over the controversial tidal barrage. 🖳www.cardiffharbour.com ☎029 2046 3833 42 B1

Cardiff International Arena *Mary Ann Street, Cardiff* Indoor concert, sporting, banqueting and convention facility, hosting pop and rock concerts, opera and stand-up comedy. ☎029 2022 4488 🖳www.livenation.co.uk 63 C2

Cardiff Market *St Mary Street, Cardiff* A popular food market, with fresh produce and food goods, as well as household goods and jewellery. ☎029 2087 1214 🖳www.cardiff.gov.uk 63 B2

Channel View Centre *Jim Driscoll Way, Grangetown, Cardiff* Leisure centre with badminton and squash courts, fitness suite, dance studio, IT room, music room, arts and crafts room, darkroom, climbing wall, activities area and outdoor 5-a-side pitch. ☎029 2037 8161 🖳www.cardiff.gov.uk 41 C1

Fairwater Leisure Centre *Off Waterhall Road, Fairwater, Cardiff* Swimming pool, badminton and squash courts, sports hall, skate park, fitness suite. ☎029 2055 2210 🖳www.cardiff.gov.uk 22 B2

Llanishen Leisure Centre *Ty-Glas Avenue, Llanishen, Cardiff* Leisure pool with wave machine, badminton and squash courts, fitness suite, mini-gym and snooker room. ☎029 2076 2411 🖳www.cardiff.gov.uk 16 B4

Millennium Stadium *Westgate Street, Cardiff* The premier sports facility in the capital and home of Welsh Rugby Union, hosting rugby, large concerts and boxing matches, as well as other events. 🖳www.millenniumstadium.com ☎0870 013 8600 63 A2

New Theatre *Park Place, Cardiff* One of Cardiff's main venues for musicals, plays and panto. ☎029 2087 8889 🖳www.newtheatrecardiff.co.uk 62 B3

Ninian Park *Sloper Road, Cardiff* Home of Cardiff City FC. ☎029 2022 1011 🖳www.cardiffcityfc.premiumtv.co.uk 40 C4

Norwegian Church Arts Centre / Canolfan Gelfyddydau'r Eglwys Norwyaidd *Harbour Drive, Cardiff Bay* Formerly a Norwegian Seamen's Church, this beautiful timber building is now an arts centre, with an art gallery and the 'Norwegian Room', which is used for concerts, events, exhibitions and functions. 🖳www.norwegianchurchcardiff.co.uk ☎029 2045 4899 42 B1

Pentwyn Leisure Centre *Bryn Celyn Rd, Pentwyn, Cardiff* Leisure pool with slide and waves. Badminton and squash courts, sports hall and fitness suite. 🖳www.cardiff.gov.uk ☎029 2054 9211 18 C2

St David's Shopping Centre *St David's Way, Cardiff* Large shopping centre with more than 60 high-street names. 🖳www.stdavids-shopping.co.uk ☎029 2039 6041 63 B2

St David's Hall / Neuadd Dewi Sant *The Hays, Cardiff* Large venue hosting comedy, musicals, classical, popular and rock music, world music, jazz and lunchtime concerts. ☎029 2087 8500 🖳www.stdavidshallcardiff.co.uk 63 B2

Sherman Theatre *Senghennydd Road, Cardiff* Home of Sherman Cymru theatre company, which specializes in contemporary drama by both known and new writers. 🖳www.sherman.theatre.co.uk ☎029 2064 6901 62 B4

Sophia Gardens *Cardiff* Home of Glamorgan CCC / Canolfen Criced Genediaethol. ☎0871 2823401 🖳www.glamorgancricket.com 33 C3

▲ *The Norwegian Church Arts Centre*

Vale of Glamorgan Railway *Barry Island Station* A heritage line on Barry Island, with a small heritage centre nearby. 🖳www.valeofglamorganrailway.co.uk ☎01446 748816 55 C1

Wales Millennium Centre / Canolfan Mileniwm Cymru *Bute Place, Cardiff* Arts venue hosting a wide range of performances including stand-up comedy, opera, classical and pop music, drama, ballet and community events. Interactive art gallery. 🖳www.wmc.org.uk ☎0870 040 2000 42 B2

Welsh Hawking Centre and Children's Animal Park *Weycock Road, Barry* A large park with more than 200 birds of prey and regular flying demonstrations. Duck, geese and goldfish ponds, adventure playground and animal farm. Telephone in advance. 🖳www.barrywales.co.uk/hawkingcentre ☎01446 734687 50 A2

Welsh Institute of Sport / Athrofa Chwaraeon Cymru *Sophia Gardens, Cardiff* Important sports facility with four large halls for a wide variety of sports including gymnastics, swimming, squash and tennis. Also a rugby pitch used by the Welsh national team. ☎0845 045 0902 🖳www.welsh-institute-sport.co.uk 33 C3

Information

🛈**Cardiff Visitor Centre** *The Old Library, The Hayes, Cardiff* ☎08701 211 258 🖳www.visitcardiff.com 63 B2

Cardiff Council *County Hall, Atlantic Wharf, Cardiff* ☎029 2087 2000 🖳www.cardiff.gov.uk 42 B3

Car parking ☎029 2087 2000 🖳www.cardiff.gov.uk

Cardiff International Airport / Maes Awyr Caerdydd ☎01446 711111 🖳www.cwlfly.com 61 A2

National Rail Enquiries ☎08457 48 49 50 🖳www.nationalrail.co.uk

Cardiff buses / bus Caerdydd 🖳www.cardiffbus.com

Traveline Cymru ☎0871 200 22 33 🖳www.traveline-cymru.org.uk

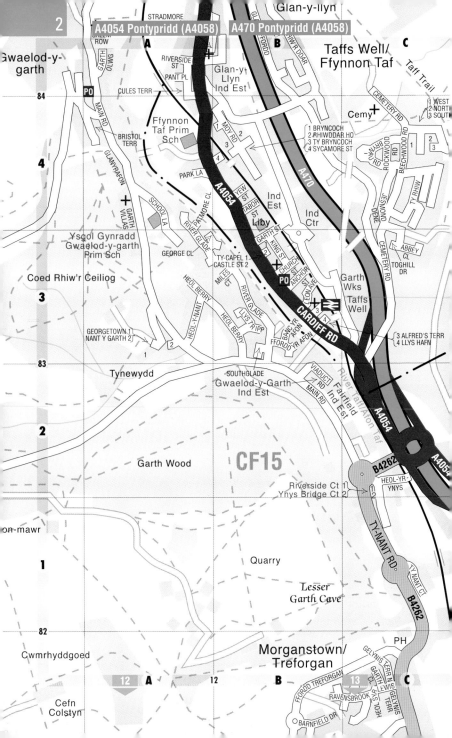

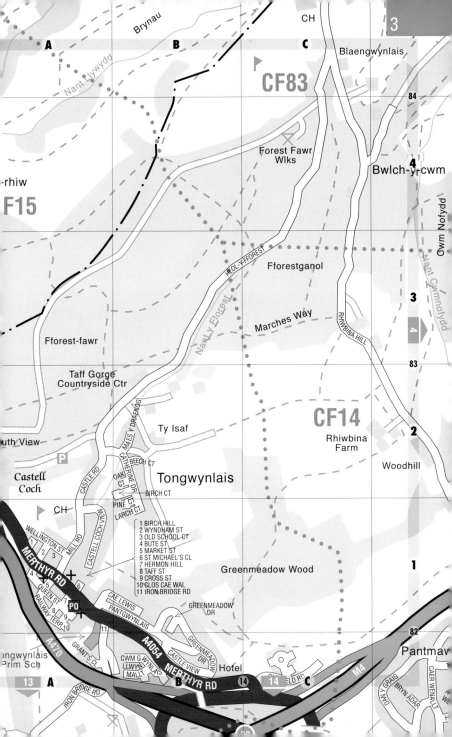

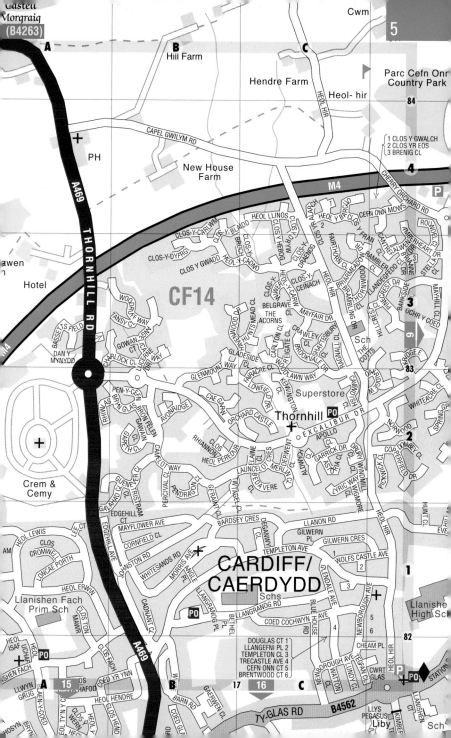

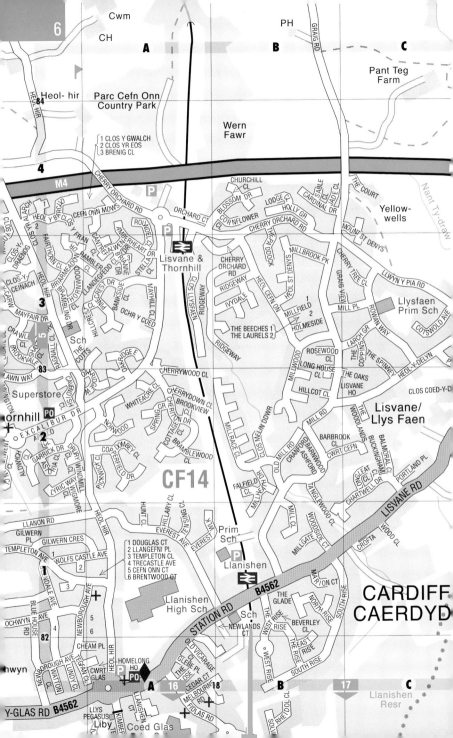

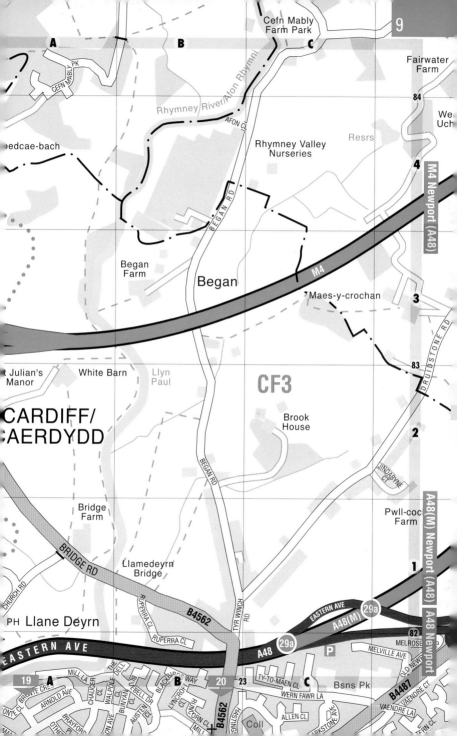

Tý'n-y-coed

TÝ'N-Y-COED RD

A
PH

B

C

Sewage
Works

Llwyn-y-brain

Y Graig

4

Coed y
Creigiau

82

Quarry

PARC-Y-BRYN

Creigiau

PARC-Y-FRO

HEOL CREIGIAU

Creigiau
Farm

CASTLE CL.

THE TERRACE

CH

TREGARTH CL

TREGARTH CT

PARC CASTELL-Y-MYNACH

PO

CLOS
DARRAN LAS

WOODLAND
CRES

Ysgol Gynradd Creigiau/
Creigiau Prim Sch

PARC CASTELL-Y-MYNACH

STATION RD

PH

3

TYNANT RD

PARC-Y-FFIN

LLYS CAPADOG

DOL-Y-FELIN

FFORDD DINERWR

LLYS ILLTYD

LLYS DYFRIG GWYNNO

LLYS GWYNNO

LLYS TEILO

MAES-YN-ANT

LLYS TUDFUL

PARC-Y-COED

MAES-Y-GOLLEN

OLD FARM LA

LLYS-Y-FFOIWG

MAES-Y-DDERWEN

MAES CADWGAN

MAES-YR-HAFOD

CLOS LLEWELLYN

GREEN
ACRE

STATION
HOS

CF15

HEOL PANT-Y-GORED

1 LLYS DEWI
2 MAES-Y-RHEDYN
3 MAES-YR-HAFOD

1

2

3

CARDIFF RD

QUEEN CHARLOTTE DR

BRUMMELL DR

Robin
Hill

2

Maes
Mawr

81

A4119 Llantrisant

THE PAD

1

A4119

CF72

A

08

B

C

Gadairwen
Farm

Henstaffe
Court

Llwynioli

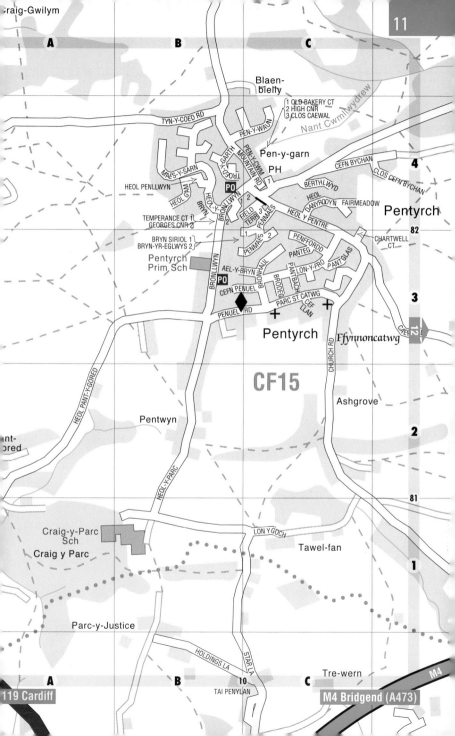

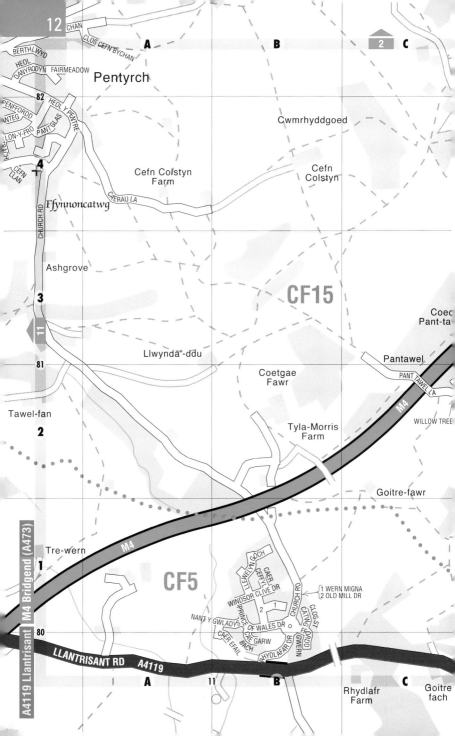

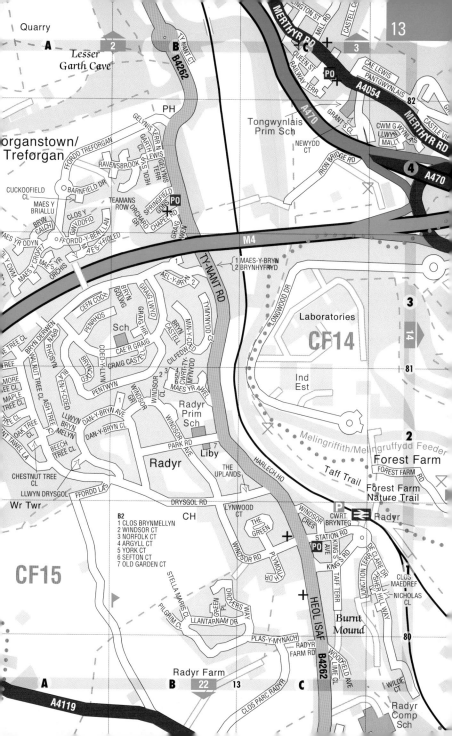

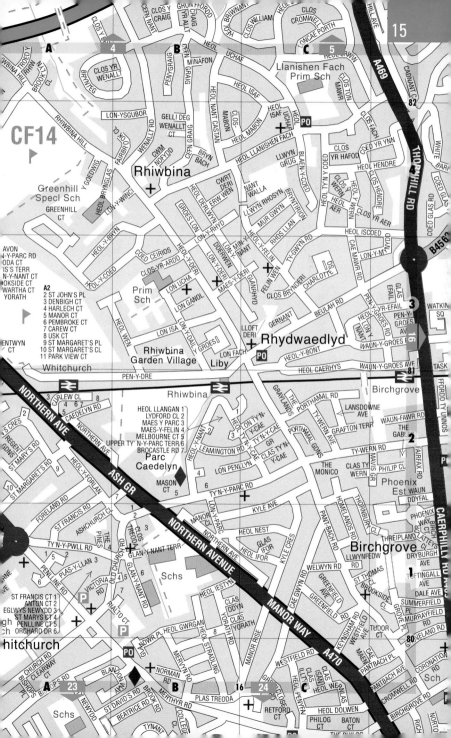

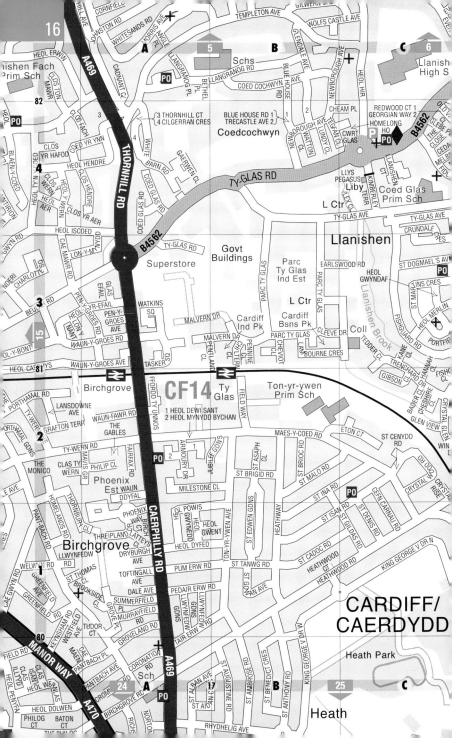

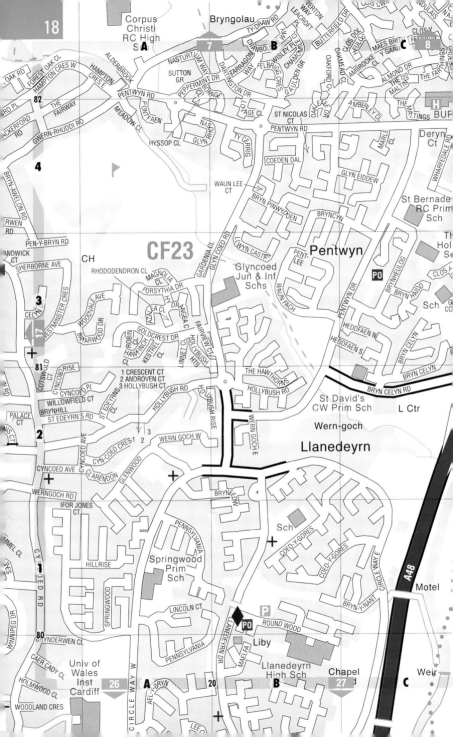

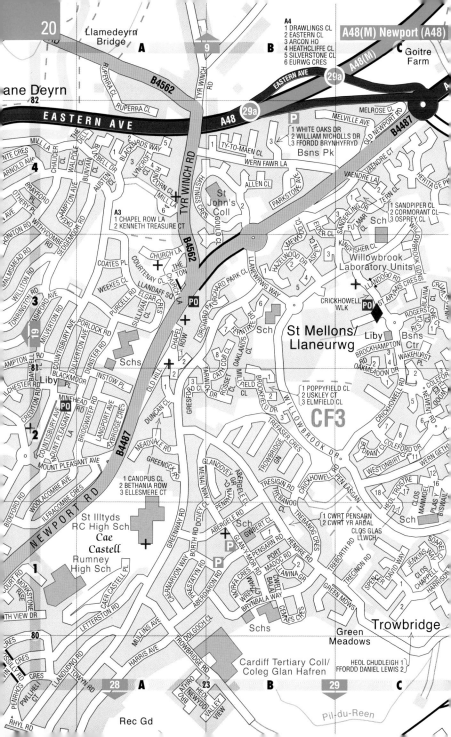

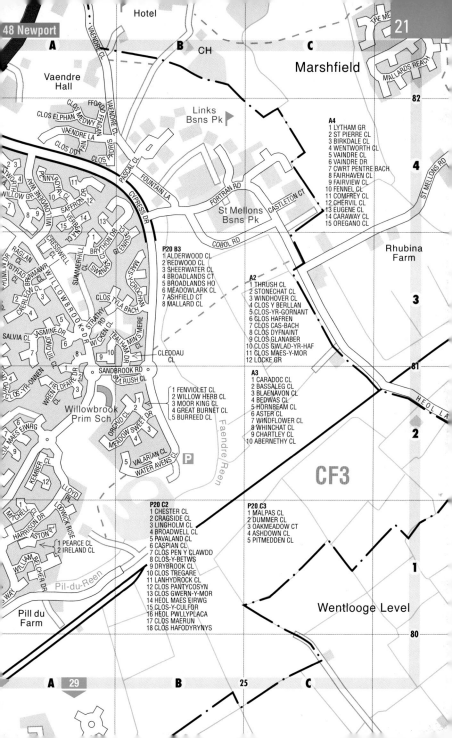

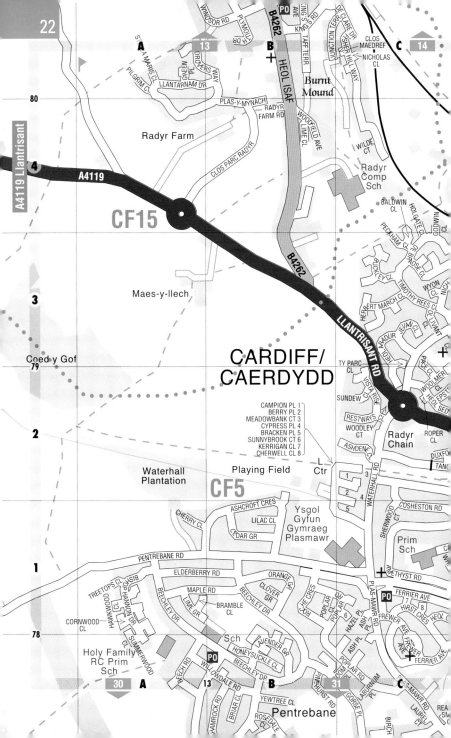

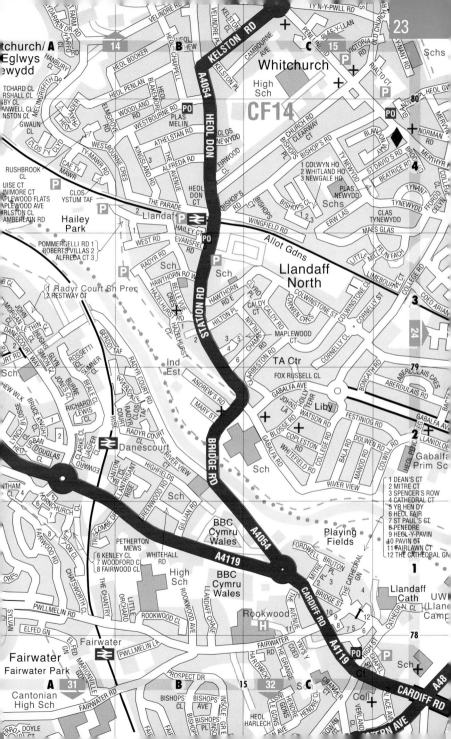

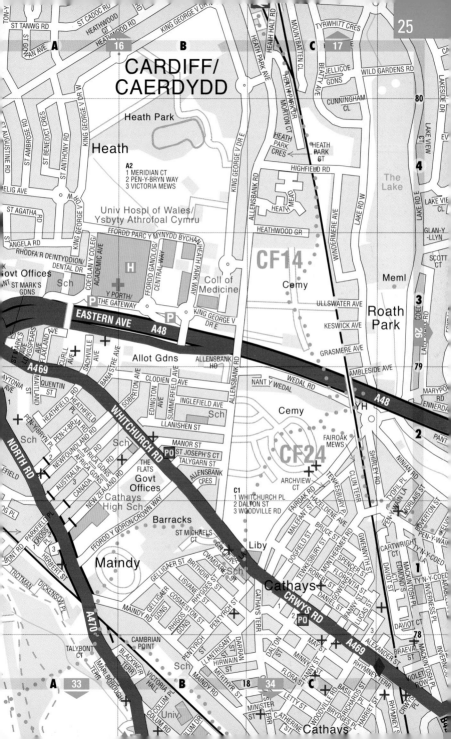

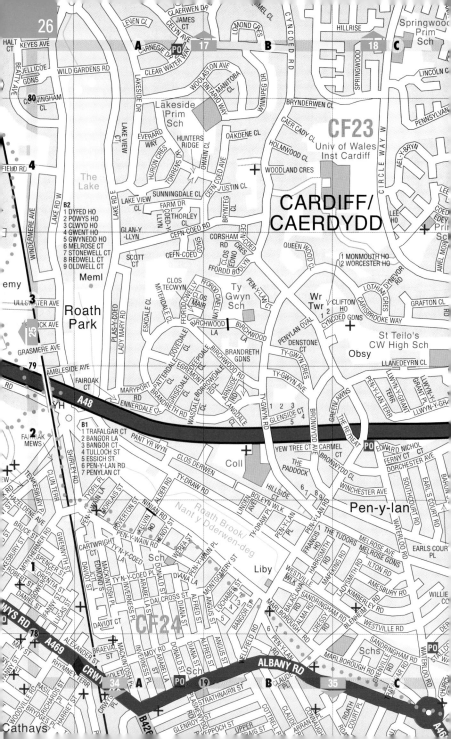

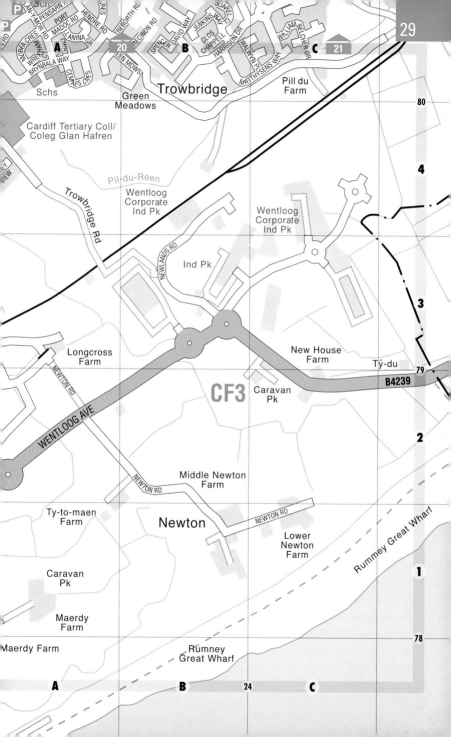

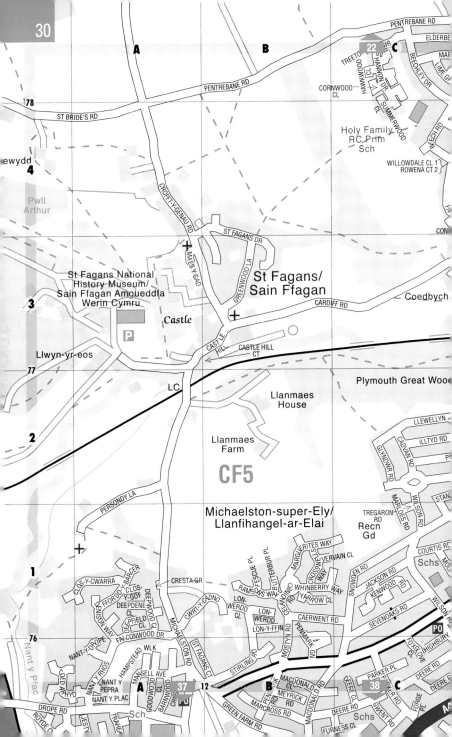

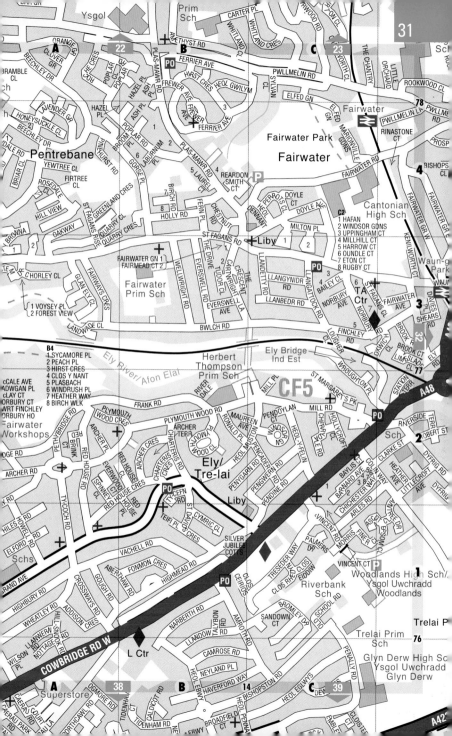

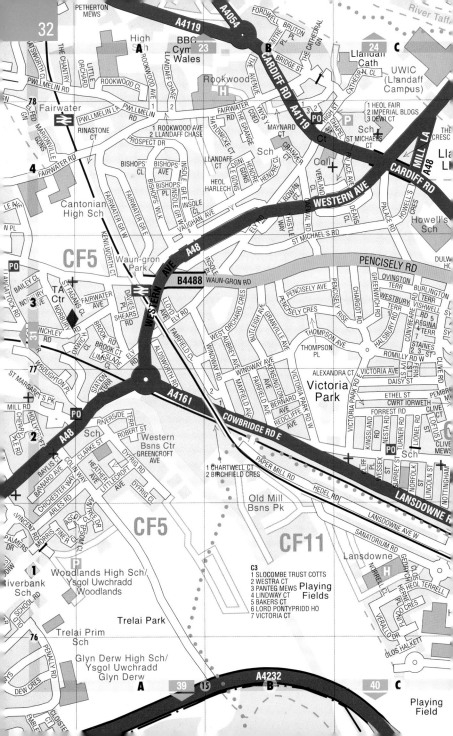

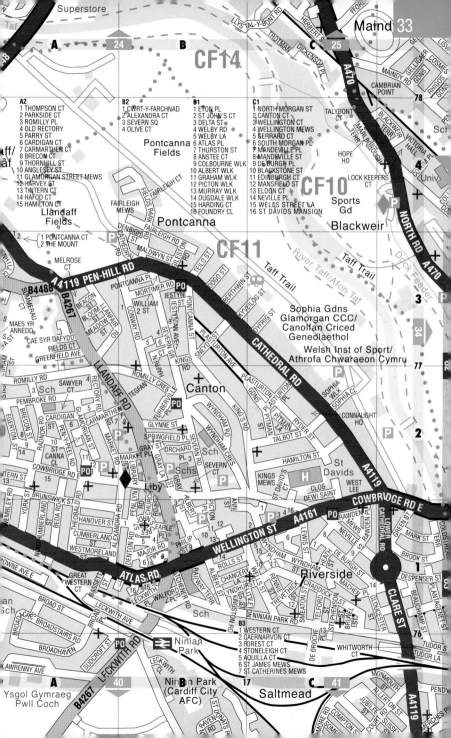

CF14

A2
1 THOMPSON CT
2 PARKSIDE CT
3 ROMILLY PL
4 OLD RECTORY
5 PARRY ST
6 CARDIGAN CT
7 CARMARTHEN CT
8 BRECON CT
9 THORNHILL ST
10 ANGLESEY ST
11 GLAMORGAN STREET MEWS
12 HARVEY ST
13 TINTERN CT
14 HAFOD CT
15 HAMILTON ST

B2
1 CWRT-Y-FARCHNAD
2 ALEXANDRA CT
3 SEVERN SQ
4 OLIVE CT

B1
1 ETON PL
2 ST JOHN'S CT
3 DELTA ST
4 WELBY RD
5 WELBY LA
6 ATLAS PL
7 THURSTON ST
8 ANSTEE CT
9 COLBOURNE WLK
10 ALBERT WLK
11 GRAHAM WLK
12 PICTON WLK
13 MURRAY WLK
14 DUGDALE WLK
15 HARDING CT
16 FOUNDRY CL

C1
1 NORTH MORGAN ST
2 CANTON CT
3 WELLINGTON CT
4 WELLINGTON MEWS
5 GERRARD CT
6 SOUTH MORGAN CT
7 MANDEVILLE PL
8 MANDEVILLE CT
9 DE BURGH PL
10 BLACKSTONE ST
11 EDINBURGH CT
12 MANSFIELD ST
13 ELDON CT
14 NEVILLE PL
15 WELLS STREET LA
16 ST DAVIDS MANSION

CF10

CF11

B3
1 WESTERN CT
2 CAERNARVON CT
3 FOREST CT
4 STONELEIGH CT
5 AQUILLA CT
6 ST JAMES MEWS
7 ST CATHERINES MEWS

Saltmead

Ysgol Gymraeg
Pwll Coch

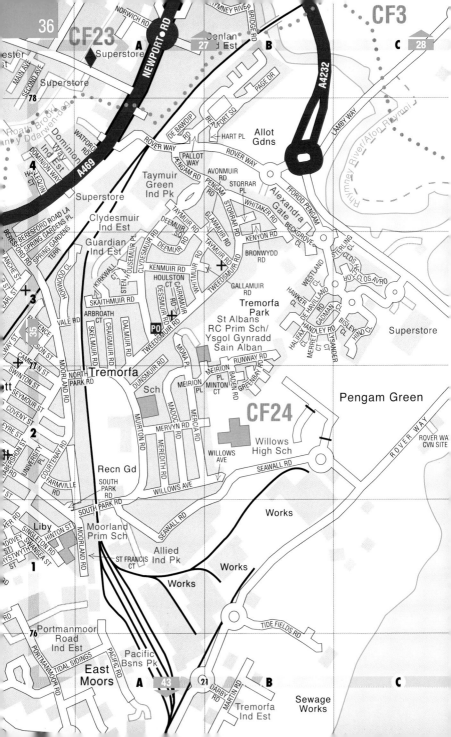

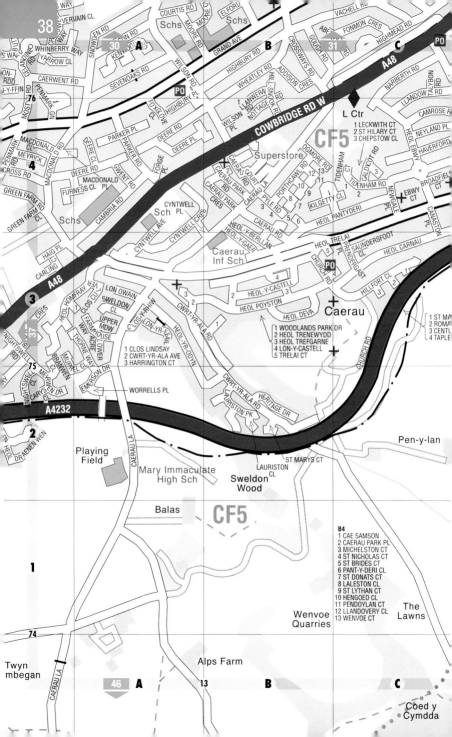

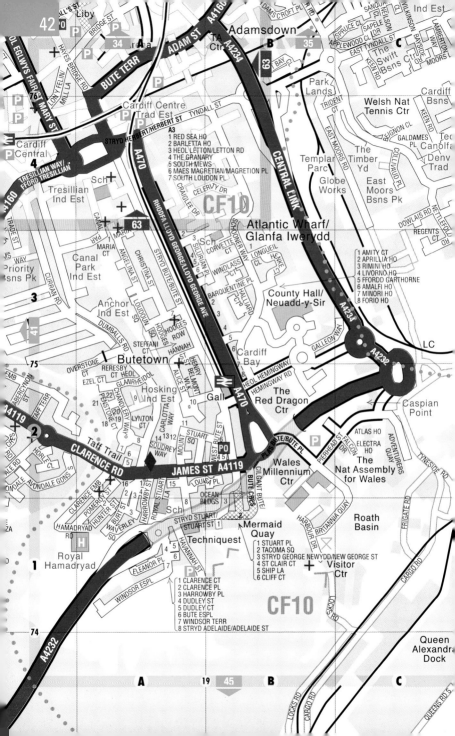

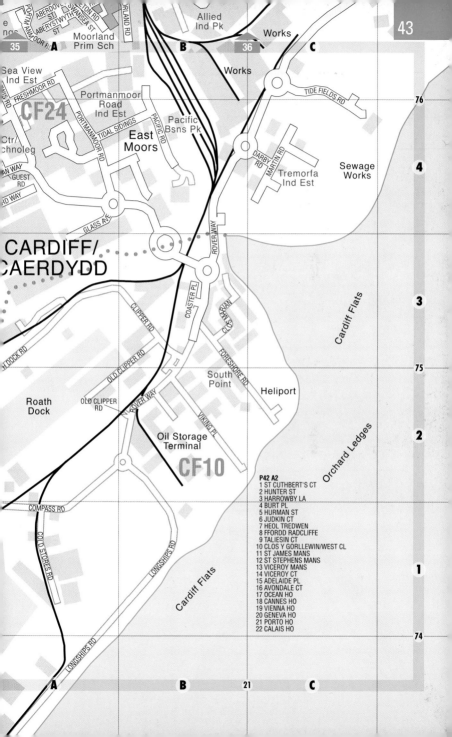

35 | **A** | **B** | **36** | **C**

Allied Ind Pk

Works

Works

Works

ABERDOVEY ST
ABERYSTWYTH ST
SWANSEA ST
MOORLAND RD

Moorland Prim Sch

PORTMANMOOR RD

Sea View Ind Est

FRESHMOOR RD

CF24

Portmanmoor Road Ind Est

TIDAL SIDINGS

PACIFIC RD

Pacific Bsns Pk

East Moors

Ctr/chnoleg

AN WAY

GUEST RD

RD WAY

GLASS AVE

PORTMANMOOR RD

TIDE FIELDS RD

76

DARBY RD

MARTIN RD

Tremorfa Ind Est

Sewage Works

4

CARDIFF/
CAERDYDD

ROVER WAY

COASTER PL

SEVERN CLO

Cardiff Flats

3

H DOCK RD

CLIPPER RD

OLD CLIPPER RD

FORESHORE RD

75

South Point

Heliport

Roath Dock

OLD CLIPPER RD

ROVER WAY

VIKING PL

Oil Storage Terminal

CF10

Cardiff Flats

Orchard Ledges

2

COMPASS RD

COLD STORES RD

LONGSHIPS RD

Cardiff Flats

1

LONGSHIPS RD

74

A | **B** | **21** | **C**

P42 A2
1 ST CUTHBERT'S CT
2 HUNTER ST
3 HARROWBY LA
4 BURT PL
5 HURMAN ST
6 JUDKIN CT
7 HEOL TREDWEN
8 FFORDD RADCLIFFE
9 TALIESIN CT
10 CLOS Y GORLLEWIN/WEST CL
11 ST JAMES MANS
12 ST STEPHENS MANS
13 VICEROY MANS
14 VICEROY CT
15 ADELAIDE PL
16 AVONDALE CT
17 OCEAN HO
18 CANNES HO
19 VIENNA HO
20 GENEVA HO
21 PORTO HO
22 CALAIS HO

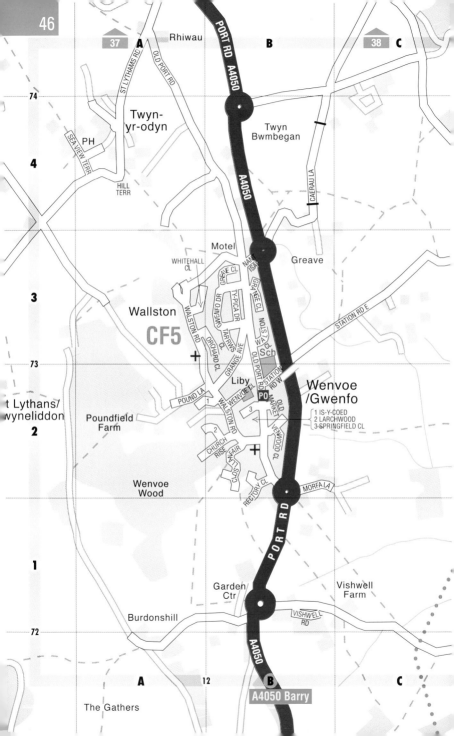

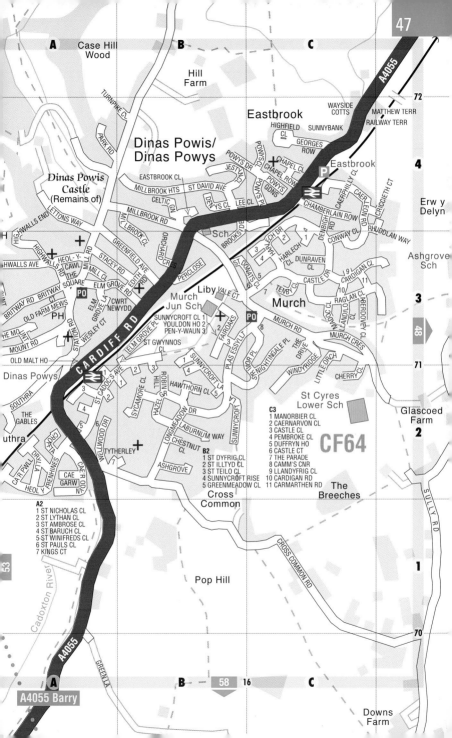

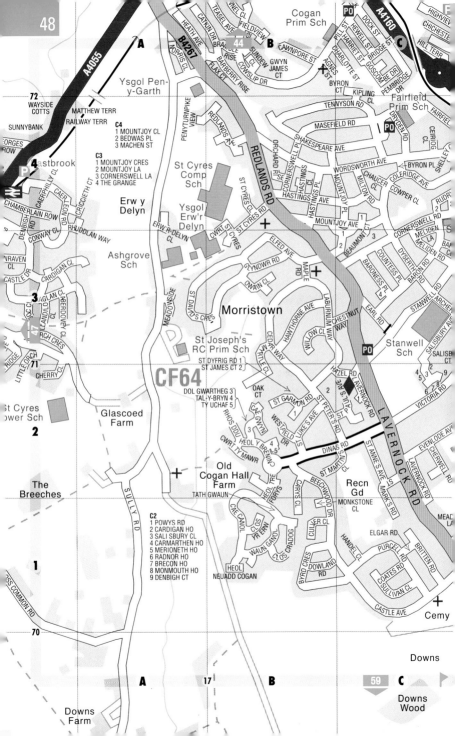

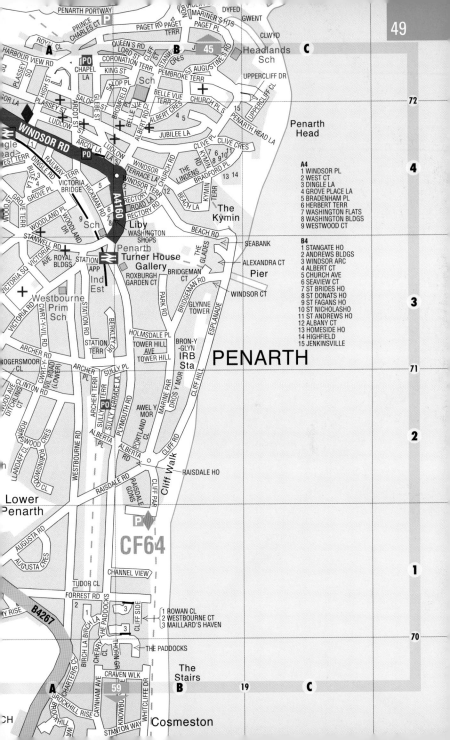

PENARTH

CF64

Lower
Penarth

Cosmeston

The
Kymin

Penarth
Head

The
Stairs

A4
1 WINDSOR PL
2 WEST CT
3 DINGLE LA
4 GROVE PLACE LA
5 BRADENHAM PL
6 HERBERT TERR
7 WASHINGTON FLATS
8 WASHINGTON BLDGS
9 WESTWOOD CT

B4
1 STANGATE HO
2 ANDREWS BLDGS
3 WINDSOR ARC
4 ALBERT CT
5 CHURCH AVE
6 SEAVIEW CT
7 ST BRIDES HO
8 ST DONATS HO
9 ST FAGANS HO
10 ST NICHOLASHO
11 ST ANDREWS HO
12 ALBANY CT
13 HOMESIDE HO
14 HIGHFIELD
15 JENKINSVILLE

1 ROWAN CL
2 WESTBOURNE CT
3 MAILLARD'S HAVEN

PENARTH PORTWAY
PRINCE CHARLES CL
ROYAL CL
HARBOUR VIEW RD
PLASSEY SQ
HIGH ST
DINGLE RD
BUTE AVE
GROVE TERR
PLASSEY ST
ARCOT ST
LUDLOW ST
WINDSOR RD
RAILWAY
VICTORIA
BRIDGE
WOODLAND PL
WOODLAND DR
VICTORIA AVE
STANWELL RD
VICTORIA SQ
VICTORIA RD
Westbourne
Prim Sch
CWRT-Y-VIL RD
ARCHER RD
ROGERSMOOR CL
CLINTON RD
DITCHLING CT
ROBINSWOOD CL
LLANDAFF CT
ROBINSWOOD CRES
WESTBOURNE RD
STATION RD
STATION TERR
BERKLEY DR
ARCHER PL
ARCHER TERR
SULLY PL
SULLY TERR
SULLY TERRACE LA
PLYMOUTH RD
ALBERTA PL
ALBERTA RD
RAISDALE RD
RAISDALE GDNS
CLIFF PAR
CLIFF WALK
AUGUSTA RD
AUGUSTA CRES
TUDOR CL
FORREST RD
CHANNEL VIEW
B4267
CHARTERS CL
BIRCH LA
BIRCH CL
CHERRY CL
THE PADDOCKS
CAYNHAM AVE
CRAVEN WLK
THORN GR
CLIFF SIDE
WHITCLIFFE DR
KNOWBURY AVE
STANTON WAY
BROCKHILL RISE
BROCKHILL WAY

PAGET RD
PAGET TERR
PAGET PL
QUEEN'S RD
LORD ST
CORONATION TERR
KING ST
CHAPEL LA
SALOP PL
BROMFIELD ST
SALOP ST
BELLE VUE CL
BELLE VUE TERR
ALBERT CRES
ALBERT RD
JUBILEE LA
Sch
STANLEY RD
CLIVE ST
CLIVE CRES
ST AUGUSTINE'S RD
PEMBROKE TERR
CHURCH PL
CHURCH RD
CHURCH TERR
CLIVE PL
THE LINDENS
BRADFORD PL
RECTORY RD
RECTORY LA
WINDSOR TERRACE LA
WINDSOR TERR
HICKMAN RD
Liby
WASHINGTON SHOPS
Penarth
Turner House
Gallery
ROXBURGH GARDEN CT
Ind Est
PARK RD
HOLMSDALE PL
TOWER HILL AVE
TOWER HILL
MARINE PAR
DROS Y MOR
CLIFF RD
CLIFF HILL
AWEL Y MOR
BRON-Y-GLYN
IRB Sta
GLYNNE TOWER
BRIDGEMAN CT
BRIDGEMAN RD
ESPLANADE
THE GLADES
SEABANK
ALEXANDRA CT
Pier
WINDSOR CT
BEACH RD
BEACH LA
KYMIN RD
KYMIN TERR
THE KYMIN

MARINER'S HTS
DYFED
GWENT
CLWYD
Headlands Sch
UPPERCLIFF DR
UPPERCLIFF CL
PENARTH HEAD LA

RAISDALE HO

THE PADDOCKS

45
59
19
72
4
3
71
2
1
70
C
A
B

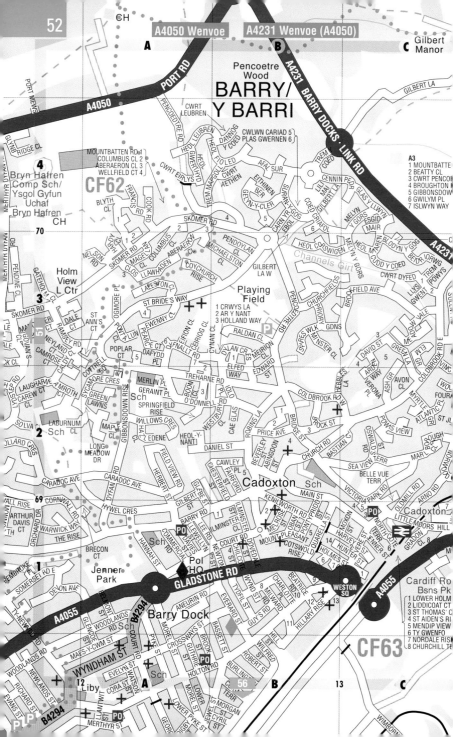

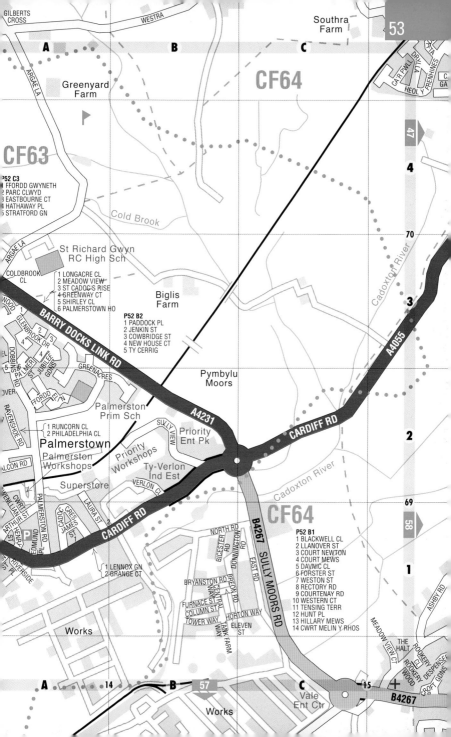

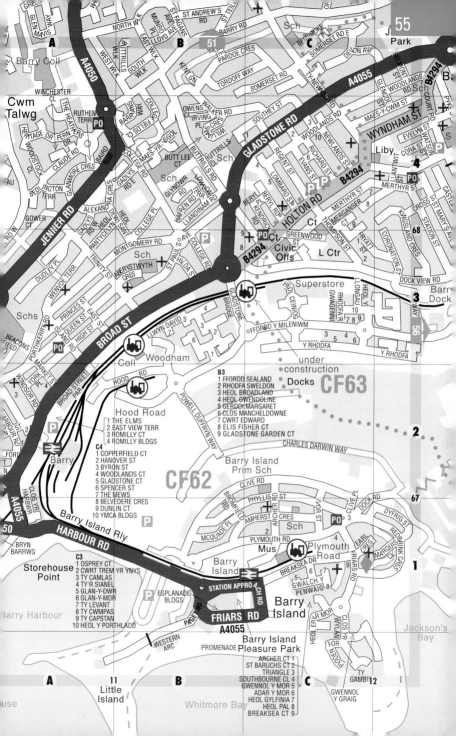

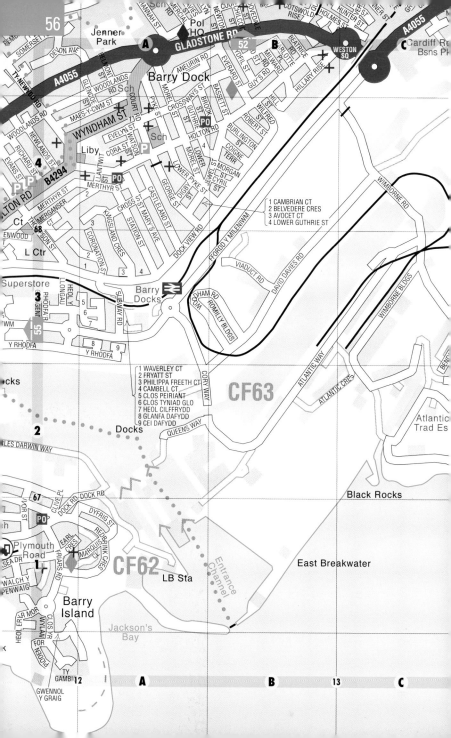

Jenner Park

Pol HQ

A

52

B

C Cardiff R
Bsns Ph

WESTON
SQ

A4055

Barry Dock

COTSWOLD
RISE

HOLMES ST

HUNTER ST

ANEURIN RD

EVERARD ST

BEATRICE

CHARLOTTE

MILWARD

HILLARY RISE

COMMERCIAL

CHICOPEE

DOVEDALE

NEWTON RD

GUY'S RD

HILL

WILFRED

A4055

T-NEWBD-RD

WOODLANDS RD

DELON AVE

SOMERSET

BELTON ST

GLENGE

GLENCOE

WOODLANDS
RD

MAES-Y-CWM ST

COURT RD

PYKE ST

MUDREL ST

CROSSWAY ST

GUTHRIE ST

BROOK ST

BASSETT ST

MILFRED

ROBERT ST

BURLINGTON

Sch

WYNDHAM ST

HOLTON RD

PO

EVANS ST

RICHARD ST

NEWLANDS ST

4

B4294

EVELYN ST

CORA ST

Sch

Liby

Sch

LLANTWIT

MERTHYR ST

P

LOWER PIKE ST

CASTLELAND ST

LOWER

MOREL ST

GEORGE ST

DIGBY ST

COIGNE
TERR

MORGAN
ST

CYRIL
ST

LOWER MORGAN ST

MERTHYR ST

PO

Ct

THE

MERGANSER

WATSON ST

TON RD

ENWOOD

L Ctr

68

CROSS ST

ST MARY'S AVE

KINGSLAND CRES

CORONATION ST

STATION ST

DOCK VIEW RD

FFORDO Y MILENIWM

VIADUCT RD

DAVID DAVIES RD

WIMBORNE RD

Superstore

3
GENI

RHODFA'R
LLONGAU

HEOL Y

5

6

7

SUBWAY RD

Barry
Docks

WM

55

Y RHODFA

8

9

Y RHODFA

WOODHAM RD

ROMILLY BLDGS

CORY WAY

1 WAVERLEY CT
2 FRYATT ST
3 PHILIPPA FREETH CT
4 CAMBELL CT
5 CLOS PEIRIANT
6 CLOS TYNIAD GLO
7 HEOL CILFFRYDD
8 GLANFA DAFYDD
9 CEI DAFYDD

CF63

ATLANTIC WAY

ATLANTIC CRES

Atlantic
Trad Es

WIMBORNE BLDGS

BENG

2

Docks

cks

LES DARWIN WAY

QUEENS WAY

Black Rocks

67

CLIVE PL

DOCK RD

DOCK RD

IVOR ST

PO

DYFRIG ST

REDBRINK CRES

East Breakwater

SEA DR

Plymouth
Road

1

EARL
CRES

FRIARS RD

MARQUIS

CF62

LB Sta

Entrance
Channel

WALCH Y
PENWAIG

Barry
Island

Jackson's
Bay

HEOL ER Y MOR

CLOS YR

WYLAN

CLOS YR

FOR

PYODEN Y

TY
GAMBI

12

GWENNOL
Y GRAIG

A

B

13

C

1 CAMBRIAN CT
2 BELVEDERE CRES
3 AVOCET CT
4 LOWER GUTHRIE ST

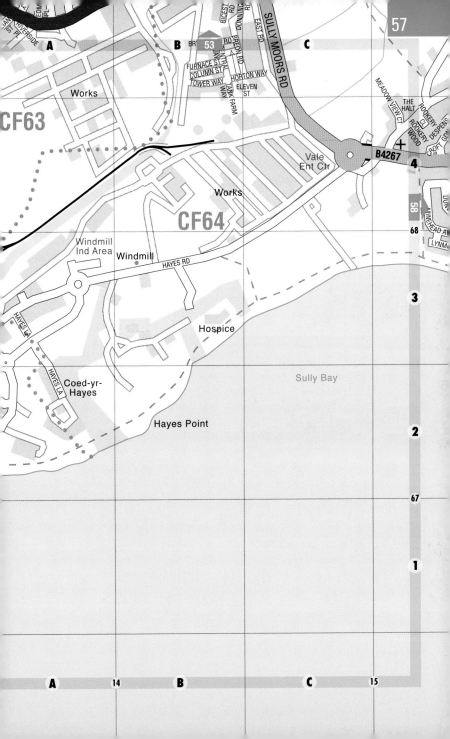

A B C

Works

CF63

BICESTER RD
DOWNING
EAST RD
SULLY MOORS RD

BR
53
BREON RD
HORTON WAY
FURNACE ST
COLUMN ST
TOWER WAY
CENTRAL RD
JANET ST
TANK FARM
ELEVEN ST

MEADOW VIEW CT
THE HALT
ROOKERY CL
ROOKERY WOOD
DESPENSER
CROFT GDN

B4267
4

Vale
Ent Ctr

58

Works

CF64

68

MINEHEAD AV
DUN
LYNM
LYNM

Windmill
Ind Area
Windmill

HAYES RD

3

Hospice

Sully Bay

HAYES LA
HAYES LA

Coed-yr-
Hayes

2

Hayes Point

67

1

A 14 B C 15

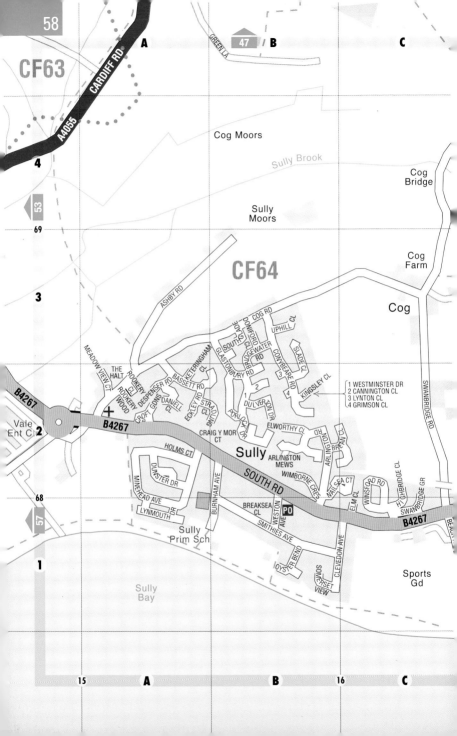

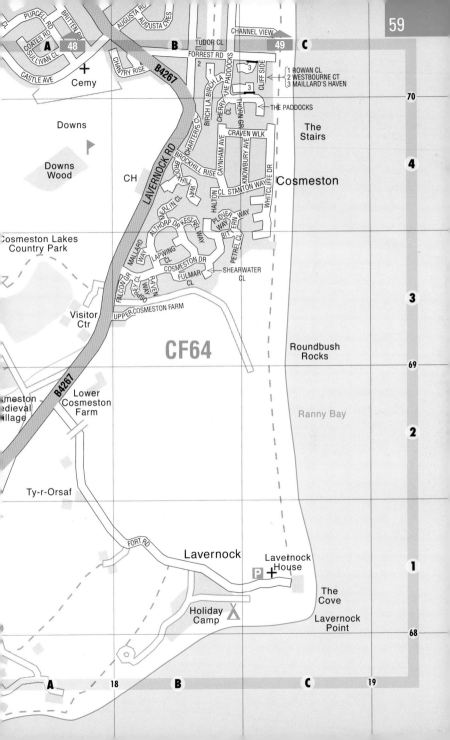

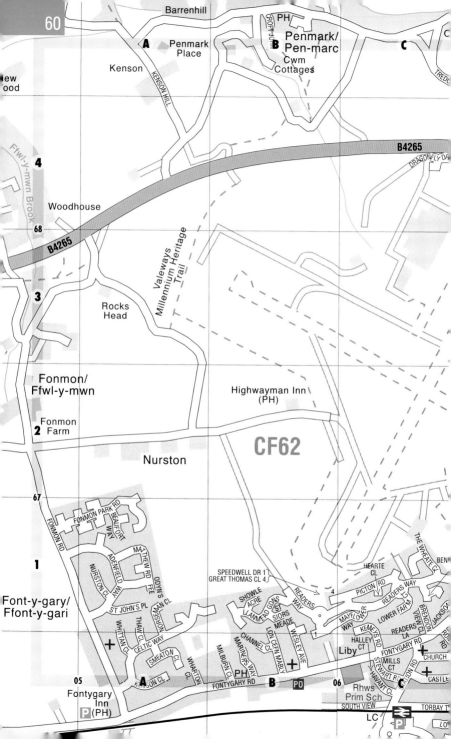

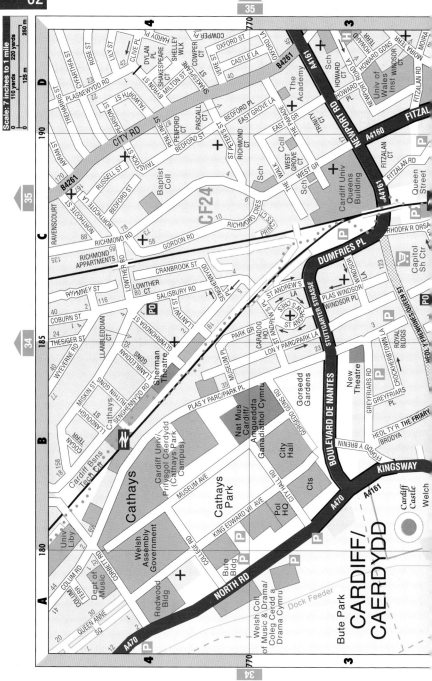

Scale: 7 inches to 1 mile

CARDIFF/CAERDYDD

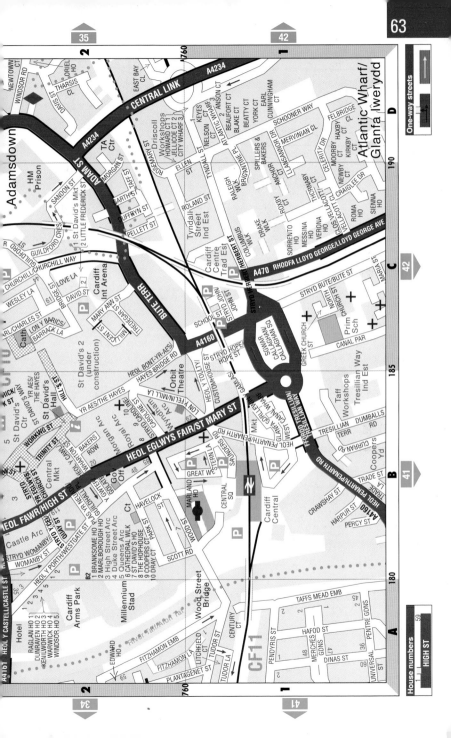

Index

Street names are listed alphabetically and show the locality, the Postcode district, the page number and a reference to the square in which the name falls on the map page

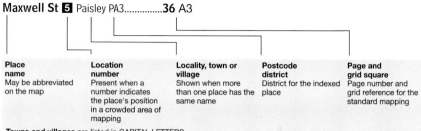

Maxwell St **Paisley PA3..............36 A3**

Place name	Location number	Locality, town or village	Postcode district	Page and grid square
May be abbreviated on the map	Present when a number indicates the place's position in a crowded area of mapping	Shown when more than one place has the same name	District for the indexed place	Page number and grid reference for the standard mapping

Towns and villages are listed in CAPITAL LETTERS

Public and commercial buildings are highlighted in magenta. **Places of interest** are highlighted in blue with a star ★

Abbreviations used in the index

Acad	**Academy**	Ct	**Court**	Hts	**Heights**	Pl	**Place**
App	**Approach**	Ctr	**Centre**	Ind	**Industrial**	Prec	**Precinct**
Arc	**Arcade**	Ctry	**Country**	Inst	**Institute**	Prom	**Promenade**
Ave	**Avenue**	Cty	**County**	Int	**International**	Rd	**Road**
Bglw	**Bungalow**	Dr	**Drive**	Intc	**Interchange**	Recn	**Recreation**
Bldg	**Building**	Dro	**Drove**	Junc	**Junction**	Ret	**Retail**
Bsns, Bus	**Business**	Ed	**Education**	L	**Leisure**	Sh	**Shopping**
Bvd	**Boulevard**	Emb	**Embankment**	La	**Lane**	Sq	**Square**
Cath	**Cathedral**	Est	**Estate**	Liby	**Library**	St	**Street**
Cir	**Circus**	Ex	**Exhibition**	Mdw	**Meadow**	Sta	**Station**
Cl	**Close**	Gd	**Ground**	Meml	**Memorial**	Terr	**Terrace**
Cnr	**Corner**	Gdn	**Garden**	Mkt	**Market**	TH	**Town Hall**
Coll	**College**	Gn	**Green**	Mus	**Museum**	Univ	**University**
Com	**Community**	Gr	**Grove**	Orch	**Orchard**	Wk, Wlk	**Walk**
Comm	**Common**	H	**Hall**	Pal	**Palace**	Wr	**Water**
Cott	**Cottage**	Ho	**House**	Par	**Parade**	Yd	**Yard**
Cres	**Crescent**	Hospl	**Hospital**	Pas	**Passage**		
Cswy	**Causeway**	HQ	**Headquarters**	Pk	**Park**		

Index of towns, villages, streets, hospitals, industrial estates, railway stations, schools, shopping centres, universities and places of interest

Abb – All

A

Abbey Cl CF15 ......2 C3
Aberaeron Cl CF62...52 A3
Aberbran Rd CF14 ...24 B2
Abercynon St CF11 ..41 C2
Aberdaron Rd CF3 ...20 B1
Aberdore Rd CF14 ...24 B2
Aberdovey Cl CF64...47 C3
Aberdovey St CF24...35 C1
Aberdulais Cres
CF14 ....24 A2
Aberdulais Rd
CF14 ....24 A2
Abergele Cl CF3 ....20 B2
Abergele Rd CF3 ...20 B1
Abernethy Cl
CF3 ....21 A3
Aberporth Rd CF14 ..24 A2
Aber St CF11 ....41 C2
Aberteifi Cl CF14 ...24 B2
Aberteifi Cres CF14 ..24 B2

Aberthaw Rd CF5....31 B1
Aberystwyth Cres
CF62 ....55 B3
Aberystwyth St
CF24 ....35 C1
Abingdon St CF63 ...52 B2
Academic Ave /
Coedlan Y Coleg
CF14 ....25 A3
Academy The CF24 ..62 D3
Acorn Gr CF23........8 B1
Acorns The CF14.....5 C3
Adamscroft Pl
CF10 ....35 A1
Adams Ct CF24 ......63 D2
ADAMSDOWN 63 D2
Adamsdown La
CF24 ....35 B1
Adamsdown Pl
CF24 ....35 B1
Adamsdown Prim Sch
CF24 ....35 B2
Adamsdown Sq
CF24 ....35 A1
Adam St CF24 ....63 C2
Adar Y Mor CF62....55 C1

Addison Cres CF5....31 A1
Adelaide Pl
CF10 ....42 A2
Adelaide St / Stryd
Adelaide CF10 .....42 A1
Adeline St CF24 .....35 C2
Adenfield Way
CF62 ....60 A1
Adventurers Quay
CF10 ....42 C2
Ael-y-Bryn
Cardiff / Caerdydd
CF23 ....26 C4
Pentyrch CF15 .....11 C3
Radyr CF15.........13 B3
Ael-y-Coed CF62 ...54 C4
Aeron Cl CF62 ......55 A4
Afal Sur CF63.......52 B4
Afan Cl CF62 ....55 A4
Afon Cl CF3 ....9 B4
Africa Gdns CF14 ...25 A2
Agate St CF24 ......35 B2
Agincourt Rd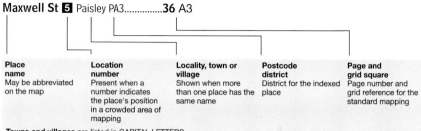
CF23 ....35 B4
Agnes St CF64......41 B1
Ainon Cl CF24 ......35 C1

Aintree Dr CF5 ......32 A1
Airport Bsns Pk
CF62 ....61 B3
Albany Ct CF64 ..49 B4
Albany Prim Sch
CF24 ....34 C4
Albany Rd CF24.....35 A4
Alberta Rd CF64 .....49 B2
Alberta Pl CF64 .....49 A2
Albert Cres CF64....49 B4
Albert Ct CF64 ...49 B4
Albert Cty Prim Sch
CF64 ....45 B1
Albert Rd CF64 .....49 B4
Albert St
Barry / Y Barri
CF63 ....53 A1
Cardiff / Caerdydd
CF11 ....33 B1
Albert Wlk CF11 ..33 B1
Alderbrook CF23 .....7 B1
Alder Rd CF23 ......26 A2
Alderwood Cl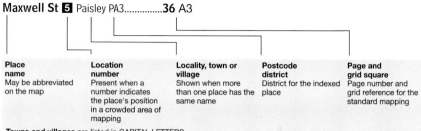
CF3 ....20 B3
Aldsworth Rd CF5 ...32 A3
Aldwych Cl CF14.....5 C2

Alexander St CF24 ...34 C4
Alexandra Cres
CF62 ....55 A4
Alexandra Ct
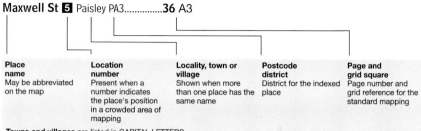 Cardiff / Caerdydd,
Canton CF5 ....33 B2
Cardiff / Caerdydd
CF5 ....32 C2
Penarth CF64 ......49 B3
Alexandra Gate
CF24 ....36 B4
Alexandra Rd CF5 ...33 A1
Alexandra Trad Est
CF3 ....28 C3
Alfreda Ct CF14.....23 B4
Alfreda Rd CF14 ....23 B4
Alfred St CF24 ......26 A1
Alfred's Terr CF15....2 B3
Alice St CF10 ....42 A2
Allan Durst Cl CF5 ..22 C3
Allen Cl CF3 ....20 B4
Allensbank Cres
CF14 ....25 B2
Allensbank Ho
CF14 ....25 B3

Allensbank Prim Sch
CF14 . . . . .25 B2
Allensbank Rd
CF14 . . . . .25 B3
Allerton St CF11 . . . . .41 B4
Allied Ind Pk CF24. . .36 A1
All Saints CIW Prim
Sch CF23 . . . . .26 C4
All Saints CW Prim
Sch CF62 . . . . .54 C4
Alltmawr Rd CF23 . . .17 C2
Allt Wen CF14 . . . . . . .14 C4
Allt Y Wennol CF23. . . .8 A1
Alma Rd CF23 . . . . .26 B1
Almond Dr CF23 . . . . . .8 A1
Althorp Dr CF64 . . . . .59 B4
Alwen Dr
Barry / Y Barri
CF62 . . . . .50 C1
Cardiff / Caerdydd
CF14 . . . . .6 A3
Amalfi Ho CF10 . . . . . .42 B3
Amber Cl CF23 . . . . .8 A1
Ambergate Dr CF23. . . .8 A1
Amberheart Dr CF14 . .6 A3
Amberley Cl CF23. . . . .18 C4
Amberwood Cl CF23. . . .8 A1
Amblecote Cl CF23 . . . .8 A1
Ambleside Ave
CF23 . . . . .25 C2
Ambrooke Cl CF23 . . . .8 A1
Amesbury Rd CF23. . . .26 C1
Amethyst Rd CF5 . . . . .22 C1
Amgueddfa
Genedlaethol
Caerdydd / National
Museum Cardiff★
CF10 . . . . .62 B4
Amherst Cres CF62 . . .55 C1
Amherst St CF11 . . . . .41 B2
Amity Ct CF10 . . . . .42 B3
Amroth Ct CF62. . . . . . .51 C2
Amroth Rd CF5 . . . . . . .31 B1
Amyas Cl CF11. . . . . . . .41 A3
Anchor Ct CF10. . . . . . .63 C1
Anchor Ind Est
CF10 . . . . .42 A3
Anchor Rd CF64 . . . . . .45 A2
Anchor St CF15. . . . . . . .9 B2
Anderson Pl CF24. . . . .35 B2
Andover Cl CF62. . . . . .50 B2
Andrew Rd CF64. . . . . .44 B1
Andrews Bldgs 2
CF64 . . . . .49 B4
Andrew's Rd CF14 . . . .23 B2
Androven Ct CF23 . . . .18 A2
Aneurin Rd CF63. . . . . .52 A1
Angelica Way CF14 . . .5 B3
Angelina St CF10 . . . . .42 A3
Angle Cl CF62 . . . . .51 C3
Angle Pl CF14 . . . . .5 C2
Anglesey St 10 CF5 . . .42 A3
Angus St CF24. . . . . . . .26 B1
Ann St CF11 . . . . .33 B1
Anson Ct CF10 . . . . . . .63 D1
Anstee Ct 8 CF5 . . . . .33 B1
Anton Ct CF14 . . . . . . .15 A1
Apollo Cl CF14. . . . . .5 C2
Appledore Rd CF14 . . .24 C3
Applewood Cl CF24. . .35 B1
Aprillia Ho CF10 . . . . .42 B3
Aquilla Ct 5 CF11 . . . .33 B3
Arabella St CF24. . . . . .26 A1
Arbroath Ct CF24. . . . . .36 A3
Archer Cres CF24. . . . .31 B2
Archer Ct CF62 . . . . . . .55 C1
Archer Pl
Cardiff / Caerdydd
CF5 . . . . .31 A2
Penarth CF64 . . . . .49 A3
Archer Rd
Barry / Y Barri
CF62 . . . . .55 C1

Archer Rd continued
Cardiff / Caerdydd
CF5 . . . . .31 B2
Penarth CF64 . . . . .49 A3
Archer Terr
Cardiff / Caerdydd
CF5 . . . . .31 B2
Penarth CF64 . . . . .49 A2
Archview Ct CF24. . . . .25 C2
Arcon Ho 3 CF3. . . . . .20 A4
Arcot La CF64 . . . . .49 A4
Arcot Lane N 7
CF64 . . . . .45 A1
Arcot St CF64. . . . . .49 A4
Arden Way CF63 . . . . .52 C2
Ardwyn CF14 . . . . .14 C4
Argyle Way CF5. . . . . . .39 A4
Argyll Ct 4 CF15 . . . .13 B2
Arles Rd CF5 . . . . .31 C1
Arlington Cres CF3 . . .19 C2
Arlington Mews
CF64 . . . . .58 B2
Arlington Rd CF64 . . . .58 B2
Armoury Dr CF14 . . . .16 A2
Arnold Ave CF3 . . . . . .19 C4
Arno Rd CF63. . . . . .52 C2
Arnside Rd CF23. . . . . .26 B2
Arran Pl CF24 . . . . .35 A4
Arran St CF24 . . . . .35 A4
Arrol St 14 CF24 . . . . .35 B1
Arthur Davis Ct
CF62 . . . . .51 C1
Arthur St
Barry / Y Barri
CF63 . . . . .53 A1
Cardiff / Caerdydd
CF24 . . . . .35 C3
Arundel Pl CF11 . . . . . .40 C2
Ar-y-Nant CF63 . . . . . .52 A2
Ascot Cl CF5. . . . . .32 A1
Asgog St CF24 . . . . .35 B1
Ashburton Ave CF3 . . .19 C3
Ashby Rd CF64 . . . . . . .58 A3
Ashchurch Ct CF14. . . .15 A1
Ashcroft Cres CF5 . . . .22 B1
Ashdene Ct CF5. . . . . . .22 C2
Ashdown Cl 4 CF3 . . .20 C3
Ashfield St 7 CF3 . . . .20 B3
Ashford CF64 . . . . .6 B2
Ash Gr
Barry / Y Barri
CF63 . . . . .52 C2
Cardiff / Caerdydd
CF14 . . . . .15 B2
Cardiff / Caerdydd,
Culverhouse Cross
CF5 . . . . .37 C2
Llandough / Llandochau
CF64 . . . . .44 B2
Ashgrove CF64. . . . . . . .47 B2
Ashgrove Sch CF64. . . .48 A3
Ash Pl CF5 . . . . .22 C1
Ash Tree Cl CF15 . . . . . .9 B2
Ash Tree Ct CF23 . . . . . .8 B3
Ashwood Ct 6
CF24 . . . . .35 A3
Aspen Cl CF3 . . . . .20 B3
Aster Cl 6 CF3 . . . . . . .21 A3
Aston Pl CF3 . . . . .21 A1
Astoria Cl CF14 . . . . . . .5 C2
Athelstan Rd CF14 . . . .23 B4
Athrofa Chwaraeon
Cymru / Welsh Inst
of Sport CF11. . . . . . .33 C3
Atlantic Cres CF63. . . .56 C2
Atlantic Pl CF63 . . . . . .52 C2
Atlantic Trad Est
CF63 . . . . .56 C2
Atlantic Way CF63 . . . .56 B2
Atlantic Wharf
CF10 . . . . .63 D1
ATLANTIC WHARF /
GLANFA
IWERYDD. 42 B3

Atlas Ho CF10 . . . . .42 C2
Atlas Pl 6 CF5 . . . . . . .33 B1
Atlas Rd CF5 . . . . .33 B1
Attfield Cl CF23. . . . . . .27 A1
Aubrey Ave CF5. . . . . . .32 B3
Augusta Cres CF64. . . .49 A1
Augusta Rd CF64 . . . . .49 A1
Augusta St CF24 . . . . . .35 A2
Austen Cl CF3 . . . . .20 A4
Australia Rd CF14. . . . .25 A2
Avenue Ind Pk
CF23 . . . . .19 A4
Avenue The
Cardiff / Caerdydd
CF5 . . . . .23 C1
Cardiff / Caerdydd,
Rumney / Rhymni
CF3 . . . . .28 B2
Cardiff / Caerdydd,
Whitchurch CF14 . . . .23 B4
Avoca Pl CF11 . . . . .41 A3
Avocet Ct CF63 . . . . . . .56 A4
Avon Cl CF63 . . . . .52 C2
Avondale Cres
CF11 . . . . .41 C2
Avondale Ct 16
CF10 . . . . .42 A2
Avondale Gdns
CF11 . . . . .41 C2
Avondale Gdns S
CF11 . . . . .41 C2
Avonmuir Rd CF24. . . .36 B4
Avonridge CF14. . . . . . . .5 B2
Avonridge CF14 . . . . . . .5 B2
Awbery Ho CF62. . . . . . .51 A1
Awel Mor CF23 . . . . . . .26 C3
Awel y Mor CF64. . . . . .49 B2
Axbridge Cres CF3. . . .20 A2
Axminster Rd CF3 . . . .35 C4
Aylesbury Mans 2
CF14 . . . . .14 C2
Azalea Cl CF23. . . . . . . .18 A3

B

Baber Cl CF23 . . . . .27 A1
Bacton Rd CF14 . . . . . .24 A2
Baden Powell Prim
Sch CF24 . . . . .36 A2
Baden Rd CF24 . . . . . . .36 B2
Bader Cl CF14 . . . . .16 C2
Bailey Cl CF5 . . . . .31 C3
Baird Rise CF62 . . . . . . .55 A4
Bakers Ct 5 CF5 . . . . . .32 C3
Bakers Row CF10 . . . . .63 B2
Balaclava Rd CF23 . . . .26 B1
Bala Rd CF14 . . . . .23 C2
Baldwin Cl CF5 . . . . . . .22 C3
Ball La CF3 . . . . .19 A2
Ball Rd CF3. . . . . .19 B2
Balmoral Cl CF14 . . . . . .6 C2
Balmoral Ct CF62 . . . . .50 C3
Baltimore Cl CF23 . . . . .8 B2
Bampton Rd CF3 . . . . . .19 C3
Banastre Ave CF14. . . .25 A2
Banc Yr Afon CF15. . . . .2 B3
Bangor Ct 3 CF24 . . . .26 B1
Bangor La 2 CF24. . . . .26 B1
Bangor St CF24 . . . . . . .26 B1
Bankside Cl CF14. . . . . . .6 A3
Banwell Pl CF3 . . . . . . .19 C2
Baptist Ct CF24 . . . . . . .25 C2
Barberry Rise CF64 . . .44 B1
Barbrook Cl CF14 . . . . . .6 B2
Bardsey Cres CF14. . . . .5 C1
Bargoed St CF11. . . . . . .41 C2
Barletta Ho 2
CF10 . . . . .42 A3
Barmouth Rd CF3. . . . .28 A3
Barnard Ave CF5. . . . . .31 C2
Barnfield Cl CF23 . . . . . .8 C1
Barnfield Dr CF15. . . . .13 A4
Barnstaple Rd CF3. . . .19 C2
Barnwood CF14 . . . . . . .6 B2

Barnwood Cres
CF5 . . . . .37 B4
Baron Cl CF64 . . . . .48 C3
Baroness Pl CF64 . . . . .48 C3
Baron Rd CF64. . . . . . . .48 C3
Baron's Court Rd
CF23 . . . . .26 C1
Barquentine Pl
CF10 . . . . .42 B3
Barrack La / Lon Y
Barics CF10. . . . . .63 C2
Barrians Way CF62. . . .55 B4
Barrington Rd 3
CF14 . . . . .24 A4
Barry Coll
Barry / Y Barri
CF62 . . . . .50 A2
Barry / Y Barri, Cwm
Talwg CF62. . . . . .51 A1
Barry Coll (Annexe)
CF62 . . . . .61 B3
Barry Comp Sch
CF62 . . . . .51 A2
Barry Coll Heritage
Skills Training Ctr
CF62 . . . . .55 B3
BARRY DOCK 52 A1
Barry Docks Link Rd
CF63 . . . . .53 A3
Barry Docks Sta
CF63 . . . . .56 A3
Barry Hospl The
CF62 . . . . .51 A2
BARRY ISLAND 55 C1
Barry Island Pleasure
Pk★ CF62 . . . . .55 B1
Barry Island Prim Sch
CF62 . . . . .55 C2
Barry Island Rly★
CF62 . . . . .55 A1
Barry Island Sta
CF62 . . . . .55 B1
Barry Rd
Barry / Y Barri CF62,
CF63 . . . . .51 B1
Llandough / Llandochau
CF64 . . . . .44 B2
Barry Sta CF62 . . . . . . .55 A2
Basil Pl CF24 . . . . .34 B4
Bassaleg Cl 2 CF3. . . .21 A3
Bassett Rd CF64 . . . . . .58 A2
Bassetts Field CF14 . . . .5 A3
Bassett St
Barry / Y Barri
CF63 . . . . .56 B4
Cardiff / Caerdydd
CF5 . . . . .33 A1
Bastian Cl CF63. . . . . . .52 C2
Batchelor Rd CF14 . . . .24 C2
Baton Ct CF14 . . . . .24 B4
Baylis Ct CF5 . . . . .31 C2
Baynton Cl CF5 . . . . . . .23 A2
Bayside Rd CF24. . . . . .35 B1
BBC Cymru Wales
CF5 . . . . .23 B1
Beach La CF64 . . . . .49 B4
Beach Rd CF64 . . . . . . .49 B4
Beaconsfield Ho
CF62 . . . . .55 B3
Beacon St CF11. . . . . . .33 A3
Beale Cl CF5 . . . . .23 A2
Beatrice Rd
Barry / Y Barri
CF63 . . . . .52 B1
Cardiff / Caerdydd
CF14 . . . . .24 A4
Beatty Ave CF23 . . . . . .17 A1
Beatty Cl 2 CF62. . . . . .52 A3
Beatty Ct CF10. . . . . . . .63 D1
Beauchamp St
CF11 . . . . .34 A1
Beaufort Ct CF10 . . . . .63 D1
Beaufort Sq CF24. . . . . .36 B4

Beaufort Way CF62 . . .60 A1
Beaumaris Rd CF3. . . .28 A3
Beaumont Cl CF62. . . .50 C2
Beaumont Ct CF24. . . .48 C3
Beckgrove Cl CF24. . . .36 B3
Beda Rd CF5 . . . . .33 A1
Bedavere Cl CF14. . . . . .5 C2
Bedford Pl CF24 . . . . . .62 D4
Bedford St CF24 . . . . . .62 C4
Bedlington Terr
CF62 . . . . .55 A4
Bedwas Cl 4 CF3. . . . .21 A3
Bedwas Pl 2 CF64. . . .48 C4
Bedwas St CF11 . . . . . .41 A3
Beech Ct CF15. . . . . .3 B2
Beecher Ave CF11 . . . .41 B1
Beeches The CF14 . . . . .6 B3
Beech Ho CF14 . . . . . . .14 B3
Beechley Dr CF5. . . . . . .31 A4
Beech Rd CF5 . . . . .30 C4
Beech Tree Cl
CF15 . . . . .13 A2
Beechwood Dr
CF64 . . . . .48 B2
Beechwood Rd CF15. . .2 C4
BEGAN 9 B3
Began Rd CF3 . . . . .9 B4
Beidr Iorwg CF63. . . . . .52 C3
Beignon Cl CF24. . . . . . .42 C4
Belgrave Cl CF14 . . . . . .5 C3
Belgrave Ct 1
CF11 . . . . .34 A1
Belle Vue Cl CF64 . . . . .49 B4
Belle Vue Cres
CF14 . . . . .23 B3
Belle Vue Terr
Barry / Y Barri
CF63 . . . . .52 C2
Penarth CF64 . . . . .45 B1
Bell St CF62 . . . . .54 C3
Belmont St CF63. . . . . .52 A1
Belmont Wlk CF10. . . . .42 A2
Belvedere Cres 6
CF63 . . . . .55 C4
Bendrick Rd CF63. . . . .56 C3
Benecrofte CF62. . . . . . .60 C1
Beresford Ct CF24 . . . .35 C3
Beresford Rd CF24 . . . .35 C3
Beresford Road La
CF24 . . . . .35 C3
Berkeley Sq CF5 . . . . . .37 C2
Berkley Dr CF64 . . . . . .49 A3
Bernard Ave CF5. . . . . .32 B2
Berrymead Rd
CF23 . . . . .17 B3
Berry Pl CF5. . . . . .22 C2
Berthlwyd CF15. . . . . . . .11 C4
Berthwin St CF11. . . . . .33 B3
Bertram St CF24 . . . . . .35 C3
Beryl Pl CF62 . . . . .55 C4
Beryl Rd CF62 . . . . .55 C4
Bessborough Dr
CF11 . . . . .41 A3
Bessemer Cl CF11 . . . .40 C2
Bessemer Close
Workshops CF11. . . . .40 B2
Bessemer Rd CF11. . . . .40 C3
Bethania Row CF3. . . . .20 A4
Bethel Pl CF14 . . . . .5 B1
Bethlehem Ct CF24 . . .35 C2
Bettws-y-Coed Rd
CF23 . . . . .17 B3
Beulah Rd CF14. . . . . . .15 C3
Bevan Pl CF14 . . . . .24 C2
Beverley Cl CF14. . . . . . .6 B1
Beverley St CF63. . . . . .52 B2
Bicester Rd CF3. . . . . . .53 B1
Bideford Rd CF3 . . . . . .19 C1
Birch Ct
Cardiff / Caerdydd
CF14 . . . . .16 A1

Birch Ct continued
Tongwynlais CF15......3 B2
Birchfield Cres CF5 . . 32 B2
Birch Gr CF62 . . . . 54 C1
BIRCHGROVE 16 A1
Birchgrove Prim Sch
CF14 . . . . .24 C4
Birchgrove Rd
CF14 . . . . .24 C4
Birchgrove Sta
CF14 . . . . .16 A2
Birch Hill CF15 . . . . . . .3 A1
Birch La CF64. . . . . . . .49 A1
Birch Rd CF5 . . . . .31 B4
Birch Wlk **8** CF5 . . . .31 B4
Birchwood Gdns
CF14 . . . . .24 B3
Birchwood La CF23 . .26 B3
Birchwood Rd
CF23 . . . . .26 B3
Birkdale Cl **3** CF3 . . .21 A4
Bishop Childs CW
Prim Sch CF3. . . . . . .20 C3
Bishop Hannon Dr
CF5 . . . . .22 A1
Bishop of Llandaff CW
High Sch CF5. . . . . . .23 B1
Bishops' Ave CF5 . . . .32 A4
Bishops Cl CF14 . . . . .23 C4
Bishops' Cl CF5. . . . . .32 A4
Bishops Ct CF14 . . . . .23 C4
Bishops Pl CF14 . . . . .23 C4
Bishops' Pl CF5. . . . . .32 A4
Bishop's Rd CF14 . . . .23 C4
Bishop St CF11 . . . . . .41 A3
Bishopston Rd CF5 . .39 A4
Bishops' Wlk CF5 . . . .32 A4
Bisley Cl CF24 . . . . . . .36 C3
Bittern Way CF64 . . . .59 B4
Bittern Wood Ho
CF62 . . . . .51 C2
Blackberry Dr CF62 . .50 C1
Blackberry Way **7**
CF23 . . . . .8 B1
Blackbirds Way
CF3 . . . . .20 A4
Blackmoor Pl CF3 . . .19 C2
Black Oak Rd CF23 . .17 C4
Blackstone St **10**
CF11 . . . . .33 C1
Blackton La CF62 . . . .61 C3
BLACKWEIR 33 C4
Blackweir Terr
CF10 . . . . .34 A4
Blackwell Cl **1**
CF63 . . . . .52 B1
Blaenavon Cl **3**
CF3 . . . . .21 A3
Blaenclydach Pl **4**
CF11 . . . . .41 B3
Blaenclydach St
CF11 . . . . .41 B3
Blaen-y-Coed
Cardiff / Caerdydd
CF14 . . . . .15 C4
Radyr CF15. . . . . . . .13 A2
Blagdon Cl CF3. . . . . .19 B1
Blaina Cl CF3. . . . . . . .20 C3
Blaise Pl CF11 . . . . . . .41 A2
Blake Ct CF10 . . . . . . .63 D1
Blanche St CF24 . . . . .35 C3
Blandings Ct CF23 . . .17 C2
Blandon Way CF14 . .24 A4
Blanthorn Ct **1**
CF14 . . . . .14 C2
Blenheim Cl CF62 . . .50 C2
Blenheim Rd CF23. . .26 C1
Blethin Cl CF5 . . . . . . .23 A3
Blodyn Y Gog CF63. .52 C3
Bloom St CF11. . . . . . .33 A1
Blosse Rd CF14 . . . . . .23 C2

Blossom Dr CF14 . . . . .6 B4
Bluebell Dr CF3. . . . . .20 A4
Blue House Rd CF14 . .5 C1
Blyth Cl CF62 . . . . .52 A4
Bodnant Cl CF3. . . . . .20 C2
Boleyn Wlk CF23. . . . .26 B1
Boncath Rd CF14 . . . .23 C2
Booker St CF24 . . . . . .35 C3
Boon Cl CF63. . . . . . . .52 A2
Borage Cl CF23 . . . . . . .7 C1
Borough Ave CF62 . .51 B3
Borrowdale Cl
CF23 . . . . .26 B2
Borth Rd CF3 . . . . .20 A1
Boswell Cl CF3 . . . . . .19 B4
Boulevard De Nantes
CF10 . . . . .62 B3
Boverton St CF23 . . . .26 A1
Bowley Ct CF24. . . . . .35 C1
Bow St CF5. . . . . .37 C2
Brachdy Cl CF3 . . . . . .28 A2
Brachdy La CF3 . . . . . .28 A2
Brachdy Rd CF3 . . . . .28 A2
Bracken Pl CF5 . . . . . .22 C1
Bradenham Pl **5**
CF64. . . . . .49 A4
Bradford Pl CF64 . . . .49 B4
Bradford St CF11 . . . .41 C2
Bradley St CF24. . . . . .35 C3
Braeval St CF24. . . . . .34 C4
Bramble Ave CF64 . . .51 A1
Bramble Cl CF5. . . . . .22 A1
Bramble Rise CF64 . .44 B1
Bramblewood Cl
CF14 . . . . .6 A2
Brambling Dr CF14 . . .5 C3
Bramshill Dr CF23 . . .8 C1
Brandreth Gdns
CF23 . . . . .26 B2
Brandreth Rd CF23 . .26 A2
Brangwyn Cl **4**
CF64. . . . . .44 C1
Branksome Ho **1**
CF10 . . . . .63 B2
Branwen Cl CF5 . . . . .37 C2
Braunton Ave CF3 . . .19 C2
Braunton Cres CF3 . .19 B2
Brayford Pl CF3. . . . . .19 C4
Breaksea Cl CF64. . . .58 B1
Breaksea Ct CF62 . . .55 C1
Breaksea Dr CF62. . . .55 C1
Brean Cl CF64 . . . . . . .58 C2
Brecon Ct
Barry / Y Barri
CF63 . . . . .52 A1
8 Cardiff / Caerdydd
CF5 . . . . .33 A2
Brecon Ho **7** CF64 . .48 C2
Brecon St CF5 . . . . . . .33 A2
Brendon Cl **3** CF3 . .19 C2
Brendon View Cl
CF62 . . . . .60 C1
Brenig Cl
Barry / Y Barri
CF62 . . . . .50 C1
Cardiff / Caerdydd
CF14 . . . . .6 A3
Brentwood Ct CF14 . .6 A1
Breon Rd CF64. . . . . . .53 B1
Brianne Dr CF14. . . . . .6 A3
Briar Cl CF5 . . . . .31 A4
Briarmeadow Dr
CF14 . . . . .5 C3
Briartree Manor **6**
CF24 . . . . .35 B3
Briarwood Dr CF23 . .18 A3
Brickyard Bsns Pk
CF14 . . . . .24 C2
Bridgeman Ct CF64 . .49 B3
Bridgeman Rd
CF64 . . . . .49 B3
Bridge Rd
Cardiff / Caerdydd CF5,
CF14 . . . . .23 B2

Bridge Rd continued
Cardiff / Caerdydd, Llane
Deyrn CF3 . . . . .9 A1
Bridge St
Barry / Y Barri
CF63 . . . . .52 B2
Cardiff / Caerdydd
CF10 . . . . .63 C2
Cardiff / Caerdydd,
Llandaff / Llandaf
CF5 . . . . .23 C1
Penarth CF64 . . . . . . .44 C1
Bridgewater Rd
CF64 . . . . .58 B3
Bridgwater Rd CF3 . .20 A2
Brigantine Pl CF10. . .63 D1
Brindley Rd CF11 . . . .40 C1
Bristol Terr CF15. . . . . .2 A4
Britannia Quay
CF10 . . . . .42 B2
Brithdir St CF24 . . . . .25 B1
British Legion Dr
CF3 . . . . .28 A4
Britten Rd CF64. . . . . .48 C1
Britway Ct CF64 . . . . .47 A3
Britway Rd CF64 . . . . .47 A3
Broadacres CF11 . . . .33 A1
Broad Cl CF62 . . . . . . .54 B4
Broadfield Ct CF5. . . .38 C4
Broadhaven CF11. . . .40 B4
Broadlands Ct **4**
CF3 . . . . .20 B3
Broadlands Ho **5**
CF3 . . . . .20 B3
Broad Pl CF11 . . . . . . .33 A1
Broad St
Barry / Y Barri
CF62 . . . . .55 A3
Cardiff / Caerdydd
CF11 . . . . .33 A1
Broadstairs Rd
CF11 . . . . .33 A1
Broad Street Par
CF62 . . . . .55 A2
Broadway CF24. . . . . .35 B3
Broadwell Cl **4**
CF3 . . . . .20 C2
Bro Athro CF3 . . . . . . .28 A4
Brocastle Rd CF14 . . .15 B2
Brockhampton Rd
CF3 . . . . .20 C3
Brockhill Rise CF64 . .59 B4
Brockhill Way CF64 . .59 B4
Brock St CF63 . . . . . . .52 B2
Brodeg CF15 . . . . .11 C3
Bromfield Pl CF64 . . .45 B1
Bromfield Rd CF62. . .55 B1
Bromfield St CF11 . . .41 B2
Bromley Dr CF5. . . . . .31 C1
Bromsgrove St
CF11 . . . . .41 B2
Bron Awelon CF62 . . .54 B2
Bron Felen CF15. . . . .11 C3
Bronhaul CF15. . . . . . .11 C3
Bronllwyn CF15. . . . . .11 B3
Bronte Cl CF3 . . . . . . .19 C4
Bronte Cres CF3 . . . . .19 C4
Bronwydd Ave
CF23 . . . . .26 B2
Bronwydd Cl CF23 . . .26 C2
Bronwydd Rd CF24 . .36 B4
Bron-y-Glyn CF64 . . .49 B3
Bron-y-Mor CF62. . . .54 C1
Brook Ct
Cardiff / Caerdydd,
Fairwater CF5 . . . . . .32 A3
Cardiff / Caerdydd,
Riverside CF11 . . . . .34 A1
Brookfield Ave
CF63 . . . . .52 C3
Brookfield Dr CF3 . . .20 B2
Brooklands Terr
CF5 . . . . .31 B2

Brooklyn Cl CF14 . . . . .4 B1
Brook Rd
Cardiff / Caerdydd
CF5 . . . . .32 A1
Cardiff / Caerdydd,
Whitchurch CF14 . . .24 A4
Brookside CF64. . . . . .47 B4
Brookside Cl CF14 . . .16 A1
Brookside Ct **6**
CF14 . . . . .15 B1
Brook St
Barry / Y Barri
CF63 . . . . .56 A4
Cardiff / Caerdydd
CF11 . . . . .34 A1
Brookvale Dr CF14 . . .5 C3
Brookview Cl CF14. . .6 A2
Broom Pl CF5 . . . . .31 B4
Broughton Pl **4**
CF63 . . . . .52 A3
Browning Cl CF3. . . . .19 B3
Bruce Knight Cl
CF5 . . . . .23 A2
Bruce St CF24 . . . . . . .25 C1
Brummell Dr CF15 . . .10 C1
Brundall Cres CF3 . . .37 C3
Brunel Cl CF63 . . . . . .53 A3
Brunel St CF11 . . . . . .33 C1
Brunswick St CF5. . . .33 A2
Bruton CF73 . . . . .18 C1
Bryanston Rd CF64 . .53 B1
Brydges Pl CF24 . . . . .34 B4
Bryn Adar CF14. . . . . .14 C4
Brynau Rd CF15 . . . . . .2 C1
Bryn-Awelon Rd
CF23 . . . . .17 C4
Bryn Bach CF14. . . . . .15 B4
Brynbala Way CF3 . . .20 B1
Bryn Barrwg CF62 . . .55 A1
Bryn Calch CF15. . . . .13 A4
Bryn Castell CF15 . . .13 B3
Bryn Celyn CF23 . . . .18 C3
Bryn Celyn Prim Sch
CF23 . . . . .18 C3
Bryn Celyn Rd
CF23 . . . . .18 C3
Bryncoch CF15 . . . . . . .2 B4
Bryncoed CF15 . . . . . .13 A2
Bryncyn CF23. . . . . . . .18 B4
Bryn Deri Prim Sch
CF15 . . . . .13 B3
Bryn Derwen CF15 . . .13 A3
Brynderwen Cl
CF23 . . . . .26 B4
Brynfedw CF23 . . . . . .18 B2
Bryn Glas CF14 . . . . . .5 B2
Bryn Golwg CF15 . . . .13 B3
Bryn-Gwyn Rd
CF23 . . . . .17 C3
Bryn-Hafod Prim Sch
CF3 . . . . .19 B1
Bryn Hafren Comp Sch
/ Ysgol Gyfun Uchaf
Bryn Hafren CF62. . .51 C4
Bryn Haidd CF23. . . . .18 C3
Brynheulog
Cardiff / Caerdydd
CF14 . . . . .14 C1
Cardiff / Caerdydd,
Pentwyn CF23. . . . . .18 C3
Brynhill CF23 . . . . .17 C2
Brynhill Cl CF62 . . . . .51 A3
Brynhyfryd CF15. . . . .13 B3
Brynmawr CF73 . . . . .21 A3
Bryn Pinwydden
CF23 . . . . .18 B4
Bryn Rhosyn CF15 . . .13 A3
Bryn Siriol CF15 . . . . .11 C3
Brynteg CF14. . . . . .4 B1
Brynteg Cl CF23 . . . . .26 B4
Bryntirion CF14 . . . . .15 C4
Bryn-y-Nant CF23 . . .18 C1
Bryn-yr-Eglwys
CF15 . . . . .11 C3

Brython Dr CF3. . . . . .21 A3
Buckingham Cl CF14. .6 C2
Buckingham Pl
CF62 . . . . .50 C3
Buckley Cl CF5 . . . . . .22 C3
Bull Cliff Wlk CF62. . .54 A1
Bulrush Cl CF3 . . . . . .21 B2
Bunyan Cl CF3. . . . . . .20 A4
BUPA Hospl Cardiff
CF23 . . . . .8 A1
Burgess Pl CF11 . . . . .41 A3
Burlington St CF63 . .56 B4
Burlington Terr
CF5 . . . . .32 C3
Burnaby St CF24 . . . .35 C2
Burne Jones Cl
CF5 . . . . .23 A2
Burnham Ave
Cardiff / Caerdydd
CF3 . . . . .19 C3
Sully CF64. . . . . .58 B2
Burnham Ct **8** CF3 .19 C2
Burns Cres CF62 . . . .51 C3
Burreed Cl CF3 . . . . . .21 B2
Burt Pl **4** CF10 . . . . .42 A2
Burt St CF10. . . . . .42 A1
Burwell Cl CF23 . . . . . .8 C1
Bute Cres / Cilgant
Bute CF10 . . . . .42 B2
Bute Espl CF10 . . . . . .42 A1
Bute La CF64 . . . . .49 A4
Bute Pl / Plas Bute
CF10 . . . . .42 B2
Bute St / Stryd Bute
CF10 . . . . .63 C1
Bute St CF15 . . . . .3 A1
Bute Terr CF10. . . . . . .63 C2
BUTETOWN 42 A3
Butleigh Ave CF5 . . . .32 B3
Butterbur Pl CF5 . . . .30 B1
Butterfield Dr CF23 . .7 C1
Butt Lee Ct CF62. . . . .55 B4
Buttrills Cl CF62 . . . . .55 B4
Buttrills Rd CF62 . . . .55 B4
Buttrills Wlk CF62 . . .51 B1
Bwlch Rd CF5 . . . . . . .31 B3
Byrd Cres CF64 . . . . . .48 B1
Byron Cl CF64 . . . . . . .44 C1
Byron Pl CF64 . . . . . . .48 C4
Byron St
3 Barry / Y Barri
CF62 . . . . .55 C4
Cardiff / Caerdydd
CF24 . . . . .62 D4

C

Cadman Cl CF24 . . . . .36 B3
Cadnant Cl CF14. . . . . .5 B1
Cadoc Cres CF63 . . . .53 A1
Cadoc Pl CF5 . . . . .23 A3
Cadogan Ct **3**
CF24 . . . . .34 B4
CADOXTON 52 B2
Cadoxton Com Prim
Sch CF63 . . . . .52 B2
Cadoxton Sta CF63 . .52 C1
Cadvan Rd CF5 . . . . . .30 C2
Cadwgan Pl **2** CF5 . .31 C3
Caebach Cl CF3 . . . . .37 B3
Caedelyn Rd CF14 . . .15 A2
Cae Garw
Cardiff / Caerdydd
CF14 . . . . .5 B2
Dinas Powis / Dinas
Powys CF64 . . . . .47 A2
Cae Glas CF63 . . . . . . .52 B2
Caeglas Ave CF3 . . . . .28 A3
Cae-glas Rd CF3. . . . .28 B3
Cae Gwyn CF64 . . . . .48 B2
Cae Gwyn Rd CF14. . .15 C1
Cae Leon CF62 . . . . . .51 C4
Cae Lewis CF15. . . . . . .3 A1

Cae Maen CF14......24 C4
Cae Mawr Rd CF14...15 C3
Caenewydd Cl CF5...37 B3
CAERAU...........38 C3
Caerau Com Inf Sch
CF5...............38 B3
Caerau Court Rd
CF5...............38 B4
Caerau La
Cardiff / Caerdydd
CF5...............38 A2
Pentyrch CF15......12 A4
Wenvoe / Gwenfo
CF5...............46 B4
Caerau Park Cres
CF5...............38 B4
Caerau Park Pl 2
CF5...............38 B4
Caerau Park Rd
CF5...............38 B4
Caerau Rd CF5......38 B4
Caer Cady Cl CF23...26 B4
Caer Castell Pl CF3..20 A1
Caer Ceffyl CF5......12 B4
CAERDYDD /
CARDIFF.........62 A3
Caer Efail CF5......12 B1
Caer Ffynnon CF62..54 C2
Cae'r Graig CF15....13 B2
Caerleon Cl CF3....21 A3
Caerleon Rd
Cardiff / Caerdydd
CF14.............24 C2
Dinas Powis / Dinas
Powys CF64......47 C4
Caernarvon Cl 2
CF64.............47 C3
Caernarvon Ct 2
CF11.............33 B3
Caernarvon Gdns
CF62.............51 B3
Caernarvon Way
CF3..............20 A1
Cae'r Odyn CF64.....47 C4
Caerphilly Cl CF64...47 C3
Caerphilly Rd CF14..16 A1
Caer Wenallt CF14...14 C4
Caerwent Rd CF5....30 B1
Cae Samson 1
CF5...............38 B4
Cae Syr Dafydd
CF11.............33 A3
Cae Ty Mawr CF14...23 B4
Caewal Rd CF14.....15 C3
Cae Yorath 8 CF14..15 B1
Cairnmuir Rd CF24..26 A3
Calais Ho 22 CF10....42 A4
Caldicot Rd CF5.....38 C4
Caldy Cl CF62.......51 C3
Caldy Ct CF14......23 C3
Caldy Rd CF14......23 C3
Callaghan Ct CF24...35 C2
Callaghan Sq / Sgwar
Callaghan CF10......63 C1
Cambell Ct CF63....56 A3
Cambourne Ave
CF14.............14 C1
Cambourne Cl
CF62.............50 C2
Cambria CF11......44 C2
Cambrian Ct CF63...56 A4
Cambrian Point
CF24.............25 B1
Cambrian Residential
Pk CF5...........37 C2
Cambria Rd CF5.....38 A4
Cambridge St
Barry / Y Barri
CF62.............54 C2
Cardiff / Caerdydd
CF11.............41 C2
Camelot Way CF14...5 B2
Cameron St CF24....35 C3

Camm's Cnr 8
CF64.............47 C3
Campbell Dr CF11...45 A4
Campion Pl CF5.....22 C2
Camrose Ct CF64....51 C3
Camrose Rd CF5.....38 C4
Canada Rd CF14....25 A2
Canal Par CF10......42 A3
Canal Park Ind Est
CF10.............42 A3
Canaston Pl CF5.....38 C4
Cannes Ho 18 CF10..42 A2
Cannington Ave
CF3..............19 C1
Cannington Cl
CF64.............58 B2

Canolfan = centre

Canolfan Criced
Genedlaethol /
Sophia Gdns
Glamorgan CCC
CF11.............33 C3
Canolfan Mileniwm
Cymru / Wales
Millennium Ctr
CF10.............42 B2
Canolfan Technoleg /
Techno Ctr CF24...42 C4
Canon St CF62......55 C3
Canopus Cl CF3.....20 A2
CANTON...........33 B2
Canton Ct 2 CF11...33 C1
Cantonian High Sch
CF5...............31 C4
Cantref Cl CF14......6 A3
Capel Edeyrn CF23..19 B4
Capel Gwilym Rd
CF14..............5 B4
Capital Bsns Pk
CF3..............28 C2
Capitol Sh Ctr
CF10.............62 C3
Caple Rd CF62......54 C2
Caradoc Ave CF63...52 A2
Caradoc Cl 1 CF3...23 A1
Caradog Ho CF10...62 C3
Caraway Cl 14 CF3...21 A4
Cardiff Arms Park
CF10.............63 A2
Cardiff Bay Barrage
Visitor Ctr★ CF10..45 C2
Cardiff Bay Bsns Ctr
CF24.............42 C4
Cardiff Bay Ret Pk /
Parc Manwerthu Bae
Caerdydd
Cardiff / Caerdydd
CF11.............41 B1
Cardiff / Caerdydd
CF11.............44 C1
Cardiff Bay Sta
CF10.............42 B2
Cardiff Bay Visitor
Ctr★ CF10........42 B1
Cardiff Bsns Pk
CF14.............16 B3
Cardiff Bsns Tech Ctr
CF24.............62 B4
CARDIFF /
CAERDYDD.......62 A3
Cardiff Castle★
CF10.............62 B3
Cardiff Central Sta
CF10.............63 B1
Cardiff Centre Trad
Est CF10..........63 C1
Cardiff City Hall
CF10.............62 B3
Cardiff County Hall
CF10.............42 B3

Cardiff Gate Bsns Pk
CF23.............8 B2
Cardiff Gate Ret Pk
CF23.............8 C2
Cardiff High Sch
CF23.............17 B3
Cardiff Ind Pk CF14..16 B3
Cardiff International
Airport / Maes Awyr
Caerdydd-Cymru
CF62.............61 A2
Cardiff International
Arena CF10.......63 C2
Cardiff Rd
Barry / Y Barri
CF63.............53 B1
Cardiff / Caerdydd
CF5...............32 C4
Creigiau CF15......10 C1
Dinas Powis / Dinas
Powys CF64......47 A3
St Fagans / Sain Ffagan
CF5...............30 B3
Cardiff Road Bsns Pk
CF63.............52 C1
Cardiff Royal Infmy
West Wing CF24...35 A2
Cardiff Tertiary Coll /
Coleg Glan Hafren
CF3..............29 A4
Cardiff Tertiary
College / Coleg Glan
Hafren CF24......62 A4
Cardiff Univ Bute Bldg
CF10.............62 A4
Cardiff Univ (Dept of
Music) CF10......62 A4
Cardiff Univ /
Prifysgol Caerdydd
(Cathays Park
Campus) CF10....62 B4
Cardiff Univ Queens
Building CF24.....62 C3
Cardiff Univ Redwood
Bldg CF10........62 B4
Cardigan Cl CF14...47 C3
Cardigan Ct 6 CF5..33 A2
Cardigan Ho 2
CF64.............48 C2
Cardigan Rd 10
CF64.............47 C3
Cardigan St CF5.....33 C3
Cardinal Dr CF14....6 B4
Carew Cl CF62......51 C2
Carew Ct 7 CF14...15 C2
Cargo Rd CF10.....45 C4
Carisbrooke Way
CF23.............26 C3
Carling Ct CF5......37 C3
Carlisle St CF24.....35 C2
Carlotta Way CF10...42 A2
Carlton Cl CF14......5 C3
Carmarthen Cl
CF62.............51 C2
Carmarthen Ct 7
CF5...............33 A2
Carmarthen Ho 4
CF64.............48 C2
Carmarthen Rd 11
CF64.............47 C3
Carmarthen St CF5...33 A2
Carmel Ct CF24....26 B1
Carnegie Dr CF23...17 B1
Carn-yr-Ebol CF63..52 B4
Caroline St / Stryd
Caroline CF10......63 B2
Ca'r Pwll CF64......47 A2
Carter Pl CF5.......22 C1
Cartwright Ct CF24..26 A1
Cartwright La CF5...31 B3
Carys Cl
Cardiff / Caerdydd
CF5...............37 C2
Penarth CF64.......48 B2

Caspian Cl 6 CF3...20 C2
Caspian Point CF10..42 C2
Castell Coch★ CF15..3 A2
Castell Coch View
CF15.............3 A1
Castle Arc CF10.....63 B2
Castle Ave
Cardiff / Caerdydd
CF5...............27 B2
Penarth CF64.......48 C1
Castle Cl
Creigiau CF15......10 B3
3 Dinas Powis / Dinas
Powys CF64......47 C3
Castle Cres CF3.....27 C2
Castle Ct 8 CF3....47 C3
Castle Dr CF64......47 C3
Castlefield Pl CF14..25 A2
Castle Hill CF5......30 B3
Castle Hill Ct CF5...30 B3
Castle La CF24......62 D4
Castleland St CF63..56 A4
Castle Rd CF15......3 A2
Castle Rise CF3.....27 C2
Castle St / Heol Y
Castell CF10.......63 A2
Castle St
Barry / Y Barri
CF62.............54 C3
Taffs Well / Ffynnon Taf
CF15.............2 B3
Castleton St CF3....21 C4
Castle View CF15...14 A4
Caswell Rd 4 CF3...28 A3
CATHAYS..........62 B4
Cathays High Sch
CF24.............25 A1
Cathays Sta CF10...62 B4
CATHAYS PARK....62 B4
Cath Cob Cl CF3....20 B3
Cathedral Cl CF5....24 A1
Cathedral Ct CF5....23 C1
Cathedral Gn The
CF5...............23 C1
Cathedral Rd
Cardiff / Caerdydd
CF11.............33 C3
Cardiff / Caerdydd,
Pontcanna CF11....33 B3
Cathedral Sch The
CF5...............32 C4
Cathedral View
CF14.............24 A2
Cathedral Wlk 6
CF10.............63 B2
Catherine Dr CF15...3 B2
Catherine Meazey
Flats 5 CF64......45 A1
Catherine St CF24...34 B4
Catkin Dr CF64......44 B1
Catrine CF11.......44 C2
Cavendish Cl CF14...5 C2
Cawley Pl CF63.....52 B2
Cawnpore St CF64...44 B1
Caxton Pl CF23.....19 A4
Caynham Ave CF64..59 B4
Cecil Ct 9 CF24.....35 B3
Cecil St CF24.......35 B3
Cedar Ct CF14......16 C4
Cedar Gr CF5.......22 B1
Cedar Ho CF14......14 B2
Cedar Way CF64....48 B3
Cefn Bychan CF15...11 C4
Cefn Carnau Rd
CF14.............16 C1
Cefn Coch CF15.....13 A3
Cefn Coed Ave
CF23.............26 B4
Cefn-Coed Cres
CF23.............26 B3
Cefn-Coed Gdns
CF23.............26 A3

Cefn-Coed Rd
CF23.............26 A4
Cefn Graig CF14.....15 B4
Cefn Llan CF15......11 C3
Cefn Mably Rd CF14..7 A3
Cefn Mount CF64....47 A3
Cefn Nant CF14......4 C1
Cefn Onn Ct CF14....6 A1
Cefn Onn Mdws
CF14..............6 A4
Cefn Onn Prim Sch
CF14..............5 C1
Cefn Penuel CF15...11 C3
Cefn Rd CF14.......24 B3
Cei Dafydd CF63....56 A3
Ceiriog Cl
Barry / Y Barri
CF63.............52 A3
Penarth CF64.......48 C4
Ceiriog Dr CF14.....14 C4
Celandine Rd CF5...30 B1
Celerity Dr CF10.....63 D1
Celtic Gn CF64......47 C3
Celtic Rd CF14......24 C3
Celyn Ave CF23.....17 B1
Celyn Gr CF23......17 C3
Cemaes Cres CF3...20 B1
Cemetery Rd
Barry / Y Barri
CF62.............51 C1
Taffs Well / Ffynnon Taf
CF15.............2 C3
Cennin Pedr CF63...52 C4
Central Ct 10 CF24...35 B2
CF24.............63 D2
Central Sq CF10.....63 B1
Central Way CF64...53 B1
Central Way / Ffordd
Ganolog CF14.....25 B3
Centurion Cl CF5....38 C3
Century Ct CF11....63 A1
Ceri Ave CF62......61 C1
Ceri Rd CF62.......61 A1
Chamberlain Rd
CF14.............23 C3
Chamberlain Row
CF64.............47 C4
Chamomile Cl CF23...7 C1
Chancery La CF11...33 B1
Chandlers Way
CF64.............45 A2
Chandlery Way CF10,
CF11.............42 A2
Channel View CF64..49 B1
Channel View L Ctr★
CF11.............41 C1
Channel View Rd
CF11.............41 B1
Chantry Rise CF64...49 A1
Chantry The CF5....23 B1
Chapel Cl CF64.....47 C4
Chapel La CF14.....45 A1
Chapel Rd CF15.....13 B4
Chapel Row
Cardiff / Caerdydd
CF3..............20 A3
Dinas Powis / Dinas
Powys CF64......47 C4
Chapel Row La 1
CF3..............20 A3
Chapel St CF5......32 C4
Chapel Wood CF23..27 A4
Chard Ave CF3......19 B1
Chargot Rd CF5.....32 C3
Charles Darwin Way
CF62.............55 C2
Charles Pl CF62.....55 A1

Charles St / Heol Siarl
CF10 . . . . .63 C2
Charlock Cl CF14 . . . . . 5 B3
Charlotte Pl CF63 . . . .52 B1
Charlotte Sq CF14 . . . .15 C3
Charlotte St CF64 . . . .44 C1
Charnwood Dr CF23 . . 8 B1
Charter Ave CF62 . . . .51 A3
Charteris Cl CF64 . . . .59 B4
Charteris Cres CF5 . .31 B2
Charteris Rd CF5 . . . .31 B2
Chartley Cl 9 CF3 . .21 A3
Chartwell Ct
Cardiff / Caerdydd
CF5 . . . . .32 B2
Pentyrch CF15 . . . . . . .11 C3
Chartwell Dr CF14 . . . . 6 C2
Chatsworth Cl CF5 . .23 A1
Chatterton Sq
CF11 . . . . .44 C4
Chaucer Cl
Cardiff / Caerdydd
CF3 . . . . .19 C2
Penarth CF64 . . . . .48 C4
Chaucer Rd CF62 . . . .51 C3
Cheam Pl CF14 . . . . . .16 C4
Cheddar Cres CF3 . .19 B1
Chepstow Cl CF5 . . .38 C4
Cheriton Cl CF3 . . . .27 C3
Cheriton Dr CF14 . . . . 6 A2
Cherry Cl
Cardiff / Caerdydd
CF5 . . . . .22 A1
Dinas Powis / Dinas
Powys CF64 . . . . .47 C2
Penarth CF64 . . . . .59 B4
Cherrydale Rd CF5. .31 C2
Cherrydown Cl CF14 . . 6 A2
Cherry Orchard Rd
CF14 . . . . 6 A4
Cherry Tree Cl CF14 . . 6 C3
Cherrywood Cl CF14 . . 6 A2
Chervil Cl 12 CF3 . . .21 A4
Cherwell Cl CF5 . . . .22 C1
Cherwell Rd CF64 . . .48 C2
Cheshire Cl CF14 . . .16 C2
Chester Cl 1 CF3. . .20 C2
Chesterfield St
CF63 . . . . .52 B2
Chester Pl CF11 . . . .41 B3
Chester St CF11 . . . .41 B3
Chesterton Rd CF3. .19 B3
Chestnut Cl CF64 . . .47 B2
Chestnut Rd CF5. . . .31 B4
Chestnut Tree Cl
CF15 . . . . .13 A2
Chestnut Way CF64 . .48 C3
Cheviot Cl CF14 . . . .16 B3
Chichester Rd
CF64 . . . . .44 C1
Chichester Way
CF5 . . . . .31 C2
Chilcote St CF63 . . . .52 B1
Chiltern Cl CF14 . . . .16 B3
Chorley Cl CF5 . . . . .31 A3
Christina St CF10 . . . .42 A2
Christ The King RC
Prim Sch / Ysgol
Gynradd RC Crist y
Brenin CF14 . . . . 6 B1
Chumleigh Cl CF3 . .27 C4
Church Ave 5
CF64 . . . . .49 B4
Church Cl CF14 . . . . . 7 A3
Churchfields CF63 . .52 B3
Churchill Cl CF14 . . . . 6 A4
Churchill Terr
CF63 . . . . .52 C1
Churchill Way / Ffordd
Churchill CF10 . . . . . .63 C2
Church La CF3 . . . . . .20 A3

Church Pl S CF64 . . . .45 B1
Church Rd
Barry / Y Barri
CF63 . . . . .52 B2
Cardiff / Caerdydd,
Caerau CF5 . . . . .38 B3
Cardiff / Caerdydd,
Canton CF5 . . . . .33 B1
Cardiff / Caerdydd
CF5 . . . . .38 C3
Cardiff / Caerdydd,
Lisvane / Llys Faen
CF14 . . . . 7 A3
Cardiff / Caerdydd, Llane
Deyrn CF3 . . . . 9 A1
Cardiff / Caerdydd,
Pentwyn CF23. . . . . . .19 A4
Cardiff / Caerdydd,
Rumney / Rhymni
CF3 . . . . .28 A3
Cardiff / Caerdydd,
Whitchurch CF14 . . . .23 C4
Penarth CF64 . . . . . . .49 B4
Pentyrch CF15 . . . . . .11 C3
St Fagans / Sain Ffagan
CF5 . . . . .12 B1
Church Rise CF5. . . .46 B2
Church St / Stryd yr
Eglwys CF10 . . . . . . .63 B2
Church St CF15 . . . . . 2 B3
Church Terr CF23 . . .35 B4
Church View Cl
CF64 . . . . .44 A3
Cilfedw CF15 . . . . . . .13 B3
Cilgant Bute / Bute
Cres CF10 . . . . .42 B2
Cilgerran Cres
CF14 . . . . .16 A4
Circle Way E CF23 . .18 C1
Circle Way W CF23. .26 C4
City Hall Rd CF10 . . .62 B3
City Rd CF24. . . . . . . .62 C4
City Wharf CF10 . . . .63 D1
Claerwen Dr CF23 . .17 B1
Clarbeston Rd
CF14 . . . . .23 C3
Clare Gdns 3 CF11 . .34 A1
Claremont Ave CF3 . .28 A4
Claremont Cres
CF3 . . . . .28 A4
Clarence Ct CF10 . . .42 A1
Clarence Emb
CF10 . . . . .42 A2
Clarence Mews
CF10 . . . . .41 C1
Clarence Pl CF10 . . .42 A1
Clarence Rd CF10. . .42 A2
Clarendon CF23 . . . .18 A2
Clarendon Rd CF23 . .26 C3
Clare Pl 4 CF11 . . . .34 A1
Clare Rd CF11 . . . . . .41 B4
Clare St CF11 . . . . . . .34 A1
Clarke St CF5. . . . . . .32 A2
Clas Dyfrig 1 CF14 . .24 A3
Clas Gabriel 3
CF14 . . . . .24 A3
Clas Heulog CF14 . .24 A4
Clas Illtyd CF14 . . . . .24 B4
Clas Isan CF14 . . . . .24 B4
Clas Odyn CF14. . . . .15 B1
Clas Teilo 2 CF14. . .24 A3
Clas Tynewydd
CF14 . . . . .24 A4
Clas Ty'n-y-Cae
CF14 . . . . .15 C2
Clas Ty Wern CF14 . .15 C2
Clas Yorath CF14. . . .15 B1
Claude Pl CF24 . . . . .35 A4
Claude Rd
Barry / Y Barri
CF62 . . . . .55 A4
Cardiff / Caerdydd
CF24 . . . . .35 A4
Claude Rd W CF62. . .55 A3

Claverton Way CF23 . .7 C1
Claymore Pl CF11. . .45 A4
Clear Water Way
CF23 . . . . .17 B1
Clearway Ct CF14 . . .23 C4
Cleddau Cl CF3 . . . . .21 B3
Cledwen Cl CF62 . . .54 B4
Cleeve Dr CF14 . . . . .16 B3
Clement Pl CF62 . . . .54 C1
Clevedon Ave CF64 . .58 B1
Clevedon Ct 5
CF3 . . . . .19 C2
Clevedon Rd CF3 . . .19 C2
Cliff Ct CF10 . . . . .42 B2
Cliff Hill CF64. . . . . . .49 B2
Cliff Par CF64 . . . . . . .49 B2
Cliff Pl CF5 . . . . .32 C2
Cliff Rd CF64 . . . . . . .49 B2
Cliff Side CF64. . . . . .49 B1
Cliff St CF64 . . . . .45 B1
Cliff Wood View
CF62 . . . . .54 A1
Clifton Cl 1 CF24. . .35 B2
Clifton Ho CF3 . . . . .26 C3
Clifton Mews 2
CF24 . . . . .35 B2
Clifton St
Barry / Y Barri
CF62 . . . . .55 A2
Cardiff / Caerdydd
CF24 . . . . .35 B2
Clinton Rd CF14 . . . .49 A2
Clipper Rd CF10 . . . .43 B3
Clive Cres CF64. . . . .49 B4
Clive Ct CF5 . . . . .32 C2
Clive La
Cardiff / Caerdydd
CF11 . . . . .41 B2
1 Penarth CF64 . . . .44 C1
Clive Mews CF5 . . . .32 C2
Clive Pl
Barry / Y Barri
CF62 . . . . .55 C1
Cardiff / Caerdydd
CF24 . . . . 62 D4
Penarth CF64 . . . . . . .49 B4
Clive Rd
Barry / Y Barri
CF62 . . . . .55 C2
Cardiff / Caerdydd
CF5 . . . . .32 C2
Clive St CF11 . . . . . . .41 B2
Clodien Ave CF14 . . .25 B2
Cloister Ct CF5 . . . . .39 A4
Clonakilty Way CF23 . .8 B2
Clos Alyn CF3 . . . . . . 8 A1
Clos Avro CF24 . . . . .36 C3
Clos Berriew 5
CF14 . . . . .24 A3
Clos Brynderi CF14 . .15 C3
Clos Brynmellyn 1
CF15 . . . . .13 B2
Clos Caewal CF15. . .11 C4
Clos Cae Wal CF15. . .3 A1
Clos Cas-Bach 7
CF3 . . . . .21 A2
Clos Cefni CF62. . . . .50 C1
Clos Ceirios CF5 . . . .31 B1
Clos Cemmaes 6
CF14 . . . . .24 A3
Clos Chappell CF3 . .20 C1
Clos Coed Hir CF14 . .14 C2
Clos Coedydafarn
CF14 . . . . 7 A2
Clos Cornel CF14 . . .24 A4
Clos Corris 9
CF14 . . . . .24 A3
Clos Cradog CF64. . .48 B1
Clos Cromwell CF14 . .5 A1
Clos Culver CF5 . . . .38 A3
Clos Cwm Barri
CF62 . . . . .54 B3
Clos Cwm Crcunant
CF23 . . . . 8 A1

Clos Cwm Du CF23. . .8 A1
Clos Darran Las
CF15 . . . . .10 B2
Clos Dyfan CF23 . . . .26 B3
Clos Derwen CF3 . . .26 A2
Clos Dewi Saint
CF11 . . . . .33 C2
Clos Dol Heulog
CF23 . . . . 8 A1
Clos Dyfnaint 8
CF3 . . . . .21 A2
Clos Edno CF23. . . . .26 B3
Clos Eiddiw CF5 . . . .31 C1
Clos Elphan CF3 . . . .21 A4
Close The CF14 . . . . .16 C4
Clos Fach CF14 . . . . .15 C4
Clos Gedrych CF11. .32 C1
Clos Glanaber 9
CF3 . . . . .21 A2
Clos Glas Llwch
CF3 . . . . .20 C1
Clos Gwern-y-Mor 13
CF3 . . . . .20 C2
Clos Gwlad-yr-Haf 10
CF3 . . . . .21 A2
Clos Gwy CF23. . . . . . 8 A1
Clos Hafodyrynys 18
CF3 . . . . .20 C2
Clos Hafren 6 CF3 . .21 A2
Clos Halkett CF11. . .40 A4
Clos Hector CF24 . . .36 C3
Clos Hendre CF14 . . .16 A4
Clos Lindsay CF5 . . .37 C3
Clos Llanfair CF5 . . .46 B2
Clos Llawhaden
CF62 . . . . .52 A3
Clos Llewellyn
CF15 . . . . .10 B1
Clos Llysfaen CF14. . .6 A3
Clos-Mabon CF14 . . .15 B4
Clos Maedref CF15. . .14 A1
Clos Maerun 17
CF3 . . . . .20 C2
Clos Maes-y-mor 11
CF3 . . . . .21 A2
Clos Mair CF23 . . . . .26 A3
Clos Mancheldowne
6 CF62 . . . . .55 B3
Clos Manmoel CF3. . .20 C2
Clos Marian CF10. . . .43 B3
Clos Medwy CF3. . . .21 A4
Clos Meifod 7
CF14 . . . . .24 A3
Clos Melin Ddwr
CF14 . . . . 6 B2
Clos Menter CF14. . . .24 C2
Clos Nant Coslech
CF23 . . . . 7 C1
Clos Nant Ddu CF23. . .8 A1
Clos Nanteos CF23. . .19 B4
Clos Nant Glaswg
CF23 . . . . 7 C1
Clos Nant Mwlan
CF23 . . . . 8 A1
Clos Nant Y Cor
CF23 . . . . 8 A1
Clos Nant Y Cwm
CF23 . . . . 8 A1
Clos Newydd CF14. . .23 B4
Clos Padrig CF3 . . . .21 A4
Clos Pantycosyn 12
CF3 . . . . .20 C2
Clos Parc Radyr
CF15 . . . . .22 B4
Clos Peiriant CF63. . .56 A3
Clos Pen Y Clawdd 7
CF3 . . . . .20 C2
Clos Rhedyn CF5 . . .31 C1
Clos Rhiannon CF14 . .5 A1
Clos St Catwg CF5 . .12 B1
Clos Synod 8
CF14 . . . . .24 A3
Clos Taf CF5 . . . . . . .23 B2
Clos Tawe CF62 . . . . .50 C1

Clos Tecwyn CF23. . .26 A3
Clos Ton Mawr CF14 . .5 A1
Clos Tregare 10
CF3 . . . . .20 C2
Clos Treoda CF14 . . .15 B1
Clos Ty Bronna
CF5 . . . . .31 A3
Clos Ty Clyd CF14 . . .23 A4
Clos Tyla Bach CF3. .21 B3
Clos Tyniad Glo
CF3 . . . . .56 A3
Clos Vellacott /
Vellacott Cl CF10 . .63 C1
Clos William CF14 . . .5 A1
Clos Y Berllan 4
CF3 . . . . .21 A2
Clos-y-Betws 8
CF3 . . . . .20 C2
Clos-y-Blaidd CF14. . .5 B4
Clos-y-Broch CF14. . .5 C3
Clos Y Bryn CF14. . . . 4 B1
Clos-y-Carlwm CF14 . .5 B4
Clos-y-Ceinach
CF14 . . . . 5 C3
Clos Y Craig CF14 . . .4 C1
Clos-y-Culfor 15
CF3 . . . . .20 C2
Clos-y-Cwarra CF5. .30 A1
Clos-y-Draenog
CF14 . . . . 5 C3
Clos Y Dryw CF14 . . .5 C4
Clos-y-Dyfrgi CF14. . .5 B3
Clos Y Ffynnon CF23. .8 A1
Clos Y Fran CF14. . . . 5 C4
Clos Y Gamlas
CF14 . . . . .14 B2
Clos Y Gelyn CF23. . .18 C3
Clos-y-Gof CF5. . . . .30 A1
Clos Y Gorllewin /
West CF10. . . . . . . .42 B2
Clos Y Gwadd CF14. . .5 B3
Clos Y Gwalch CF14. . .5 C4
Clos y Gwyddfid
CF15 . . . . .13 A4
Clos Y Hebog CF14. . .5 C4
Clos Y Mynydd
CF15 . . . . .13 A3
Clos Y Nant 4 CF5. . .31 B4
Clos Yr Aer CF14. . . .15 C4
Clos Yr Alarch CF14. . .5 C4
Clos-Yr-Ardd CF14 . .15 B3
Clos Yr Eos CF14. . . . 5 C4
Clos yr Erw CF64. . . .48 B1
Clos-y-Gornant 5
CF3 . . . . .21 A2
Clos Yr Hafod CF14 . .15 C4
Clos Yr Harbwr
CF62 . . . . .55 A1
Clos-y-Rhiw CF5 . . .38 A3
Clos-yr-Onnen
CF3 . . . . .21 A2
Clos Yr Wenallt
CF14 . . . . 4 C1
Clos Yr Wylan
CF62 . . . . .55 C1
Clos Ystum Taf
CF14 . . . . .23 A4
Clos Y Wern CF14 . . .15 C4
Clos-y-Wiwer CF14. . .5 C3
Clovelly Cres CF3 . . .19 A1
Clover Gr CF5 . . . . . .22 B1
Clun Terr CF24 . . . . .25 C2
Clwyd CF64. . . . . .45 C1
Clwyd Ho 3 CF23. . .26 B2
Clydach St CF11 . . . .41 C3
Clydesmuir Ind Est
CF24 . . . . .36 A4
Clydesmuir Rd
CF24 . . . . .36 A3
Clyde St 2 CF24. . . . .35 B1
Clyro Pl CF14 . . . . . .23 C3
Coaster Pl CF10 . . . .43 B3
Coates Pl CF3 . . . . . .20 A3
Coates Rd CF64. . . . .48 C1

Cobol Rd CF3 . . . . 21 B3
Coburn St CF24 . . . . . . 34 C4
Coed Arhyd CF5 . . . . . 37 A4
Coed Arian CF14 . . . . . 24 A3
Coed Bach CF62 . . . . . 50 C2
Coed Briwnant CF14 . . 5 A1
Coedcae St CF11 . . . . 41 B3
Coed Ceirios CF14 . . . 15 B3
Coed Cochwyn Ave
CF14 . . . . 5 C1
Coed Criafol CF63 . . . 52 B4
Coed Edeyrn CF23 . . . 26 C4
Coeden Dal CF23 . . . 18 B4
Coed Glas Prim Sch
CF14 . . . . 16 C4
Coed Glas Rd CF14 . . 16 A4
Coedlan Y Coleg /
Academic Ave
CF14 . . . . 25 A3
Coed Mawr CF62 . . . 50 C2
Coedriglan Dr CF5 . . 37 A3
Coed Y Capel CF62 . . 50 C2
Coed-y-Fellin CF62 . . 54 C4
Coed-y-Gores
CF23 . . . . 18 B1
Coed-y-Llyn
Cardiff / Caerdydd
CF23 . . . . 26 A4
Radyr CF15 . . . . 13 A3
Coed Yr Odyn CF62 . . 54 B2
Coed Yr Ynn CF14 . . 16 A4
Coed Y Wenallt
CF14 . . . . 4 C1
COG 58 C3
COGAN 44 B1
Cogan Ct CF64 . . . . . 44 B2
Cogan Hill CF64 . . . . 44 B2
Cogan Pill Rd CF64 . . 44 B2
Cogan Prim Sch
CF64 . . . . 44 B1
Cogan Sta CF64 . . . . 44 B2
Cogan Terr CF24 . . . . 62 B4
Cog Rd CF64 . . . . 58 B3
Coigne Terr CF63 . . . 56 B4
Coity Cl CF3 . . . . 21 A3
Colbourne Wlk 9
CF11 . . . . 33 B1
Colchester Ave
CF23 . . . . 27 A1
Colchester Ct CF23 . 26 C1
Colchester Est
CF23 . . . . 27 A1
Colchester Factory Est
CF23 . . . . 35 C4
COLCOT 51 A2
Colcot Prim Sch
CF62 . . . . 51 B4
Colcot Rd CF62 . . . . 51 A1
Coldbrook Cl CF63 . . 53 A3
Coldbrook Rd E
CF63 . . . . 52 C3
Coldbrook Rd W
CF63 . . . . 52 B2
Cold Stores Rd
CF10 . . . . 43 A1
Coldstream Terr
CF11 . . . . 34 A1
Coleford Dr CF3 . . . . 21 B2

Coleg = college

Coleg Cerdd a Drama
Cymru / Welsh Coll
of Music & Drama
CF10 . . . . 62 A3
Coleg Glan Hafren /
Cardiff Tertiary Coll
CF3 . . . . 29 A4
Coleg Glan Hafren /
Cardiff Tertiary
College CF24 . . . . . 62 C3
Coleridge Ave
CF64 . . . . 48 C4

Coleridge Cres
CF62 . . . . 51 B3
Coleridge Rd CF11 . . 40 C1
Colin Way CF5 . . . . . 31 C2
Collard Cres CF62 . . 51 C2
College Cl CF14 . . . . 24 A4
College Fields Cl
CF62 . . . . 55 B4
College Pl CF62 . . . . 55 B4
College Rd
Barry / Y Barri
CF62 . . . . 55 B3
Barry / Y Barri, Cwm
Talwg CF62 . . . . . . 55 B4
Cardiff / Caerdydd
Cathays CF10 . . . . . 62 B4
Cardiff / Caerdydd
Llandaff North
CF14 . . . . 24 A3
Cardiff / Caerdydd
CF14 . . . . 24 A4
5 Cardiff / Caerdydd
CF14 . . . . 24 A4
Cardiff / Caerdydd
Llandaff North
CF14 . . . . 24 A3
Collivaud Pl CF24 . . . 42 C4
Columbus Cl CF62 . . 52 A3
Columbus Wlk
CF10 . . . . 63 C1
Colum Dr CF10 . . . . . 34 A4
Colum St CF64 . . . . . 53 B1
Colum Pl CF10 . . . . . 34 A4
Colum Rd CF10 . . . . . 34 A4
Colum Terr CF10 . . . 62 A4
Colwill Rd CF14 . . . . 24 A2
Colwinstone Cl
CF14 . . . . 23 C3
Colwinstone St
CF14 . . . . 23 C3
Colwyn Ho CF14 . . . 23 C4
Colwyn Rd CF3 . . . . . 28 B3
Comet St CF24 . . . . . 35 A2
Comfrey Cl 11 CF3 . . 21 A4
Commercial Rd
CF63 . . . . 52 A1
Compass Rd CF10 . . 43 A1
Compton St CF11 . . . 41 A4
Conifer Ct CF5 . . . . . 30 C4
Connaught Ho
CF11 . . . . 33 C2
Connaught Rd
CF24 . . . . 35 A4
Constant Cl CF11 . . . 45 A4
Constellation St
CF24 . . . . 35 B2
Conway Cl CF24 . . . . 47 C3
Conway Dr CF62 . . . . 50 C1
Conway Rd CF11 . . . 33 B3
Conybeare Rd
Cardiff / Caerdydd
CF5 . . . . 32 C3
Sully CF64 . . . . 58 B2
Cook Rd CF62 . . . . . . 52 A4
Coopers Ct 9 CF10 . 63 B2
Coopers Yd CF10 . . . 63 B1
Copleston Rd CF14 . . 23 C2
Copperfield Ct 1
CF62 . . . . 55 C4
Copperfield Dr CF14 . 6 A2
Copper St CF24 . . . . 35 B2
Coppins The CF14 . . . 6 C3
Copse Wlk CF23 . . . . 8 B2
Copthorne Way
CF5 . . . . 37 B2
Cora St CF63 . . . . . . 56 A4
Corbett Rd
Cardiff / Caerdydd
CF10 . . . . 62 A4
Llandough / Llandochau
CF64 . . . . 44 A2
Corinthian Ct CF64 . 44 A1
Cork Dr CF23 . . . . 8 B2
Cormorant Cl CF3 . . 20 C4
Cornelly Cl CF14 . . . . 23 C3

Cornelly St CF14 . . . 23 C3
Cornerswell La 3
CF64 . . . . 48 C3
Cornerswell Pl
CF64 . . . . 48 B4
Cornerswell Rd
CF64 . . . . 48 C4
Cornfield Cl CF14 . . . 5 B1
Cornflower Cl CF14 . . 5 B1
Corn Glas CF63 . . . . 52 C3
Cornish Cl CF11 . . . . 41 C2
Cornwall St CF11 . . . 41 A3
Cornwall Rd CF62 . . 51 C1
Cornwall Rise CF62 . 51 C1
Cornwall St CF11 . . . 41 B4
Cornwood Cl CF5 . . . 22 C1
Coronation Rd
CF14 . . . . 24 C4
Coronation St CF63 . 56 A3
Coronation Terr
CF64 . . . . 45 B1
Corporation Rd
CF11 . . . . 41 C2
Corpus Christi RC
High Sch CF23 . . . . . 7 B1
Corsham Rd CF24 . . 26 B3
Corvette Ct CF10 . . . 42 B3
Corwen Cres CF14 . . 23 C3
Cory Pl CF11 . . . . 45 A4
CORYTON 14 B3
Coryton Cl CF14 . . . . 14 C3
Coryton Cres CF14 . . 14 C3
Coryton Dr CF14 . . . . 14 B3
Coryton Halt CF14 . . 14 C2
Coryton Prim Sch
CF14 . . . . 14 B3
Coryton Rise CF14 . . 14 B3
Cory Way CF63 . . . . . 56 A2
Cosheston Rd CF5 . . 22 C1
COSMESTON 59 B3
Cosmeston Dr
CF64 . . . . 59 B3
Cosmeston Lakes Ctry
Pk★ CF64 . . . . 59 C4
Cosmeston Lakes Ctry
Pk Visitor Ctr★
CF64 . . . . 59 A3
Cosmeston Medieval
Village★ CF64 . . . . 59 A2
Cosmeston St CF24 . 25 B1
Cosslett Pl CF11 . . . 41 C2
Cotswold Ave CF14 . . 6 C3
Cotswold St CF23 . . 17 C2
Cotswold Rise
CF63 . . . . 52 B1
Cottage Cl CF14 . . . . 6 A2
Cottrell Rd
2 Cardiff / Caerdydd
CF14 . . . . 24 A4
Cardiff / Caerdydd,
Roath / Y Rhath
CF24 . . . . 35 A4
Cottrell Sq CF11 . . . 40 B1
Cotts The CF14 . . . . . 5 C3
Countess Pl CF14 . . 48 C3
Countisbury Ave
Cardiff / Caerdydd
CF3 . . . . 19 C2
Cardiff / Caerdydd
CF3 . . . . 19 C3
Court Cl CF14 . . . . . . 24 B3
Courtenay Cl CF3 . . 20 A3
Courtenay Rd
9 Barry / Y Barri
CF63 . . . . 52 B1
Cardiff / Caerdydd
CF24 . . . . 35 C2
Courtis Rd CF5 . . . . . 30 C1
Courtlands CF62 . . . . 54 C2
Court Mews 4
CF63 . . . . 52 B1
Court Newton 3
CF63 . . . . 52 B1

Court Rd
Barry / Y Barri, Barry
Dock CF63 . . . . 56 A4
Barry / Y Barri, Cadoxton
CF63 . . . . 52 B1
Cardiff / Caerdydd
CF11 . . . . 41 B4
Cardiff / Caerdydd,
Gwaun Treoda
CF14 . . . . 24 B3
Court Specl Sch The /
Ysgol-y-Llys CF14 . . 6 B1
Court The
Cardiff / Caerdydd,
Lisvane / Llys Faen
CF14 . . . . 6 C4
4 Cardiff / Caerdydd,
Roath / Y Rhath
CF24 . . . . 35 B4
Courtyard The 15
CF24 . . . . 35 B1
Coveny St CF24 . . . . 35 C2
Cowbridge Rd E
Cardiff / Caerdydd,
Canton CF5 . . . . . . 33 A2
Cardiff / Caerdydd,
Victoria Park CF5 . . 32 B2
Cowbridge Rd W
CF5 . . . . 38 B4
Cowbridge St 3
CF63 . . . . 52 B2
Cowper Cl CF64 . . . . 48 C4
Cowper Ct CF24 . . . . 62 D4
Cowper Pl CF24 . . . . 62 D4
Cowslip Cl CF23 . . . . 8 B1
Cowslip Dr CF64 . . . 44 B1
Coychurch Rise
CF63 . . . . 52 A3
Craddock St CF11 . . 33 C1
Cradoc Rd CF14 . . . . 24 B4
Cragside CF3 . . . . . . 20 C2
Craig Castell CF15 . . 13 B3
Craiglee Dr CF10 . . . 63 C1
Craigmuir Rd CF24 . . 36 A3
Craig Y Mor Ct
CF64 . . . . 58 B2
Craig-y-Parc Sch
CF15 . . . . 11 B1
Craig Yr Allt CF14 . . . 4 C1
Cranberry Way
CF23 . . . . 7 C1
Cranbrook St CF24 . . 62 C4
Cranford CF14 . . . . . . 6 B2
Cranleigh Rise CF3 . 27 C4
Cranmer Ct CF5 . . . . 32 B4
Cranwell Cl 4 CF14 . . 5 C3
Craven Wlk CF64 . . . 59 C4
Crawford Dr CF23 . . . 8 B1
Crawley Cl CF14 . . . . 5 C3
Crawshay St CF10 . . 63 B1
Crediton Rd CF3 . . . . 19 C2
CREIGIAU 10 A3
Creigiau Prim Sch /
Ysgol Gynradd
Creigiau CF15 . . . . 10 A3
Crescent Ct CF23 . . 18 A3
Crescent The
Barry / Y Barri
CF62 . . . . 54 B4
Cardiff / Caerdydd
CF5 . . . . 31 B3
Cardiff / Caerdydd,
Culverhouse Cross
CF5 . . . . 37 C2
Cardiff / Caerdydd,
Llandaff / Llandaf
CF5 . . . . 32 C4
Cressfield Dr CF23 . . 8 C1
Cresswell Cl CF3 . . . 21 A4
Cresswell Ct CF62 . . 51 C3
Cressy Rd CF23 . . . . 26 B1
Cresta Gr CF5 . . . . . 30 A1

Criccieth Ct CF64 . . . 47 C4
Criccieth Rd CF3 . . . 28 B3
Crickhowell Rd
CF3 . . . . 20 C2
Crickhowell Wlk
CF3 . . . . 20 C3
Crockherbtown La
CF10 . . . . 62 B3
Croes Cadarn CF23 . . 8 A2
Croescadarn Cl 8
CF23 . . . . 8 B1
Croescadarn Rd
CF23 . . . . 8 A1
Croffta CF64 . . . . 47 A2
Crofta CF14 . . . . 6 C1
Croft Gdns CF64 . . . 58 A2
Crofts St CF24 . . . . . 35 A3
Cromwell Rd CF14 . . 24 C4
Cross Common Rd
CF64 . . . . 47 C1
Crossfield Rd CF62 . . 54 C3
Cross Pl CF14 . . . . . . 25 A1
Cross St
Barry / Y Barri
CF63 . . . . 56 A4
Tongwynlais CF15 . . . 3 A1
Crossways Rd CF5 . . 31 A1
Crossways St CF63 . 56 A4
Crosswells Way
CF5 . . . . 30 C2
Crown Way / Ffordd Y
Goron CF14 . . . . . . 25 A1
Croyde Ave CF3 . . . . 19 C2
Crumlin Dr CF3 . . . . 21 A3
Crundale Cres
CF14 . . . . 16 C4
Crwys La CF63 . . . . . 52 B3
Crwys Lofts 4
CF24 . . . . 34 C4
Crwys Mews 1
CF24 . . . . 34 B4
Crwys Pl CF24 . . . . . 34 C4
Crwys Rd CF24 . . . . . 34 C4
Crystal Ave CF23 . . . 17 A1
Crystal Ct CF11 . . . . 41 B3
Crystal Glen CF14 . . 16 C2
Crystal Rise CF14 . . 16 C2
Crystal Wood Rd
CF14 . . . . 16 C2
Cuckoofield Cl
CF15 . . . . 13 A4
Cudd Y Coed CF63 . . 52 C3
Culver Cl CF64 . . . . . 48 B1
Culver Cross CF5 . . . 37 B3
CULVERHOUSE
CROSS 37 C1
Cumberland St CF5 . 33 A1
Cumnock Pl CF24 . . 35 B1
Cumnock Terr 4
CF24 . . . . 35 B1
Cumrae St 7 CF24 . 35 B1
Cunningham Cl
CF23 . . . . 25 C4
Curlew Cl CF14 . . . . . 15 A2
Curll Ave CF14 . . . . . 25 A3
Curran Emb CF10 . . 41 C3
Curran Rd CF10 . . . . 41 C3
Custom House Pl 1
CF64 . . . . 45 B1
Customhouse St /
Heol Y Tollty
CF10 . . . . 63 B1
Cwlwm Cariad
CF63 . . . . 53 B4
Cwm Barry Way
CF62 . . . . 54 C3
Cwmcarn Cl CF3 . . . 20 C3
Cwm-Cidy La CF62 . 54 A3
Cwmdare St CF24 . . 25 B1
Cwm Gwynlais
CF15 . . . . 14 A4

Cwm Nofydd CF14 . . . . . 15 B4
Cwm Parc CF62. . . . . . . 54 C4
CWM TALWG. 55 A4
Cwrt Aethen CF63 . . . 52 B4
Cwrt Bala CF3 . . . . 20 B1
Cwrt Boston CF24 . . . . 27 C1
Cwrt Brynteg CF15. . . 13 C1
Cwrt Cefn CF14 . . . . . . 6 C2
Cwrt Coles CF24 . . . . . 27 C1
Cwrt Deri CF14 . . . . . 15 B4
Cwrt Dewi Sant **1**
  CF24 . . . . 35 A1
Cwrt Dyfed CF63. . . . 52 C3
Cwrt Edward **7**
  CF62 . . . . 55 B3
Cwrt Eglwys Newydd
  CF14 . . . . 15 A1
Cwrt Eirlys CF63 . . . . 52 A4
Cwrt Finchley **5**
  CF5. . . . . 31 C3
Cwrt Glas CF14 . . . . . 16 C4
Cwrt Gwenllian
  CF63 . . . . 53 A1
Cwrt Heol Casnewydd
  5 CF24 . . . . 35 B4
Cwrt Iorweth CF5. . . . 32 C2
Cwrt Leubren CF3 . . 52 A4
Cwrt Llandough
  CF64 . . . . 44 A2
Cwrt Melin Y Rhos **14**
  CF63 . . . . 52 B1
Cwrt Newydd CF64 . . 47 B3
Cwrt Pencoedtre **3**
  CF63 . . . . 52 A3
Cwrt Pensarn CF3 . . 20 B1
Cwrt Pentre Bach **7**
  CF3 . . . . 21 A4
Cwrt Roberts CF5. . . 37 C3
Cwrt St Cyres CF64 . 48 B4
Cwrt Trem Yr Ynys **2**
  CF63 . . . . 55 C3
Cwrt Ty Mawr CF64 . 48 B2
Cwrt-Ty-Mynydd
  CF15 . . . . 13 B2
Cwrt-y-Cadno CF5 . 30 A1
Cwrt-y-Farchnad **1**
  CF5. . . . . 33 B2
Cwrt-yr-Ala Ave
  CF5. . . . . 38 A3
Cwrt-yr-Ala Jun Sch
  CF5. . . . . 38 A4
Cwrt-yr-Ala Rd
  CF5. . . . . 38 B2
Cwrt Yr Ardal CF3. . 20 B1
Cwrt-y-Vil Rd
  CF64 . . . . 49 A3
Cwrt-y-Vil Road
  (Lower) CF64 . . . . . 49 A2
Cyfarthfa St CF24 . . 62 D4
Cymmer St CF11. . . . 41 B3
Cymric Cl CF5 . . . . . . 31 B1
Cynan Cl CF63 . . . . . 52 B3
CYNCOED 17 B2
Cyncoed Ave CF23 . 18 A2
Cyn-Coed Cres
  CF23 . . . . 18 A2
Cyncoed Gdns
  CF23 . . . . 26 B3
Cyncoed Pl CF23. . . 17 C2
Cyncoed Rd CF23 . . 17 C1
Cyncoed Rise CF23 . 17 C2
Cyntwell Ave CF5 . . 38 A3
Cyntwell Cres CF5 . 38 A4
Cyntwell Pl CF5. . . . 38 A4
Cynulliad
  Cenedlaethol Cymru /
  Nat Assembly for
  Wales The CF10. . . . 42 B2
Cypress Dr CF3 . . . . . 21 B4
Cypress Pl CF5 . . . . . 22 C2
Cyril Cres CF24 . . . . . 35 B3

Cyril St CF63 . . . . 56 B4

D

Dafydd Pl CF63 . . . . . 52 A3
Daisy St CF5. . . . . . . 32 C2
Dalcross St CF24 . . . 26 A1
Dale Ave CF14 . . . . . . 16 A1
Dale Ct CF62 . . . . 51 C3
Dalmuir Rd CF24 . . . 36 A3
Dalton Ct **2** CF24 . . . 34 B4
Dalton St
  2 Cardiff / Caerdydd,
  Cathays CF24 . . . . . 25 C1
  Cardiff / Caerdydd
  CF24 . . . . 34 B4
Danescourt Halt
  CF5. . . . . 23 A2
Danescourt Jun & Inf
  Sch CF5 . . . . 23 A2
Danescourt Way
  CF5. . . . . 23 A3
Daniell Cl CF64 . . . . 58 A2
Daniel St
  Barry / Y Barri
  CF63 . . . . 52 B2
  Cardiff / Caerdydd
  CF24 . . . . 25 C1
Dannog Y Coed
  CF23 . . . . 52 B4
Dan-y-Bryn Ave
  CF15 . . . . 13 A2
Dan-y-Bryn Cl
  CF15 . . . . 13 B2
Dan-y-Coed Cl
  CF23 . . . . 17 B2
Dan-y-Coed Rd
  Cardiff / Caerdydd
  CF23 . . . . 17 B2
  Cardiff / Caerdydd
  CF23 . . . . 17 C2
Dan-y-Coed Rise
  CF23 . . . . 17 B2
Dan Y Graig CF14 . . . 14 C4
Dan Y Mynydd CF14. . 5 A3
Dan-Yr-Heol CF23. . . 17 B2
Darby Rd CF24. . . . . . 43 C4
Darran St CF24 . . . . . 34 A4
Dartington Dr CF23 . . 7 C1
David Davies Rd
  CF63 . . . . 56 B3
David St
  Barry / Y Barri
  CF63 . . . . 52 C3
  Cardiff / Caerdydd
  CF10 . . . . 63 C2
Davies Pl CF5. . . . . . . 32 A3
Davies St CF63 . . . . . 52 A1
Daviot Ct CF24. . . . . . 26 A1
Daviot St CF24 . . . . . . 26 A1
Davis St CF24. . . . . . . 63 D2
Davis's Terr **4**
  CF14 . . . . 15 B1
Davnic Cl **5** CF63. . . 52 B1
Dawan Cl CF62 . . . . . 55 A4
Deans Cl CF5. . . . . . . 32 C4
Deans Ct CF62 . . . . . 60 C1
Dean's Ct CF5 . . . . . . 23 C1
De Bawdip Rd
  CF24 . . . . 36 A4
De Braose Cl CF5 . . 22 C3
De Burgh Pl **9**
  CF11 . . . . 33 C1
De Burgh St CF11 . . 33 C1
De Clare Dr CF15 . . 14 A1
De Croche Pl CF11. . 33 C1
Deemuir Rd CF24 . . . 36 A3
Deemuir Sq CF24 . . . 36 A3
Deepdale Cl CF23. . . 26 A3
Deepdene Cl CF5 . . 30 A1
Deepfield Cl CF5 . . . 30 A1
Deepwood Cl CF5. . . 30 A1
Deere Cl CF5 . . . . 38 A4

Deere Pl CF5 . . . . 38 A4
Deere Rd CF5. . . . . . . 38 A4
Deganwy Cl CF14 . . . 5 C1
De Havilland Rd
  CF24 . . . . 36 B3
Dell The CF3. . . . . 20 A4
Delta St **3** CF11 . . . . 33 B1
Denbigh Ct
  3 Cardiff / Caerdydd
  CF14 . . . . 15 A2
  9 Penarth CF64 . . . 48 C2
Denbigh Rd CF64 . . . 47 C4
Denbigh St CF11. . . . 33 B1
Denbigh Way CF62. . 51 C2
Denison Way CF5. . . 30 A1
Denstone Ct CF24 . . 26 B3
Dental Dr / Rhodfa'r
  Deintyddion CF14. . 25 A1
Denton Rd CF5 . . . . . 33 B1
Denvale Trad Pk
  CF24 . . . . 42 C4
Denys Cl CF64 . . . . . . 47 B4
Deri Cl CF23 . . . . 27 A1
Dering Rd CF23. . . . . . 8 C1
Deri Rd CF23 . . . . 26 C1
Derwen Rd CF23. . . . 17 C4
Derwent Cl CF14. . . . 5 C2
Deryn Ct CF23. . . . . . 18 C4
Despenser Gdns **5**
  CF11 . . . . 34 A1
Despenser Pl **6**
  CF11 . . . . 34 A1
Despenser Rd CF64 . 58 A2
Despenser St CF11. . 34 A1
Dessmuir Rd CF24 . . 36 A3
Devon Ave CF63 . . . . 51 C1
Devon Pl CF11. . . . . . 41 B3
Devon St CF11. . . . . . 41 A3
Dew Cres CF5 . . . . . . 39 A4
Dewi Ct CF5 . . . . 32 B4
Diamond St CF24 . . . 35 B2
Diana La CF24 . . . . . . 26 A1
Diana St CF24 . . . . . . 26 A1
Dickens Ave CF3 . . . . 19 B3
Digby Cl **3** CF5. . . . 23 A2
Digby St CF63 . . . . . . 56 A4
Dinas Pl CF11 . . . . . . 41 B3
DINAS POWIS / DINAS
  POWYS. 47 B4
Dinas Powis Inf Sch
  CF64 . . . . 47 B4
DINAS POWYS /
  DINAS POWIS. . . . 47 B4
Dinas Powys Sta
  CF64 . . . . 47 A2
Dinas Rd CF64. . . . . . 48 C2
Dinas St CF11 . . . . . . 63 A1
Dingle Cl CF62. . . . . . 54 B1
Dingle La **3** CF64. . . 49 A4
Dingle Rd CF64 . . . . . 49 A4
Dingle Road Sta
  CF64 . . . . 49 A4
Ditchling Ct CF64 . . . 49 A2
Dobbins Rd CF63 . . . 53 A2
Dochdwy Rd CF64 . . 44 B2
Dock Rd CF62 . . . . . . 55 C1
Dock St CF64 . . . . 44 C1
Dock View Rd CF63 . 56 A3
Doe Cl CF23 . . . . 27 A1
Dogfield St CF24 . . . 25 C1
Dogo St CF11. . . . . . . 33 B3
Dolgoch Cl CF3. . . . . 20 A1
Dol Gwartheg CF64 . 48 B2
Dolwen Rd CF14 . . . . 23 C1
Dol-y-Felin CF15. . . . 10 A2
Dombey Cl CF14 . . . . 6 A2
Dominion Bsns Ctr
  CF24 . . . . 35 C4
Dominion Way
  CF24 . . . . 35 C4
Dominion Way Ind Est
  CF24 . . . . 35 C4
Donald St CF24 . . . . . 26 A1
Doniford Cl CF64 . . . 58 B3

Donnington Rd
  CF64 . . . . 53 B1
Dorchester Ave
  CF23 . . . . 26 C2
Dorchester Mans **5**
  CF14 . . . . 14 C2
Doreen Ford Ct
  CF24 . . . . 35 C3
Dorothy Ave CF62. . . 51 B3
Dorothy Cl CF62 . . . . 51 B3
Dorset Ave CF63 . . . . 51 C1
Dorset St CF11 . . . . . . 41 B3
Douglas Cl CF5 . . . . . 23 A2
Douglas Ct CF14. . . . 5 C1
Dovedale Cl CF23 . . 26 A3
Dovedale St CF63 . . 52 B1
Dovey Cl
  Barry / Y Barri
  CF62 . . . . 50 C3
  Cardiff / Caerdydd
  CF3 . . . . 20 A1
Dowlais Rd CF24. . . . 42 C4
Dowland Rd CF64. . . 48 B1
Dowlands Way CF3 . 27 C2
Downfield Cl CF64 . . 44 B2
Downton Grange
  CF3 . . . . 28 B2
Downton Rd CF3. . . . 28 A2
Downton Rise CF3 . . 28 A2
Doyle Ave CF5 . . . . . . 31 C4
Doyle Ct CF5 . . . . 31 C4
Dragonfly Dr CF62 . . 60 C4
Drake Wlk CF10 . . . . 63 C1
Drawlings Cl **1**
  CF3 . . . . 20 A4
Dray Ct **10** CF10. . . . 63 B2
Driscoll Ct **8** CF24. . 35 B3
Driscoll Workshops
  CF10 . . . . 63 D2
Drive The
  Cardiff / Caerdydd
  CF5. . . . . 31 B3
  Dinas Powis / Dinas
  Powys CF64 . . . . 47 C3
Drope Rd CF5 . . . . . . 37 A4
Drope Terr CF5 . . . . . 37 A4
Dros y Mor CF64 . . . . 49 B2
Dros-y-Morfa CF3. . . 28 B2
Drovers Way CF15 . . 13 B1
Drury Cl CF14 . . . . . . 5 C2
Drybrook Cl **9** CF3 . 20 C2
Dryburgh Ave CF14 . 16 A1
Dryden Cl CF3 . . . . . . 19 B3
Dryden Rd CF64 . . . . 48 C4
Dryden Terr CF62 . . . 51 C3
Drylla CF64 . . . . 47 A2
Drysgol Rd CF15. . . . 13 B1
Dudley Cl CF10 . . . . . 42 A1
Dudley Pl CF62 . . . . . 55 A3
Dudley St CF10 . . . . . 42 A1
Duffryn Ave CF23 . . . 17 B2
Duffryn Cl CF23. . . . . 17 B2
Duffryn Ho **5** CF64 . 47 C3
Duffryn Rd CF23 . . . . 17 C2
Duffryn St CF24 . . . . 63 C2
Dugdale Wlk **14**
  CF11 . . . . 33 C1
Duke St / Heol Y Dug
  CF10 . . . . 63 B2
Duke Street Arc **4**
  CF10 . . . . 63 B2
Dulverton Ave CF3 . . 20 A3
Dulverton Dr CF64 . . 58 B2
Dulwich Gdns CF5 . . 33 A3
Dulwich Ho CF5 . . . . 33 A3
Dumballs Rd CF10 . . 42 A3
Dumfries Pl CF10. . . 62 C3
Dummer Cl **2** CF3. . 20 C3
Dunbar Cl CF23. . . . . 8 B1
Duncan Cl CF3 . . . . . 20 A1
Dungarvan Dr CF23 . 8 B1
Dunkery Cl CF3 . . . . . 19 B1
Dunleavy Dr CF11. . . 44 B3
Dunlin Ct **9** CF63. . . 55 C4

Dunraven Cl CF64. . . . 47 C3
Dunraven Ho CF10. . . 63 A2
Dunraven Rd CF11. . . 40 C4
Dunraven St CF62 . . 54 C2
Dunsmuir Rd CF24. . . 36 A2
Dunster Dr CF64 . . . . 58 A2
Dunster Rd CF3. . . . . 20 A3
Durham St CF11 . . . . 41 B3
Durleigh Cl CF3 . . . . 19 C3
Durlston Cl **5**
  CF14 . . . . 23 B3
Duxford Cl CF5 . . . . . 22 C2
Dyfan Rd CF63. . . . . . 52 A2
Dyfed CF64 . . . . 45 B1
Dyfed Ho **1** CF23 . . 26 B2
Dyffryn Pl CF62 . . . . . 51 A2
Dyfnallt Rd CF63. . . . 52 A3
Dyfrig Cl CF5 . . . . 32 A2
Dyfrig Rd CF5 . . . . . . 32 A2
Dyfrig St
  Barry / Y Barri
  CF62 . . . . 56 A1
  Cardiff / Caerdydd
  CF11 . . . . 33 C3
Dylan Cl CF64 . . . . . . 44 B2
Dylan Cres CF63 . . . . 52 B3
Dylan Pl CF24 . . . . . . 62 D4
Dynevor Rd CF23 . . . 26 C3
Dyserth Rd CF64 . . . . 48 C3

E

Earl Cres CF62. . . . . . 55 C1
Earl Cunningham Ct
  CF10 . . . . 63 D1
Earle Pl CF5 . . . . 33 B1
Earl La CF11. . . . . 41 B1
Earl Rd CF64 . . . . 48 C3
Earls Court Pl CF23 . 26 C1
Earl's Court Rd
  CF23 . . . . 26 C1
Earl St CF11 . . . . 41 B1
Earlswood Rd CF14 . 16 B3
East Bay Cl CF10. . . . 35 A1
Eastbourne Ct **3**
  CF63 . . . . 52 C3
EASTBROOK. 47 C4
Eastbrook Cl CF64 . . 47 B4
Eastbrook Sta
  CF64 . . . . 47 C4
Eastern Ave CF23 . . 27 A2
Eastern Bsns Pk The
  CF3 . . . . 20 B4
Eastern Cl **2** CF3. . 20 A4
Eastgate Bsns Pk
  CF3 . . . . 28 B1
East Gr CF24. . . . . . . 62 D3
East Grove La CF24 . 62 D3
EAST MOORS. 43 B4
East Moors Bsns Pk
  CF24 . . . . 43 B4
East Moors Rd
  CF24 . . . . 42 C4
East Point CF3 . . . . . 28 C2
East Rd CF64 . . . . 53 C1
East Rise CF14. . . . . . 17 A4
East Tyndall St
  CF24 . . . . 35 B1
East View Terr
  CF62 . . . . 55 A2
East Wlk CF62 . . . . . . 51 B1
Ebwy Ct CF5. . . . . 38 C4
Eckley Rd CF64 . . . . . 58 A2
Eclipse St CF24 . . . . . 35 A2
Eddystone Cl CF11. . 41 A3
Edgehill Ave CF14 . . 5 A1
Edgehill Ct CF14. . . . 5 B1
Edinburgh Ct **11**
  CF11 . . . . 33 C1
Edington Ave CF14. . 25 B2
Edith Rd CF64 . . . . . . 47 B3
Edmond's Ct CF24 . . 26 A1
Edmund Pl CF63. . . . 53 A1

Edward Clarke Cl
CF5 . . . . .23 A2
Edward Ho CF11. . . . . .63 A2
Edward Nicholl Ct
CF23 . . . . .26 C2
Edward St CF63. . . . . . .52 B2
Egerton St CF5 . . . . . . .33 A2
Egham St CF5 . . . . .33 A2
Eglwys Newydd Prim
Sch CF14. . . . . .15 B1
Eglwys Wen Prim Sch
CF14 . . . . .23 C4
Egremont Rd CF23. . .26 A2
Eider Cl CF3 . . . . .20 B4
Eifion Cl CF63. . . . . . .52 A3
Eithinen Ber CF63 . . .52 B4
Elaine Cl CF14. . . . . .5 C2
Elan Cl CF62. . . . . .50 C1
Elan Rd CF14 . . . . .17 A3
Elderberry Rd CF5 . . .22 A1
Elder Wood Cl
CF23 . . . . .27 A3
Eldon Ct 13 CF11. . . . .33 C1
Eleanor Pl CF10 . . . . . .42 A1
Electra Ho CF10 . . . . . .42 C2
Eleven St CF64 . . . . . . .53 B1
Elfed Ave CF64 . . . . . . .48 B3
Elfed Gn CF5 . . . . .23 A1
Elfed Way CF63. . . . . . .52 B2
Elford Rd CF5 . . . . .31 A1
Elgar Cres CF3 . . . . . . .20 A3
Elgar Rd CF64 . . . . . . .48 C1
Elis Fisher Ct 8
CF62 . . . . .55 B3
Elizabethan Ct
CF64 . . . . .44 B2
Elizabeth Ave CF62 . .51 B3
Ellen St CF10 . . . . .63 C2
Ellesmere Ct CF3 . . . .20 A2
Ellwood Cl CF3 . . . . . . .20 C2
Elm Cl CF64 . . . . .58 C1
Elmfield Cl CF3. . . . . . .20 B2
Elm Gr CF63 . . . . .52 C3
Elm Grove La CF5. . . . .47 A3
Elm Grove Pl CF64 . . .47 B3
Elmgrove Rd CF14 . . .23 A4
Elm Grove Rd CF5 . . .47 A3
Elm Ho CF14. . . . . .14 B2
Elm St CF24 . . . . .35 A3
Elms The
Barry / Y Barri
CF62 . . . . .55 A2
Cardiff / Caerdydd
CF24 . . . . .35 A3
Elm Street La CF24. . .35 A3
Elmwood Cl
CF5 . . . . .31 C3
Elworthy Cl CF14 . . . .58 B2
Ely Bridge Ind Est
CF5 . . . . .31 C3
Ely Rd
Cardiff / Caerdydd
CF5 . . . . .32 B4
Cardiff / Caerdydd,
Llandaff / Llandaf
CF5 . . . . .32 B4
ELY / TRE-LAI 31 B2
Emblem Cl CF14 . . . . .39 A4
Emerald St CF24. . . . . .35 B3
Emerson Dr CF5 . . . . .38 A2
Emsworth Ct CF23 . . .17 C2
Enbourne Dr 5
CF23 . . . . .8 B1
Enfield Dr CF62 . . . . . .50 C2
Ennerdale Cl CF23. . . .26 A2
Epsom Cl CF5 . . . . .32 A1
Epstein Cl CF5. . . . . . . .22 C2
Erskine Ct CF24. . . . . . .35 C3
Erw Las CF14 . . . . .23 C4
Erw'r-Delyn Cl
CF64 . . . . .48 A4
Erw Wen CF14 . . . . . . .15 B4
Esgid Mair CF63 . . . . .52 C4
Eskdale Cl CF23 . . . . . .26 A3

Esplanade CF64 . . . . .49 B3
Esplanade Bldgs
CF62 . . . . .55 B1
Essich St 5 CF24 . . . . .26 B1
Ethel St CF5 . . . . .32 C2
Eton Ct
Cardiff / Caerdydd
CF14 . . . . .16 C2
7 Cardiff / Caerdydd,
Ely / Tre-lai CF5 . . . . .31 C2
Eton Pl 1 CF5. . . . . . . .33 B1
Eton St CF62 . . . . .54 C2
Eugene Cl 13 CF3 . . . .21 A4
Eurwg Cres 6 CF3. . .20 A4
Evansfield Rd CF14 . .23 B3
Evans St CF12 . . . . .55 C4
Evelian Ct CF14. . . . . . .24 C3
Evelyn St CF63. . . . . . . .56 A4
Evenlode Ave CF64 . .48 C2
Evenlode Prim Sch
CF64 . . . . .48 C2
Evenwood Cl CF23 . . . .8 A1
Everard St CF63 . . . . . .52 B1
Everard Way CF23 . . .26 A4
Everest Ave CF14 . . . . .6 A1
Everest Wlk CF14 . . . . .6 A1
Everswell Ave CF5 . . .31 B3
Everswell Rd CF5 . . . .31 B3
Everwood Ct CF5 . . . . .31 A2
Ewbank Cl CF63 . . . . . .52 C3
Ewenny Cl CF5 . . . . . . .52 A3
Ewenny Rd CF14 . . . . .17 A3
Excalibur Dr CF14 . . . .5 C2
Excelsior Ind Est
CF14 . . . . .24 C2
Excelsior Rd CF14 . . .24 B2
Exeter Mans 6
CF14 . . . . .14 C2
Exford Cres CF3 . . . . . .19 A1
Eyre St CF24. . . . . .35 C2
Ezel Ct CF10 . . . . .42 A2

F

Faber Way CF11 . . . . . .40 C3
Fairacre Cl CF14 . . . . . . .5 C2
Fairbrook Cl CF14 . . .15 B4
Fairfax Rd CF14. . . . . . .16 A2
Fairfield Ave CF5 . . . . .32 B2
Fairfield Cl CF5. . . . . . .32 A3
Fairfield Ind Est
CF15 . . . . .2 B2
Fairfield Prim Sch
CF64 . . . . .48 C4
Fairfield Rd CF64 . . . .48 C4
Fairford St CF63 . . . . . .52 B2
Fairhaven Cl 8
CF3 . . . . .21 A4
Fairlawn Ct CF5 . . . . . .23 C1
Fairleigh Ct CF11 . . . . .33 B4
Fairleigh Mews
CF11 . . . . .33 B4
Fairleigh Rd CF11. . . . .33 B3
Fairmead Ct CF5. . . . . .31 B3
Fairmeadow CF15 . . . .11 C4
Fairoak Ct CF23. . . . . . .26 A2
Fairoak Mews
CF24 . . . . .25 C2
Fairoak Rd CF24 . . . . . .25 C1
Fairoaks CF64 . . . . .47 B3
Fairthorn Cl CF14. . . . . .5 C3
Fairview Cl 9 CF3 . . . .21 A4
Fairview Ct CF23. . . . . .18 B3
FAIRWATER. 31 C4
Fairwater Ave CF5 . . .32 A3
Fairwater Gn CF5. . . . .31 A3
Fairwater Gr E CF5 . .32 A4
Fairwater Gr W
CF5 . . . . .32 A4
Fairwater Prim Sch
CF5 . . . . .31 B3
Fairwater Rd CF5 . . . .31 C4
Fairwater (Tyllgoed)
Halt CF5. . . . . .31 C4

Fairwater Workshops
7 CF5 . . . . .31 C3
Fairways Cres CF5. . . .31 A3
Fairway The CF23 . . . . .7 A1
Fairwood Cl CF5. . . . . .23 A1
Fairwood Rd CF5 . . . .23 A1
Falcon Dr CF10 . . . . . . .42 C2
Falcon Gr CF64 . . . . . . .59 B3
Falcon Rd CF63. . . . . . .53 A2
Falconwood Dr
CF5 . . . . .30 A1
Falfield Cl CF14. . . . . . . .6 B2
Fanny St
Cardiff / Caerdydd,
Cathays CF24 . . . . . . .34 B4
Cardiff / Caerdydd
CF24 . . . . .25 C1
Farlington Ct CF3. . . .27 C3
Farm Dr CF23. . . . . .26 A4
Farmhouse Way
CF5 . . . . .38 A3
Farmleigh CF3 . . . . . . .28 A3
Farmville Rd CF24 . . .35 C2
Farthings The CF23 . . .8 A1
Felbridge Cl CF10. . . .63 D1
Felbrigg Cres CF23 . . .7 C1
Felin Fach CF14 . . . . . .24 A3
Felin Lon Fferm
CF62 . . . . .54 C3
Felin Wen CF14. . . . . . .15 C3
Felsted Cl 2 CF23 . . . .8 A1
Fennel Cl
10 Cardiff / Caerdydd
CF3 . . . . .21 A4
Penarth CF64 . . . . .44 B1
Fenviolet Cl CF3. . . . . .21 B2
Ferndale St CF11 . . . . .41 B3
Fern Dr CF62 . . . . .55 A4
Fern Pl CF5 . . . . .31 B4
Fern St CF5 . . . . .32 C2
Ferns The 4 CF64 . . . .45 B1
Ferntree Dr CF3 . . . . . .20 B1
Ferny Ct CF23 . . . . .26 C2
Ferrier Ave CF5 . . . . . . .31 B4
Ferry La 7 CF64. . . . . .45 B1
Ferry Rd CF11 . . . . .44 C4
Fescue Pl CF5 . . . . .30 B1
Festiniog Rd CF14 . . .23 C2

Ffordd = road, way

Fford Churchill /
Churchill Way
CF10. . . . . .63 C2
Ffordd Bodlyn
CF23 . . . . .26 B3
Ffordd Brynhyfryd
CF3 . . . . .20 B4
Ffordd Celyn CF14 . . .24 A4
Ffordd Cwellyn
CF23 . . . . .26 A3
Ffordd Cwell Yn
CF23 . . . . .26 B3
Ffordd Cwm Cldl
CF62 . . . . .54 B4
Ffordd Daniel Lewis
CF3 . . . . .20 C1
Ffordd Dinefwr
CF15 . . . . .10 A2
Ffordd Elin CF63. . . . . .53 A2
Ffordd Ffagan CF3. . . .21 A4
Ffordd Ganolog /
Central Way CF15 . . .25 B3
Ffordd Garthorne
CF10. . . . . .42 B3
Ffordd Gwyneth 1
CF63 . . . . .52 C3
Ffordd Las CF15 . . . . .13 A2
Ffordd Morgannwg
CF14 . . . . .14 B2
Ffordd Parc Y Mynydd
Bychan / Heath Park
Way CF14. . . . . .25 B3

Ffordd Pengam
CF24 . . . . .36 B4
Ffordd Radcliffe 8
CF10. . . . . .42 A2
Ffordd Sealand 1
CF62 . . . . .55 B3
Ffordd Treforgan
CF15 . . . . .13 A4
Ffordd Tresillian /
Tresillian Way
CF10. . . . . .63 B1
Ffordd Ty Unnos
CF14 . . . . .16 A2
Ffordd-y-Barcer
CF5 . . . . .30 A1
Ffordd-y-Berllan
CF5 . . . . .13 A3
Ffordd y Brenin
CF10. . . . . .62 B3
Ffordd Y Goron /
Crown Way CF14. . . . .25 A1
Ffordd y Mileniwm
CF63 . . . . .56 B3
Ffordd Yr Afon CF15 . .2 B3
Fforest Dr CF62. . . . . . .54 B3
Fforest View CF62. . . .54 B3
Ffynnon Taf Prim Sch
CF15 . . . . .2 A4
Fidlas Ave CF14. . . . . . .17 A3
Fidlas Rd CF14. . . . . . . .17 A3
Fieldfare Dr CF3. . . . . .21 A2
Fielding Cl CF3 . . . . . . .19 B3
Fields Ct CF11 . . . . .33 A3
Fields Park Rd
CF11 . . . . .33 B4
Field Terr CF15 . . . . . . .11 C4
Fieldview Cl CF64. . . .44 B1
Field View Rd CF63. . .52 A2
Field Way CF14 . . . . . .16 B2
Finchley Rd CF5 . . . . . .31 C3
Finnimore Ct 2
CF14 . . . . .23 B3
Firs Ave CF5. . . . . .30 C4
Firstbrook Cl CF23 . . .27 A1
Firtree Cl CF5 . . . . .31 A4
Firwood Cl CF14 . . . . .23 B4
Fisher Hill Way
CF15 . . . . .14 A1
Fishguard Cl CF14 . . .17 A3
Fishguard Rd CF14. . .16 C3
Fishpond Rd CF3 . . . . .19 B2
Fitzalan Ct CF24 . . . . .62 C3
Fitzalan High Sch
CF11 . . . . .32 C1
Fitzalan Pl CF24 . . . . . .62 D3
Fitzalan Rd
Cardiff / Caerdydd
CF24 . . . . .62 C3
Cardiff / Caerdydd
CF24 . . . . 62 D3
Fitzhamon Emb
CF11 . . . . .63 A2
Fitzhamon La CF11 . .63 A2
Fitzroy St
Cardiff / Caerdydd
CF24 . . . . .34 B4
Cardiff / Caerdydd
CF24 . . . . .34 C4
Flatholm Ho CF11. . . .45 A3
Flats The CF14 . . . . . . .25 B2
Flax Ct CF64. . . . . .44 B1
Flaxland Ave CF14 . . .25 B3
Fleet Way CF11 . . . . . . .41 A2
Flindo Cres CF11 . . . . .32 C1
Flint St CF14. . . . . .25 A1
Flora St CF24 . . . . .34 B4
Florence Ave CF62. . . .51 B3
Florence St CF24 . . . . .35 C3
Florentia St CF24 . . . .25 A1
Fonmon Cres CF5. . . . .31 B1
Fonmon Park Rd
CF62 . . . . .60 A1
Fonthill Pl CF11 . . . . . .41 A3
Fontigarry Rd CF3 . . .28 B3

Fordwell CF5 . . . . .23 C1
Foreland Rd CF14. . . .15 A1
Foreshore Rd CF10 . .43 B3
Forest Ct 3 CF11. . . . .33 B3
Forester Way CF23. . . .8 B2
FOREST FARM 14 A2
Forest Farm Nature
Trail★ CF14 . . . . .14 A2
Forest Farm Rd
Cardiff / Caerdydd
CF14 . . . . .14 B1
Radyr CF14. . . . . .14 A2
Forest Fawr Wlks★
CF83. . . . . .3 C4
Forest Oak Cl CF23 . . .7 A1
Forest View CF5 . . . . .31 A3
Forge Pl CF5 . . . . .38 A4
Forio Ho CF10 . . . . .42 B2
Forrest Rd
Cardiff / Caerdydd
CF5 . . . . .32 C2
Penarth CF64 . . . . .49 A1
Forrest St CF11 . . . . . . .41 B2
Forster St 8 CF23 . . . .52 B1
Forsythia Dr CF3 . . . . .18 A3
Fortran Rd CF3 . . . . . . .21 B4
Fort Rd CF64 . . . . .59 B1
Fort St CF24. . . . . .35 C3
Foster Dr CF23 . . . . . . .27 A1
Foundry Cl 16 CF11 . .33 B1
Fountain La CF24 . . . .21 B4
Fouracres Cl CF63 . . . .52 C2
Four Elms Ct 1
CF24 . . . . .35 A2
Four Elms Rd 2
CF24 . . . . .35 B3
Foxberry Cl CF23 . . . . .8 C1
Foxglove Cl CF5 . . . . . .38 A4
Foxglove Rise CF64 . .44 B1
Fox La CF24 . . . . .35 C3
Fox Russell Cl
CF14 . . . . .23 C2
Fox St CF24. . . . . .35 C3
Francis Ho CF23 . . . . . .26 B1
Francis Rd CF62 . . . . . .52 A4
Franklen Rd CF14. . . .24 B4
Franklen St 5
CF11 . . . . .41 B3
Frank Rd CF5. . . . . .31 B2
Frederick St CF10. . . . .63 C2
Fremington Pl CF3. . . .19 C1
Freshmoor Rd
CF24 . . . . .35 C1
Frewer Ave CF5. . . . . . .22 C1
Friars Rd
Barry / Y Barri, Barry
Island CF62. . . . . .55 B1
Barry / Y Barri
CF62 . . . . .55 C1
Friary The CF10. . . . . . .62 B3
Frigate Rd CF10 . . . . . .42 C1
Fryatt St CF63 . . . . .55 C3
Fulmar Cl
Cardiff / Caerdydd
CF3 . . . . .20 C4
Penarth CF64 . . . . .59 B3
Furnace St CF64 . . . . . .53 B1
Furness Cl CF5 . . . . . . .38 A4

G

GABALFA. 24 C1
Gabalfa Ave CF14 . . . .23 C2
Gabalfa Prim Sch
CF14 . . . . .24 A2
Gabalfa Rd CF14 . . . . .23 C2
Gabalfa Workshops
CF14 . . . . .24 C2
Gables The
Cardiff / Caerdydd
CF14 . . . . .16 A2

Gables The *continued*
Dinas Powis / Dinas
Powys CF64 ....47 A2
Gadlys Rd E CF62 ....55 B4
Gadlys Rd W CF62 ...55 A4
Gaen St CF62 ....54 C3
Gaerwen Cl CF14 .....16 A4
Gainsborough Ct 2
CF64 ....44 C1
Gainsborough Rd 6
CF64 ....44 C1
Galahad Cl CF14 ......5 B2
Galdames Pl CF24 ....42 C4
Gallamuir Rd CF24 ...36 A3
Galleon Way CF10 ...42 B3
Galston St 5 CF24 ...35 B2
Gardenia Cl CF23 .....18 A3
Garesfield St CF24 ...35 B2
Gareth Cl CF14 ....5 B2
Garrick Dr CF14 ....5 C2
Garth Cl CF15........13 B4
Garth Pl CF14........24 C2
Garth St
Cardiff / Caerdydd
CF24 ....63 C2
Taffs Well / Ffynnon Taf
CF15 ....2 B3
Garth Villas CF15......2 A4
Garth Wks CF15 ......2 C3
Gaspard Pl CF62 .....54 C1
Gateholm Cl CF62 ...51 C3
Gateside Cl CF23 ....8 B2
Gateway The / Y
Porth CF14 ....25 A3
Gaulden Gr CF23 .....7 C1
Gawain Cl CF14 ....5 B2
Gelli Deg CF14.......15 B4
Gelligaer Gdns
CF24 ....25 B1
Gelligaer La CF24....25 B1
Gelligaer St CF24....25 B1
Gelynis Terr CF15 ...13 B4
Gelynis Terr N
CF15 ....13 B4
Gelyn-y-Cler CF63...52 B4
Geneva Ho 20 CF10 ..42 C4
George Cl CF15.......2 A3
George Ct 7 CF24 ...35 B4
Georges Cnr CF15 ...11 B4
Georges Row CF64...47 C4
George St CF63......56 A4
Georgetown CF15 ....2 A3
Georgian Way
CF14 ....16 C4
Geraint Cl CF14.......5 B2
Geraint Pl CF63......52 A2
Gerddi Margaret 5
CF62 ....55 B3
Gerddi Taf CF15 .....23 A3
Gerddi Ty Celyn
CF14 ....14 C3
Gernant CF14........15 C3
Gerrard Ct 5 CF11 ..33 C1
Gerry Galvin Ct
CF24 ....35 C2
GIBBONSDOWN 51 C2
Gibbonsdown Cl 5
CF63 ....52 A3
Gibbonsdown Rise
CF63 ....52 A2
Gibson Cl CF14.......16 C2
Gilbert La CF63 ......52 B4
Gilbert La W CF63 ...52 B3
Gilbert Pl CF14 ......24 B2
Gilbert St CF63 ......54 C2
Gileston Rd CF11 ....33 B3
Gillian Rd CF5 ......23 B1
Gilwern Cres CF14 ...5 C1
Gilwern Pl CF14 ......5 C1
Gladeside Cl CF14 ...5 C3
Glades The CF64.....49 B3

Glade The CF14 ....6 B1
Gladstone Bridge
CF62 ....55 B3
Gladstone Ct 5
CF62 ....55 C4
Gladstone Garden Ct
9 CF62 ....55 B3
Gladstone Prim Sch
Barry / Y Barri
CF62 ....55 B4
Cardiff / Caerdydd
CF24 ....25 B1
Gladstone Rd CF62...55 C4
Gladys St 5 CF24....34 B4
Glamorgan St
Barry / Y Barri
CF62 ....54 C2
Cardiff / Caerdydd
CF5 ....33 A2
Glamorgan Street
Mews 11 CF5 ....33 A2
Glandovey Gr CF3 ...20 B2
Glandwr Pl CF14......24 A4
Glan Ely Cl CF5 .....31 A3
Glanfa Dafydd
CF63 ....56 A3
Glanfa Gorllewin Y
Gamlas / West
Canal Wharf
CF10 ....63 B1
GLANFA IWERYDD /
ATLANTIC
WHARF 42 B3
Glan Hafren CF62....54 B1
Glanmore Cres
CF62 ....55 A4
Glanmuir Rd CF24 ...36 B4
Glanrhyd CF14.......15 C3
Glan Rhymni CF24 ...27 C1
Glan-y-Dwr 5
CF63 ....55 C3
Glan-y-Ilyn CF23 ....26 A3
Glan-y-Mor
6 Barry / Y Barri,
Barry Dock CF63....55 C3
Barry / Y Barri CF63..54 B1
Glan-y-Mor Rd
CF3 ....20 B1
Glan-y-nant Ct 5
CF14 ....15 B1
Glan-y-Nant Rd
CF14 ....15 B1
Glan-y-Nant Terr
CF14 ....15 B1
Glanyrafon CF15.....2 A4
Glan-yr-Afon Prim
Sch / Ysgol Gynradd
Glan-yr-Afon
CF3 ....19 B3
Glas Canol CF14 .....24 A3
Glas Efail CF14 ......16 A3
Glas Ifor CF14 ....15 C1
Glaslyn Cl CF62......54 C4
Glass Ave CF24 ......43 A4
Glastonbury Rd
CF64 ....58 B2
Glastonbury Terr
CF3 ....19 B2
Glas Y Llwyn CF63 ..52 C4
Glas-y-Pant CF14 ...14 C3
Glebe Pl CF14 ....16 C4
Glebe St
Barry / Y Barri
CF63 ....52 A2
Penarth CF64 ......49 A4
Glen Afric Cl CF62 ..51 A1
Glenbrook Dr CF63 ..53 A3
Glencoe St CF63.....52 A1
Glendale Ave CF14...5 C1
Glendower Ct CF14 ..14 C1
Glen Mavis Way
CF62 ....51 A1

Glenmount Way
CF14 ....5 B2
Glenrise Cl CF3......21 B3
Glenroy St CF24 .....35 A4
Glenside Ct CF24 ....26 B1
Glen View CF14 ......16 C2
Glenwood CF23.......18 A2
Glenwood Cl CF63 ...53 A3
Globe Ctr The CF24 ..35 A4
Globe Works CF24...42 C4
Glossop Rd CF24 .....35 A2
Gloucester Cl CF62 ..51 C1
Gloucester St CF11 ..34 A1
Glynbridge Cl CF62 ..51 C4
Glyncoed Jun & Inf
Schs CF23 ....18 B3
Glyn Coed Rd CF23 ..18 B3
Glyn Collen CF23 ....19 A3
Glyn Derw High Sch /
Ysgol Uwchradd
Glyn Derw CF5 ......39 A4
Glyndwr Rd
Barry / Y Barri
CF62 ....55 B4
Cardiff / Caerdydd
CF5 ....30 C2
Penarth CF64 ......49 A4
Glyn Eiddew CF23 ...18 C4
Glynne St CF11 ......33 B2
Glynne Tower CF64 ..49 B3
Glynrhondda St
CF24 ....62 C4
Glyn Rhosyn CF23 ...18 A3
Glyn Rhymni CF3 ....28 B2
Glyn Simon Cl CF5 ..23 A2
Glynstell Cl CF11 ...40 C2
Glynstell Ind Est
CF11 ....41 A2
Godwin Cl CF15......22 C4
Golate / Y Gwter
CF10 ....62 C3
Goldcrest Dr CF23 ...18 A3
Goldsland Pl CF62...54 C4
Goldsmith Cl CF3 ...19 B3
Gold St CF24 ....35 B2
Goodwick Cl CF62 ...51 C3
Goodwick Rd CF3....28 B3
Goodwood Cl CF5 ....37 B4
Gordon Rd CF24 .....62 C4
Gorsedd Gardens Rd
CF10 ....62 B3
Gorse Pl CF5 ....31 B4
Goscombe Dr CF64 ..44 C1
Gough Rd CF5 ....31 A1
Gould Cl CF3 ....20 B4
Gowan Ct CF14 ....5 B3
Gower Ct CF62 ......55 A4
Gower St CF24.......25 C1
Gradon Cl CF63......52 C1
Grafton Cl CF23 .....26 C3
Grafton Terr CF14....15 C2
Graham Cl CF23 .....27 A2
Graham Wlk 11
CF11 ....33 B1
Graig Hir CF15 ......13 B3
Graig Llwyn Rd CF14..7 B4
Graig-Llwyn Rd
CF14 ....7 C4
Graig Lwyd CF15.....13 B3
Graig View CF14 ......6 C3
Graig Wen CF15 .....13 B4
Granary The 4
CF10 ....42 A3
Grand Ave CF5.......36 A4
Grand The CF10......63 B2
Grange Ave CF5 .....46 B2
Grange Cl CF5 ....46 B3
Grange Ct CF63......53 A1
Grange Gdns CF11...41 B2
Grangemoor Ct
CF11 ....44 B3
Grange Pl CF11......41 C2

Grange The
Cardiff / Caerdydd
CF5 ....32 B4
4 Penarth CF64 ....48 C3
GRANGETOWN 41 B2
Grangetown Link
CF11 ....44 A4
Grange Town Prim
Sch CF11 ....41 B2
Grangetown Sta
CF11 ....41 A2
Grangewood Cl
CF23 ....8 C1
Grantham Cl CF5 ....23 A2
Grant's Cl CF15 .....13 C4
Granville Ave CF5....32 B3
Grasmere Ave
CF23 ....25 C3
Grassmere Cl CF64 ..44 B2
Gray La CF11 ....33 B2
Graylands The
CF14 ....15 C2
Gray St CF11 ....33 B2
Great Burnet Cl
CF3 ....21 B2
Great Ormes Ho
CF11 ....45 A3
Great Thomas Cl
CF62 ....60 B1
Great Western Ct
CF5 ....33 A1
Great Western La
CF10 ....63 B1
Greave Cl CF5 ....46 B3
Greek Church St
CF10 ....63 C1
Green Acre CF15.....10 B2
Greenacre Dr CF23 ...8 C2
Greenacres CF63 ....53 A2
Greenbanks Dr
CF62 ....51 A1
Greenbay Rd CF24 ..36 B2
Green Close Rd
CF14 ....24 B4
Greencroft Ave
CF5 ....32 A2
Green Farm Cl CF5 ..37 C4
Green Farm Rd
CF5 ....37 C4
Greenfield Ave
Cardiff / Caerdydd,
Birchgrove CF14 ...15 C1
Cardiff / Caerdydd,
Canton CF11 ....33 A3
Dinas Powis / Dinas
Powys CF64 ....47 B3
Greenfield Rd
Barry / Y Barri
CF62 ....51 A2
Cardiff / Caerdydd
CF14 ....15 C1
Greenhaven Rise
CF64 ....44 B2
Greenhill Cl CF14 ...15 A4
Greenhill Specl Sch
CF14 ....15 A4
Green La CF63.......52 C3
Greenland Cres
CF5 ....31 A4
Greenlawns CF23 ...26 C2
Green Lawns CF62 ..52 A2
Green Mdws CF3 ....20 B1
Greenmeadow Cl 5
CF64 ....47 B2
Greenmeadow Dr
CF15 ....14 A4
Greenock Rd CF3 ....20 A2
Green Pl CF15 ....13 B1
Green St CF11 ....34 A1
Green The
Leckwith / Lecwydd
CF11 ....40 A1
Radyr CF15 ....13 C1

Greenway Ave CF3...28 B3
Greenway Cl CF64 ...44 A3
Greenway Ct CF63 ..53 A3
Greenway Prim Sch
CF3 ....28 B4
Greenway Rd CF3....20 A1
Greenwich Rd CF5 ...32 C3
Greenwood Cl CF23 ...8 B2
Greenwood La CF5 ..30 B3
Greenwood Rd CF5 ..23 B2
Greenwood St
CF63 ....55 C3
Grenville Rd CF23....35 B4
Gresford Cl CF3......20 A2
Greyfriars Pl CF10 ..62 B3
Greyfriars Rd CF10 ..62 B3
Griffin Cl CF62.......50 C3
Grimson Cl CF64 ....58 B2
Gripoly Mills CF11 ..41 A3
Grisedale Cl CF23 ...26 A2
Groes Lon CF14......15 B4
Gron Ffordd CF14 ....4 C1
Grosvenor St CF5 ...32 C2
Grouse St CF24 .....35 A3
Groveland Rd CF14 ..16 A1
Grove Pl
Cardiff / Caerdydd
CF14 ....16 A1
Penarth CF64 ......49 A4
Grove Place La 4
CF64 ....49 A4
Grove Terr CF64......49 A4
Grove The
Barry / Y Barri
CF62 ....54 C1
Cardiff / Caerdydd
CF3 ....28 B3
Grove Way CF3......28 B3
Guardian Ind Est
CF24 ....36 A3
Guenever Cl CF14....5 B2
Guest Rd CF24.......43 A4
Guildford Cres
CF10 ....63 C2
Guildford St CF10 ...63 C2
Guildhall Pl / Plas yr
Neuadd CF10 ......63 B2
Gulf Ind Area CF11 ..41 A2
Guthrie St CF63......56 A4
Guy's Rd CF63 ......52 B1
Gwaelod-y-Garth Ind
Est CF15...........2 B2
Gwalch Y Penwaig
CF62 ....55 C1
Gwaun Cl CF14 ......23 A4
GWAUN TREODA 24 B3
Gwbert Cl CF23......20 B1
Gwendoline Pl 13
CF24 ....35 B1
Gwendoline St 12
CF24 ....35 B1
Gwenfo CW Prim Sch
CF5 ....46 B2
Gwenfo Dr CF5 ......46 B3
GWENFO /
WENVOE 46 B2
Gwenllian St CF63 ..53 A1
Gwennol Y Mor
CF62 ....55 C1
Gwennyth St CF24 ..25 C1
Gwenog Ct CF62.....54 C4
Gwent CF64 ....45 C1
Gwent Ho 4 CF23 ..26 B2
Gwent Rd CF5 ....38 A4
Gwern Rhuddi Rd
CF23 ....8 B1
Gwern-Rhuddi Rd
CF23 ....17 C4
Gwilym Pl 6 CF63 ..52 A3
Gwynant Cres CF23 ..17 B3
Gwynedd Ho 5
CF23 ....26 B2
Gwyn James Ct
CF64 ....44 B1

Habershon St CF24 ..35 C2
Hackerford Rd
CF23 ....17 C4
Hadfield Cl CF11....40 B2
Hadfield Rd CF11....40 C2
Hafan **1** CF5 ....31 C2
Hafod Ct **14** CF5 ...33 A2
Hafod St CF11 ....63 A1
Hafren Ct CF11 ......33 B3
Hafren Rd CF62.......55 B4
Haig Pl CF5 ....37 C3
Hailey Ct CF14 ....23 B3
Halifax Cl CF24 ......36 B3
Halliard Ct CF10 ....42 B3
Halsbury Rd CF5....32 C3
Halton Cl CF64 ......59 B4
Halt The CF64.......58 A2
Hamadryad Rd
CF10 ....41 C1
Hamilton Ct **15** CF5 .33 A2
Hamilton St CF11 ....33 C2
Hammond Way
CF23 ....27 A1
Hampstead Wlk
CF5 ....37 B4
Hampton Court Rd
CF23 ....27 A2
Hampton Cres E
CF23 ....7 B1
Hampton Cres W
CF23 ....7 A1
Hampton Rd CF14 ...24 C4
Hanbury Cl CF14 .....14 B1
Handel Cl CF64 ......48 C1
Handley Rd CF24 ....36 B3
Hannah Cl CF14 .....16 C2
Hannah St
Barry / Y Barri
CF63 ....52 A2
Cardiff / Caerdydd
CF10 ....42 A3
Hanover Ct
Barry / Y Barri
CF63 ....53 A2
9 Cardiff / Caerdydd
CF14 ....14 C2
Hanover St
2 Barry / Y Barri
CF62 ....55 C4
Cardiff / Caerdydd
CF5 ....33 A1
Hansom Pl CF11 .....41 A3
Harbour Dr CF10 ....42 B1
Harbour Rd
Barry / Y Barri, Barry
Island CF62.........55 A1
Barry / Y Barri
CF62 ....55 A2
Harbour View Rd
CF64 ....45 A1
Harding Cl **15** CF11 ..33 B3
Hardwicke Ct CF5 ...32 B4
Hardy Cl CF62 ....52 A3
Hardy Pl CF24 ....62 D4
Harefield Cl CF23 .....8 C1
Harford Cl CF14 .....14 B1
Harlech Cl CF64 .....47 C3
Harlech Ct **4** CF14 ..15 A2
Harlech Dr CF64 .....47 C3
Harlech Gdns CF62 ..51 B3
Harlech Ho CF15.....13 C2
Harlech Rd CF3......28 B3
Harlequin Ct CF24 ...35 C4
Harold St CF24 ......35 C3
Harpur St CF10 ......63 B1
Harriet St
Cardiff / Caerdydd
CF24 ....34 C4
Penarth CF64 ....44 C1
Harrington Ct CF5 ..38 A3
Harris Ave CF3 ......28 C4

Harrismith Rd CF23 ..26 B1
Harrison Dr CF3 .....21 A1
Harrison Way CF11 ..44 C4
Harrowby La **8**
CF10 ....42 A2
Harrowby Pl CF10 ...42 A1
Harrowby St CF10 ...42 A1
Harrow Ct **5** CF5 ...31 C2
Hartland Ho CF11....45 A3
Hartland Rd CF3.....19 A1
Hartley Pl CF11 .....41 A3
Hart Pl CF24........36 B4
Harvey St
Barry / Y Barri
CF63 ....52 C1
12 Cardiff / Caerdydd
CF5 ....33 A2
Hastings Ave CF64 ..48 B4
Hastings Cl CF64 ...48 B4
Hastings Cres CF3 ..20 A4
Hastings Pl CF64 ...48 B4
Hathaway Pl **4**
CF63 ....52 C3
Hatherleigh Rd
CF3 ....27 C3
Haul Fryn CF14 ......14 C4
Havannah St CF10 ...42 A1
Havelock Pl CF11 ...41 B3
Havelock St CF10 ...63 B2
Havenwood Dr CF14 ..5 B3
Haverford Way CF5 ..38 C4
Hawfinch Cl CF23 ...18 A3
Hawker Cl CF24 .....36 B3
Hawkwood Cl CF5 ...22 A1
Hawthorn Cl CF64 ...47 B2
Hawthorne Ave
CF64 ....48 B3
Hawthorn Inf Sch
CF14 ....23 B3
Hawthorn Jun Sch
CF14 ....23 B3
Hawthorn Rd CF62 ..54 C3
Hawthorn Rd E
CF14 ....23 B3
Hawthorn Rd W
CF14 ....23 B3
Hawthorns The
CF23 ....18 B2
Haxby Ct CF10 ......63 B1
Hayes Bridge Rd /
Heol Bont-yr-Aes
CF10 ....63 C2
Hayes La CF64.......57 A3
Hayes Rd CF64.......57 B3
Hayes The / Yr Aes
CF10 ....63 B2
Hazeldene Ave
CF24 ....25 C1
Hazel Gr CF64 ....47 B2
Hazelhurst Ct CF14 ..23 B4
Hazelhurst Rd CF14 ..23 B3
Hazel Pl CF5........22 C1
Hazel Rd CF14 ......36 B3
Hazel Tree Cl CF15 ..13 A2
Hazelwood Dr CF3...20 B3
Hazledene Cl CF5....52 A2
Hazlitt Cl CF3.......19 C4
Headlands Sch
CF64 ....45 B1
Hearte Cl CF62 ......60 C1
HEATH...........25 A4
Heath Ave CF64.....44 A1
Heathbrook CF23....17 A2
Heathcliffe Cl **4**
CF3 ....20 A4
Heather Ave CF5.....32 A2
Heathers The CF62...55 A4
Heather Way **7**
CF5 ....31 B4
Heathfield Dr CF62...51 B2
Heathfield Pl CF14...25 A4
Heathfield Rd CF14 ..25 A4
Heath Halt Ct CF23 ..17 A1

Heath Halt Rd CF14,
CF23 ....17 A1
Heath High Level Sta
CF23 ....17 A1
Heath Low Level Sta
CF23 ....17 A1
Heath Mead CF14...25 C4
Heath Park Ave
CF14 ....17 A1
Heath Park Cres
CF14 ....25 C4
Heath Park Ct
CF14 ....25 C4
Heath Park Dr
CF14 ....17 A1
Heath Park La
Cardiff / Caerdydd,
Cyncoed CF23 .....17 A1
Cardiff / Caerdydd,
Heath CF14........24 C4
Heath Park Way /
Ffordd Parc Y
Mynydd Bychan
CF14 ....25 B3
Heath St CF11 ......33 C1
Heathway CF14 .....16 B1
Heathwood Ct
CF14 ....16 B1
Heathwood Gr
CF14 ....25 C4
Heathwood Rd
CF14 ....16 B1
Hebbles La CF63.....52 B2
Heddfaen N CF23 ...18 C3
Heddfaen S CF23 ...18 C3
Hedel Rd CF11.......32 B2
Helen Pl CF24 ....35 B3
Helen St CF24 ......35 B3
Hellas Dr CF62......50 C3
Hemingway Rd / Heol
Hemingway CF10 ..42 B2
Hendre Cl CF5.......32 B4
Hendre Gdns CF5....32 B4
Hendre Rd CF3 .....20 B1
Hendy St CF23.......26 A1
Hengoed CF15 ......13 A4
Henke Ct CF10.......42 B3
Henllys Rd CF23.....17 C3
Henry St
Barry / Y Barri
CF63 ....53 A1
Cardiff / Caerdydd
CF10 ....42 A3
Heol Aer CF14 ......15 C4
Heol Amlwch CF14...24 A3
Heol Aradur CF5.....22 C3
Heol Berry CF15 ....19 B3
Heol Blakemore
CF14 ....14 C1
Heol Bont-yr-Aes /
Hayes Bridge Rd
CF10 ....63 C2
Heol Booker CF14 ...14 C1
Heol Briwnant CF14...14 A4
Heol Broadland **3**
CF62 ....55 B3
Heol Brynglas
CF14 ....15 A4
Heol Caerhys CF14...15 C3
Heol Camddwr CF23 ..8 C1
Heol Carnau CF5 ....38 C3
Heol Carne CF14 ....24 B4
Heol Cattwg CF14...24 A3
Heol Cefn On CF14 ..16 B3
Heol Ceiniog CF63...55 C3
Heol Chappell
CF14 ....14 C1
Heol Chudleigh
CF23 ....20 C1
Heol Cilffrydd CF63 ..56 A3
Heol Coed Cae
CF14 ....24 B3
Heol Collen CF5 ....37 C2

Heol Corswigen
CF63 ....52 B3
Heol Danyrodyn
CF15 ....11 C4
Heol Dennant CF5 ..31 C4
Heol Derlwyn CF14 ..15 B4
Heol Deva CF5.......38 B3
Heol Dewi Sant
Barry / Y Barri
CF62 ....55 B4
Cardiff / Caerdydd
CF14 ....16 A2
Heol Dolwen CF14...24 B4
Heol Don CF14 ......23 B4
Heol Don Ct CF14...23 B4
Heol Draenen Wen
CF5 ....37 C2
Heol Dyfed CF14....16 A1
Heol Ebwy CF5 .....38 C4
Heol Eglwys CF5....39 A4
Heol Eglwys Fair / St
Mary St CF10 ......63 B2
Heol Erwin CF14.....5 A1
Heol Eryr Mor
CF62 ....55 C1
Heol Esgyn CF23....17 A2
Heol Fair CF5........23 C1
Heol Fawr / High St
CF10 ....63 B2
Heol Ffynnon Wen
CF14 ....14 C4
Heol Fioled CF63 ...52 B4
Heol Gabriel CF14 ..24 B3
Heol Gam CF15 .....11 B4
Heol Glandulais
CF23 ....8 A1
Heol Glanrheidol CF10,
CF11 ....42 A2
Heol Glaslyn CF23 ...8 C1
Heol Gwendoline **4**
CF62 ....55 B3
Heol Gwent CF14 ...16 A1
Heol Gwerthyd
CF63 ....52 A4
Heol Gwilym CF5 ...22 C1
Heol Gwrgan CF14 ..15 B1
Heol Gwyndaf CF14...16 A2
Heol Gwynedd
CF14 ....16 A1
Heol Gylfinir CF62...55 C1
Heol Harlech CF5....32 B4
Heol Hemingway /
Hemingway Rd
CF10 ....42 B2
Heol Hendre CF14 ..16 A4
Heol Hir
Cardiff / Caerdydd
CF14 ....5 C3
Cardiff / Caerdydd
CF14 ....6 A1
Heol Homfray CF5...37 C3
Heol Iestyn CF14....15 B1
Heol Ifor CF14 ......15 C1
Heol Isaf
Cardiff / Caerdydd
CF14 ....5 A1
Radyr CF15.........13 C1
Heol Iscoed CF14 ...15 C4
Heol Letten / Letton
Rd **3** CF10 ......42 A3
Heol Leubren CF62 ..52 A4
Heol Lewis CF14 ....15 C4
Heol Llangan CF14...15 B2
Heol Llanishen Fach
CF14 ....15 C4
Heol Llinos CF14....5 C4
Heol Mabon CF14...15 C4
Heol Madoc CF14 ...24 B4
Heol Maes Eirwg **14**
CF3 ....20 C2
Heol Maes Eirwg
CF3 ....21 A2
Heol Mathew CF14...14 C1
Heol Merlin CF14....16 C3

Heol Miaren CF63....52 C3
Heol Moor CF62 .....54 B3
Heol Muston CF5 ....31 B2
Heol Mynydd Bychan
CF14 ....16 A2
Heol Nant Castan
CF14 ....15 B4
Heol Nest CF14 .....15 C1
Heol Neuadd Cogan
CF64 ....48 B1
Heol Newydd CF3...28 C4
Heol Pal CF62 ......55 C1
Heol Pantycelyn
Barry / Y Barri
CF62 ....55 A3
Cardiff / Caerdydd
CF14 ....14 C3
Heol Pantyderi CF5..38 C4
Heol Pant-y-Gored
CF15 ....11 A2
Heol Pant y Rhyn
CF14 ....14 C3
Heol Penarth /
Penarth Rd CF11...41 A2
Heol Pencarreg
CF14 ....24 A2
Heol Penlan CF14....14 C1
Heol Penllwyn
CF15 ....11 B4
Heol Pennar CF5 ....38 C4
Heol Pentwyn CF14 ..14 C3
Heol Penyfai CF14 ..24 B4
Heol Peredur CF14 ...5 B2
Heol Pontprennau
CF23 ....8 B1
Heol Powis CF14 ....16 A1
Heol Poyston CF5...38 B3
Heol Pwllyplaca **16**
CF3 ....20 C2
Heol Rhayader
CF14 ....23 A4
Heol St Denys CF14 ..6 B3
Heol Seddon CF5....22 C2
Heol Siarl / Charles St
CF10 ....63 C2
Heol Sirhwi CF62 ...50 C1
Heol Solva CF5 .....39 A4
Heol Stradling
CF14 ....24 A4
Heol Syr Lewis
CF15 ....13 B4
Heol Terrell CF11 ...32 C1
Heol Tredwen **7**
CF10 ....42 A2
Heol Trefgarne
CF5 ....38 B3
Heol Tre Forys
CF64 ....48 B2
Heol Trelai CF5 .....38 B3
Heol Trenewydd
CF5 ....38 B3
Heol Trostre CF3 ...20 C2
Heol Ty Ffynnon
CF23 ....8 A1
Heol Ty'n-y-Cae
CF14 ....15 C2
Heol Ty'n Y Coed
CF14 ....15 C4
Heol Ty'r Brodya
CF10 ....62 B3
Heol Uchaf CF14....4 C1
Heol Urban CF5 .....23 C2
Heol Waun Y Nant
CF14 ....24 A3
Heol Wen CF14 .....15 B3
Heol Wernlas CF14 ..24 A4
Heol Y Barcud CF14 ..5 C4
Heol-y-Berllan
CF5 ....38 B3
Heol-y-Bont CF14 ...15 C3
Heol Y Brenin CF64 ..48 B2

Heol-y-Bryn
Barry / Y Barri
CF62 . . . .**54** C1
Cardiff / Caerdydd
CF14 . . . .**15** A3
Pentyrch CF15 . . . . . .**11** B4
Heol-y-Cadno CF14 . .5 C3
Heol-y-Carw CF14 . . .16 C3
Heol-y-Castell CF5 . .**38** B3
Heol Y Castell / Castle
St CF10 . . . .**63** A2
Heol-Y-Cawl CF64 . .**47** A3
Heol y Cawl /
Wharton St CF10. . . .**63** B2
Heol-y-Coed CF14. . .**15** A3
Heol Y Cwm CF15 . . .**13** A3
Heol-y-Delyn CF14 . . 6 B2
Heol-y-Delyn CF14 . . .6 C3
Heol-y-Deri CF14 . . .**15** B3
Heol Y Dug / Duke St
CF10 . . . .**63** B2
Heol-y-Felin
Cardiff / Caerdydd, Ely /
Tre-lai CF5 . . . .**31** C2
Cardiff / Caerdydd,
Rhydwaedlyd
CF14 . . . .**15** C3
Heol-y-Fforest CF14,
CF15, CF83 . . . . 3 C3
Heol-y-Forlan
CF14 . . . .**15** A2
Heol y Frenhines
CF64 . . . .**47** A2
Heol Y Frenhines /
Queen St CF10. . . . . .**62** C3
Heol-y-Gaer
Barry / Y Barri
CF62 . . . .**54** B1
Cardiff / Caerdydd
CF5 . . . .**38** B3
Heol Y Gors CF14 . . .**24** B3
Heol Y Llongau
CF63 . . . .**55** C3
Heol-y-Nant
Barry / Y Barri
CF63 . . . .**52** A2
Cardiff / Caerdydd
CF14 . . . .**15** B2
Taffs Well / Ffynnon Taf
CF15 . . . . .2 A3
Heol-y-Parc
Cardiff / Caerdydd
CF14 . . . . 8 B4
Pentyrch CF15 . . . . . .**11** B2
Heol-y-Pavin CF5 . . .**23** C1
Heol Y Pentre
CF15 . . . .**11** C4
Heol Y Porthladd 10
CF63 . . . .**55** C3
Heol Y Porth /
Westgate St CF10. . .**63** B2
Heol-Yr-Efail CF14 . .**16** A3
Heol Y Rhosog CF3 . .**28** C2
Heol-yr-Odyn CF5 . .**38** A3
Heol-yr-Ynys CF15 . . .2 C2
Heol Y Tollty /
Customhouse St
CF10 . . . .**63** B1
Heol-y-Waun CF14 . .**24** A3
Heol Y Wern CF14. . .**15** C4
Herbert March Cl
CF5 . . . .**22** C3
Herbert St / Stryd
Herbert CF10 . . . . . .**63** C1
Herbert St
Barry / Y Barri
CF63 . . . .**52** A2
Cardiff / Caerdydd
CF14 . . . .**25** A1

Herbert Terr 6
CF64 . . . .**49** A4
Herbert Thompson
Prim Sch CF5. . . . . . .**31** B2
Hereford St CF11 . . . .**41** A4
Heritage Dr
Barry / Y Barri
CF62 . . . .**55** A4
Cardiff / Caerdydd
CF5 . . . .**38** B2
Heritage Pk CF3 . . . .**20** C4
Hermon Hill CF15. . . .9 A1
Herne Pl CF11 . . . . . .**32** C1
Heron Rd CF3 . . . .**28** B3
Hewell Ct CF11 . . . . . .**41** B2
Hewell St
Cardiff / Caerdydd
CF11 . . . .**41** B2
Penarth CF64 . . . .**44** C1
Hickman Rd CF64. . . .**49** A4
Hickory Ct CF5 . . . . . .**24**...**35** B1
High Bank CF23 . . . . . . 8 C2
Highbridge CF64. .**58** C1
Highbury Pl CF5 . . . . .**38** A4
Highbury Rd CF5 . . . .**31** A1
High Cnr CF15 . . . . . .**11** C4
High Croft Wlk CF3 . .**28** A4
Highfield 14 CF64. . . .**49** A4
Highfield Cl CF14 . . . .**47** C4
Highfield Rd
Barry / Y Barri
CF62 . . . .**51** A2
Cardiff / Caerdydd CF14,
CF23 . . . .**25** C4
Highfields CF5. . . . . .**23** B2
Highlands CF3. . . . . . .**27** C2
Highlight La
Barry / Y Barri
CF62 . . . .**50** C2
Barry / Y Barri
CF62 . . . .**50** C3
Highmead Rd CF5 . . .**31** B1
High St / Heol Fawr
CF10 . . . .**63** B2
High St
Barry / Y Barri
CF62 . . . .**55** A4
Cardiff / Caerdydd
CF5 . . . .**32** B4
Penarth CF64 . . . .**45** A1
High Street Arc 3
CF10 . . . .**63** B2
High Street Prim Sch
CF62 . . . .**55** B3
Highview Rd CF64 . . .**44** C1
Highwalls Ave
CF64 . . . .**47** A3
Highwalls End
CF64 . . . .**47** A3
Highwalls Rd CF64 . .**47** A3
Hilda St CF62. . . . . . .**55** B3
Hiles Rd CF5 . . . .**31** A1
Hillary Cl CF14. . . . . . 6 A1
Hillary Mews 13
CF63 . . . .**52** B1
Hillary Rise CF63 . . . .**52** B1
Hillcot Cl CF14. . . . . . 6 A2
Hillcrest Cl CF14. . . . . 6 A3
Hillfort Cl CF5 . . . . . .**38** C3
Hillrise CF23 . . . .**18** A1
Hillside Cl CF63. . . . . .**52** C1
Hillside Ct CF24 . . . . .**26** B1
Hill-Snook Rd CF5. . .**38** B4
Hill's St CF10 . . . .**63** B2
Hill St
Barry / Y Barri
CF63 . . . .**56** B4
8 Penarth CF64 . . . .**45** B1
Hill Terr
Penarth CF64 . . . .**44** C1
Wenvoe / Gwenfo
CF5 . . . .**46** A4
Hill View CF5 . . . .**31** A4
Hilton Pl CF14 . . . . . .**23** B3

Hinchsliff Ave CF62 . .**51** A3
Hind Cl CF24 . . . .**36** C3
Hinton St CF24 . . . . . .**35** C1
Hirst Cres CF5 . . . .**22** C1
Hirwain St CF24 . . . . .**34** A4
Hodges Row CF10 . . . .**42** A3
Hodges Sq CF10 . . . . .**42** A3
Holden Rd CF11 . . . . .**40** C2
Holgate Cl CF15 . . . . .**22** C4
Holland Way CF63 . . .**52** A2
Hollies Specl Sch The
CF23 . . . .**18** C3
Hollington Dr CF23 . . . 8 B1
Hollybush Ct CF23 . . .**18** A2
HOLLYBUSH
ESTATE **14** B2
Hollybush Hts CF23 . .**18** A1
Hollybush Rd CF23. . .**18** A2
Hollybush Rise
CF23 . . . .**18** A2
Hollycroft Cl CF5 . . . .**31** C2
Holly Cl CF62. . . . .**54** C2
Holly Gr CF14. . . . . 6 B4
Holly Rd CF5 . . . .**31** B4
Hollyrood Cl CF62 . . .**50** C3
Holly Terr CF14 . . . . . .**23** C4
Holmesdale Ct
CF11 . . . .**41** B1
Holmesdale St
CF11 . . . .**41** B2
Holmeside CF14 . . . . . 6 B3
Holmes St CF63. . . . . .**52** B1
Holms Ct CF64. . . . . . .**58** A2
Holmsdale Pl CF64. . .**49** B3
Holmsview Cl CF3 . . .**28** B4
Holmview Ct CF3 . . . .**19** C1
Holmwood CF23 . .**26** B4
Holton Prim Sch
CF63 . . . .**56** A4
Holton Rd
Barry / Y Barri, Barry
Dock CF63. . . . .**56** A4
Barry / Y Barri CF62,
CF63 . . . .**55** C4
Holy Family RC Prim
Sch CF3. . . . .**30** C4
Homelands Rd
CF14 . . . .**15** C1
Homelong Ho CF14 . .**16** C4
Homeside Ho 13
CF64 . . . .**49** B4
Honeysuckle Cl
CF5 . . . .**31** A4
Honiton Rd CF3. . . . . .**19** C3
Hood Rd CF62 . . . .**55** B2
Hood Road Sta*
CF62 . . . .**55** B2
Hope Ho CF10 . . . .**33** C4
Hope St / Stryd Hope
CF10 . . . .**63** C1
Hophouse The 8
CF10 . . . .**63** B2
Horle Cl CF11 . . . .**41** C2
Hornbeam Cl 5
CF3 . . . .**21** A3
Hornchurch Cl CF5 . .**23** A1
Horton Way CF64 . . . .**53** B1
Horwood Cl CF24 . . . .**35** C3
Hosking Ind Est
CF10 . . . .**42** A2
Hotham Cl 1 CF23 . . . 8 B1
Houlston Ct CF24 . . . .**36** A3
Housman Cl CF3 . . . . .**19** C4
Howard Ct
Barry / Y Barri
CF62 . . . .**54** C3
Cardiff / Caerdydd,
Atlantic Wharf / Glanfa
Iwerydd CF10 . . . . . 63 D1
Cardiff / Caerdydd
CF10 . . . . 62 D3
Howard Gdns CF24 . .**62** D3

Howardian Cl 4
CF23 . . . .**27** A1
Howard Pl CF24 . . . . .**62** D3
Howard St CF24 . . . . .**35** B1
Howard Terr CF24. . . .**62** D3
Howell Rd CF5. . . . . . .**31** A1
Howell's Cres CF5 . . .**32** C4
Howell's Sch CF5. . . .**32** C4
Hughs Cl CF5. . . . .**23** A3
Hugon Cl 2 CF23 . . . .**27** A1
Hunt Cl CF14 . . . . 6 A1
Hunters Ridge
CF23 . . . .**26** A4
Hunter St
Barry / Y Barri
CF63 . . . .**52** C1
Cardiff / Caerdydd
CF10 . . . .**42** A1
2 Cardiff / Caerdydd
CF10 . . . .**42** A2
Huntingdon Dr CF23 . .8 B1
Hunt Pl 12 CF63. . . . . .**52** B1
Huntsmead CF14 . . . .5 C3
Hurford Pl CF23 . . . . .**17** C4
Hurman St 5 CF10 . .**42** A2
Huron Cres CF23. . . . .**26** A4
Hydrangea Cl CF23 . .**18** A3
Hyssop Cl CF23 . . . . . .**18** A4
Hywel Cres CF63. . . . .**52** A1
Hywel Dda Inf Sch
CF5 . . . .**38** A4
Hywel Dda Jun Sch
CF5 . . . .**38** A4

I

Idencroft Cl CF23 . . . . . 8 B1
Iestynian Ave CF11. . .**33** B3
Iestyn St CF11 . . . .**33** B3
Ifor Jones Ct CF23 . . .**17** C1
Ilchester Rd CF3. . . . .**19** C2
Ilex Cl CF14. . . . .**16** C4
Ilfracombe Cres
CF3 . . . .**19** C1
Illtyd Rd CF5 . . . .**30** C2
Ilminster Cl CF63 . . . .**52** B1
Ilminster St CF63 . . . .**52** B1
Ilton Rd CF23 . . . .**26** C1
Imperial Bldgs CF5 . .**32** B4
Inchmarnock St 8
CF24 . . . .**35** B1
Inglefield Ave CF14 . .**25** B2
Insole Cl CF5 . . . .**32** A4
Insole Gdns CF5 . . . . .**32** B4
Insole Gr E CF5 . . . . . .**32** A4
Insole Gr W CF5 . . . . .**32** A4
Insole Pl CF5 . . . .**32** B3
Instow CF15 . . . .**20** A2
Inverness Pl CF24. . . .**26** A1
Iolo Pl CF63 . . . .**52** B2
Ipswich Rd CF23 . . . . .**27** B1
Ireland Cl CF3 . . . .**21** A1
Ireton Cl 3 CF23 . . . . . 8 B1
Iron Bridge Rd
CF15 . . . .**13** C4
Iron St CF24 . . . .**35** B1
Irving Pl CF62 . . . .**55** B4
Island Rd CF62 . . . . . .**55** A3
Islwyn Way 7
CF63 . . . .**52** A3
Is-Y-Coed CF5. . . . . . .**46** B2
Ivor St CF62 . . . .**55** C1
Ivydale CF14. . . . . 6 B3
Ivy St
Cardiff / Caerdydd
CF5 . . . .**32** C2
Penarth CF64 . . . .**49** A4

J

Jackson Cl CF62 . . . . .**60** C1
Jackson Rd CF5 . . . . .**30** C1
Jade Cl CF14 . . . . 6 B4
James Ct CF23. . . . . . .**17** B1

James St
Barry / Y Barri
CF63 . . . .**53** A1
Cardiff / Caerdydd
CF10 . . . .**42** A2
Janet St CF24 . . . .**35** C1
Jasmine Dr CF3 . . . . . .**21** A3
Jasper Cl CF5 . . . .**23** A2
Jaycroft Cl CF23 . . . . . 8 C1
Jeffcott Pl CF64 . . . . .**45** A2
Jellicoe Ct CF10 . . . . .**63** D1
Jellicoe Gdns CF23 . .**17** A1
Jenkin St 2 CF63. . . .**52** B2
Jenkinsville 15
CF64 . . . .**49** B4
Jenkins Way CF3 . . . .**20** C1
Jenner Park Prim Sch
CF63 . . . .**52** A1
Jenner Rd CF62 . . . . . .**55** A4
Jenner St CF63 . . . . . .**52** C1
Jesmond Dene CF15 . .2 C4
Jestyn Cl
Cardiff / Caerdydd
CF5 . . . .**37** B4
Dinas Powis / Dinas
Powys CF64 . . . .**47** B4
Jevan Cl CF5 . . . .**22** C3
Jewel St CF63 . . . .**56** B4
Jim Driscoll Way
CF11 . . . .**41** C1
John Batchelor Way
CF64 . . . .**45** A2
John Morgan Cl
CF5 . . . .**23** A3
John St / Stryd John
CF10 . . . .**63** C1
Johns La CF14 . . . .**23** C2
John St
Barry / Y Barri
CF63 . . . .**53** A1
Penarth CF64 . . . .**45** B1
Johnston Rd CF14 . . . .5 B1
Jones Point Ho
CF11 . . . .**45** A3
Jonquil Cl CF3. . . . . . .**21** A3
Joseph Parry Cl
CF64 . . . .**44** B2
Jubilee Gdns
Barry / Y Barri
CF63 . . . .**53** A3
Cardiff / Caerdydd
CF14 . . . .**16** B2
Jubilee Ind Est
CF24 . . . .**35** B1
Jubilee La CF64 . . . . .**49** B4
Jubilee St CF11 . . . . . .**41** A4
Judkin Ct 6 CF10 . . .**42** A2
Junction Terr CF15. . .**13** C1
Justin Cl CF23 . . . .**26** B4

K

Kames Pl CF24 . . . . . .**35** A1
Kane Cl CF14 . . . .**16** C3
Kathleen St CF62 . . . .**54** C3
Keats Way CF62. . . . .**51** B3
Keen Rd
Cardiff / Caerdydd
CF24 . . . .**35** B1
Cardiff / Caerdydd
CF24 . . . .**42** C4
Kelston Cl CF14. . . . . .**14** C1
Kelston Pl CF14. . . . . .**14** C1
Kelston Rd CF14 . . . . .**14** C1
Kelvin Rd CF24 . . . . . .**26** A1
Kember Cl CF3 . . . .**21** A2
Kemeys Rd CF62 . . . . .**60** C1
Kemys Pl CF14. . . . . . .**24** B3
Kendrick Rd CF62. . . .**55** C4
Kenfig Rd CF14 . . . . . .**24** C3
Kenilworth Ct CF5 . . .**32** A3
Kenilworth Ho
CF10 . . . .**63** A2

Kenilworth Rd
 CF63 . . . . 52 B1
Kenley Cl CF5 . . . . . 23 A1
Kenmare Mews
 CF23 . . . . 8 B2
Kenmuir Rd CF24 . . . 36 A3
Kennedy Rise CF62 . 54 C4
Kennerleigh Rd
 CF3 . . . . 27 C4
Kenneth Treasure Ct
 2 CF3 . . . . 20 A3
Kennington Cl CF14 . . 5 C2
Kensington Ave
 CF5 . . . . 32 B2
Kent Gn CF62 . . . . . . 51 B1
Kent St CF11 . . . . 41 B2
Kenwood Rd CF5 . . . 30 C1
Kenyon Rd CF24 . . . . 36 B3
Keppoch St CF24 . . . 35 A4
Kerrigan Cl CF5 . . . . 22 C1
Kerrycroy St **10**
 CF24 . . . . 35 B1
Kestell Dr CF11 . . . . . 45 A4
Kestrel Cl CF23 . . . . . 18 A3
Kestrel Way CF64 . . . 59 B4
Keswick Ave CF23 . . 25 C3
Keteringham Cl
 CF64 . . . . 58 A2
Kewstoke Ave CF3 . . 19 B1
Kewstoke Cl CF3 . . . 19 B1
Kewstoke Pl CF3 . . . 19 B1
Keyes Ave CF23 . . . . 17 A1
Keyes Ct CF10 . . . . . 63 D1
Keynsham Rd CF14 . . 15 C1
Keyston Rd CF5 . . . . 23 A1
Kilcattan St **9**
 CF24 . . . . 35 B1
Kilcredaun Ho
 CF11 . . . . 45 A4
Kilgetty Cl CF5 . . . . . 38 B4
Kimberley Rd CF23 . . 26 C1
Kimberley Terr
 CF14 . . . . 16 C4
Kincraig St CF24 . . . . 34 C4
Kingarth St **6**
 CF24 . . . . 35 B1
King Edward VII Ave
 CF10 . . . . 62 B4
Kingfisher Cl CF3 . . . 20 C3
King George V Dr E
 Cardiff / Caerdydd
 CF14 . . . . 25 B3
 Cardiff / Caerdydd
 CF14 . . . . 25 B4
King George V Dr N
 CF14 . . . . 16 C1
King George V Dr W
 CF14 . . . . 25 A4
King's Ave CF15 . . . . 13 C1
Kings Ct **7** CF64 . . . 47 A2
Kingsland Cres
 CF63 . . . . 56 A3
Kingsland Rd
 Cardiff / Caerdydd,
 Canton CF5 . . . . 32 C2
 Cardiff / Caerdydd,
 Whitchurch / Yr
 Eglwys Newydd
 CF14 . . . . 23 B4
Kingsley Cl CF64 . . . 58 B2
Kings Mews CF11 . . . 33 C2
Kings Monkton Sch
 CF24 . . . . 62 C3
Kings Rd CF11 . . . . . 33 B3
King's Rd
 Cardiff / Caerdydd
 CF11 . . . . 33 B2
 Radyr CF15 . . . . 13 C1
King St
 Penarth CF64 . . . . . . 45 B1
 Taffs Well / Ffynnon Taf
 CF15 . . . . 2 B3

Kingston Rd CF11 . . . 33 B1
Kingsway CF10 . . . . . 62 B3
King Wood Cl CF23 . . 27 A2
Kinsale Cl CF23 . . . . . 8 B2
Kipling Cl
 Cardiff / Caerdydd
 CF3 . . . . 19 B3
 Penarth CF64 . . . . . . 44 C1
Kirkby Cl CF10 . . . . . 63 D1
Kirkwall Ct CF24 . . . 36 A3
Kirton Cl CF5 . . . . . . 23 A1
Kismet Pk CF11 . . . . 41 A2
Kitchener Prim Sch
 CF11 . . . . 33 B1
Kitchener Rd CF11 . . 33 B1
Knap Car Terr
 CF62 . . . . 54 B1
Knighton Ct **6**
 CF24 . . . . 35 B2
Knightswell Cl CF5 . . 37 C2
Knightswell Rd
 CF5 . . . . 37 C3
Knole Cl CF23 . . . . . . 8 B1
Knowbury Ave
 CF64 . . . . 59 C4
Knox Rd CF24 . . . . . . 62 C3
Kyle Ave CF14 . . . . . 15 C1
Kyle Cres CF14 . . . . . 15 C1
Kymin Rd CF64 . . . . . 49 B4
Kymin Terr CF64 . . . . 49 B4
Kyveilog St CF11 . . . 33 B3

L

Laburnum Cl CF62 . . 51 C2
Laburnum Pl CF5 . . . 31 B4
Laburnum Way
 Dinas Powis / Dinas
 Powys CF64 . . . . 47 B2
 Penarth CF64 . . . . . . 48 B3
Lady Isle Ho CF11 . . . 45 A4
Lady Margaret Ct **5**
 CF23 . . . . 27 A1
Lady Margaret's Terr
 11 CF74 . . . . 35 B1
Lady Mary Rd CF23 . . 26 C1
Ladysmith Rd CF23 . 26 C1
Lake Rd E CF23 . . . . . 26 A4
Lake Rd N CF23 . . . . 17 A1
Lake Rd W CF23 . . . . 25 C4
Lakeside Dr CF23 . . . 17 B1
Lakeside Prim Sch
 CF23 . . . . 26 A4
Lake View Cl CF23 . . 26 A4
Lake View Ct CF23 . . 26 A4
Lakin Dr CF62 . . . . . . 50 C3
Laleston Cl
 Barry / Y Barri
 CF63 . . . . 52 A3
 8 Cardiff / Caerdydd
 CF5 . . . . 38 B4
Lamberton Way
 CF24 . . . . 35 B1
Lambourne Cres
 CF14 . . . . 16 B3
Lamby Ind Pk CF3 . . 28 B1
Lamby Way CF3 . . . . 28 A1
Lamby Way
 Workshops CF3 . . . 28 B2
Landings The CF64 . . 44 C1
Landwade Cl CF5 . . . 31 A3
Langdale Cl CF23 . . . 26 B2
Langham Way
 CF11 . . . . 41 A3
Langland Rd CF3 . . . 28 B3
Langlands Rd CF63 . . 53 A2
Langport Ave CF3 . . . 20 A2
Lanhydrock Cl **11**
 CF3 . . . . 20 C2
Lansdowne Ave
 CF14 . . . . 15 C2
Lansdowne Ave E
 CF11 . . . . 33 A1

Lansdowne Ave W
 CF11 . . . . 32 C1
Lansdowne Hospl
 CF11 . . . . 32 C1
Lansdowne Prim Sch
 CF5 . . . . 32 C2
Lansdowne Rd CF5 . 32 C1
Lapwing Cl CF64 . . . 59 B3
Larch Cl CF15 . . . . . . 3 B1
Larch Gr CF14 . . . . . . 6 C3
Larch Ho CF14 . . . . . 14 B2
Larchwood CF5 . . . . 46 B2
Larkwood Ave
 CF64 . . . . 49 A2
Lascelles Dr CF23 . . . 8 C1
Latteys Cl CF14 . . . . 16 A1
Laugharne Ave CF3 . 28 B3
Laugharne Ct CF62 . 51 C2
Laugharne Rd CF3 . . 28 B3
Launcelot Cres CF14 . 5 C2
Laura St CF63 . . . . . . 53 A1
Laureate Cl CF3 . . . . 19 B3
Laurel Ct
 Barry / Y Barri
 CF62 . . . . 54 C2
 Cardiff / Caerdydd
 CF5 . . . . 31 B4
Laurels Bsns Pk The
 CF3 . . . . 28 C2
Laurels The CF14 . . . 6 B3
Lauriston Cl CF5 . . . . 38 B3
Lauriston Pk CF5 . . . 38 B2
Lavender Gr CF5 . . . . 31 A4
Lavernock
 CF64 . . . . 59 B1
Lawn The CF11 . . . . . 23 C1
Lawrenny Ave CF11 . 40 B4
Laytonia Ave CF14 . . 25 A2
Leacroft Pl CF23 . . . . 7 C1
Lead St CF24 . . . . 35 B2
Leamington Rd
 CF14 . . . . 15 B2
Leckwith Ave CF11 . . 33 A1
Leckwith Cl CF11 . . . 33 A1
Leckwith Ct CF5 . . . . 38 C4
Leckwith /
 LECWYDD
 CF11 . . . . 40 A1
Leckwith /
 LECKWITH
 MOORS 40 C2
Leckwith Pl CF11 . . . 33 B1
Leckwith Rd
 Cardiff / Caerdydd
 CF11 . . . . 40 B4
 Cardiff / Caerdydd,
 Leckwith / Leckwydd
 CF11 . . . . 40 B2
 Leckwith / Lecwydd
 CF11 . . . . 40 A1
LECWYDD /
 LECKWITH 40 A1
Lee Cl
 Cardiff / Caerdydd
 CF23 . . . . 26 C4
 Dinas Powis / Dinas
 Powys CF64 . . . . 47 B4
Lee Ct CF14 . . . . 5 A1
Lee Ho CF23 . . . . 26 C4
Lee Rd CF63 . . . . 52 A1
Lennox Gn CF63 . . . . 53 A1
Leon Ave CF15 . . . . . 2 B3
Letterston Rd CF3 . . . 20 A1
Letton Rd / Heol
 Letton **3** CF10 . . . 42 A3
Lettons Way CF64 . . 47 A4
Letty St CF24 . . . . . . 34 B4
Leven Cl CF23 . . . . . . 17 B1
Lewis Rd
 Cardiff / Caerdydd
 CF24 . . . . 35 C1
 Llandough / Llandochau
 CF64 . . . . 44 A3
Lewis St
 Barry / Y Barri
 CF62 . . . . 54 C3

Lewis St continued
 Cardiff / Caerdydd
 CF11 . . . . 33 C1
Library St CF5 . . . . . . 33 B2
Liddel Cl CF23 . . . . . . 8 C1
Liddicoat Ct CF63 . . . 52 C1
Lidmore Rd CF62 . . . 54 C4
Lilac Cl CF5 . . . . 22 B1
Lilburne Cl **4** CF23 . . 8 B1
Lili Mai CF63 . . . . 52 B4
Lily St CF24 . . . . 62 D4
Limebourne Ct
 CF14 . . . . 24 A3
Lime Cl CF15 . . . . 22 B4
Lime Gr CF5 . . . . 22 A1
Limeslade Cl CF3 . . . 32 A3
Limewood Cl CF3 . . . 20 B3
Lincoln Ct CF23 . . . . 18 A1
Lincoln St CF5 . . . . . 32 C2
Linden Ave CF23 . . . 26 B1
Linden Gr CF3 . . . . . . 28 A4
Lindens The CF64 . . . 49 B4
Lindway Ct **4** CF5 . . 32 C3
Lingholm Cl **3** CF3 . 20 C2
Links Bsns Pk CF3 . . 21 B4
Linnet Ct CF23 . . . . . 18 A3
Lionel Rd CF5 . . . . . . 32 C2
Liscum Way CF62 . . . 50 C2
Lisnagarvey Ct
 CF14 . . . . 14 C4
Lisvane Ho CF14 . . . . 6 C2
LISVANE / LLYS
 FAEN 6 C2
Lisvane Rd CF14 . . . . 6 C2
Lisvane St CF24 . . . . . 25 B1
Lisvane & Thornhill /
 Llys-faen Sta CF14 . . 6 A3
Litchfield Ct CF11 . . . 63 A1
Little Brynhill La
 CF62 . . . . 51 B3
Littlecroft Ave CF5 . . 32 A2
Little Dock St CF64 . . 44 C1
Little Frederick St
 CF10 . . . . 63 C2
Little Mill CF14 . . . . . 23 C3
Little Moors Hill
 CF63 . . . . 52 C1
Little Orch CF64 . . . . 47 C3
Little Orchard CF5 . . 23 B1
Littleton St CF11 . . . . 33 C1
Livorno Ho CF10 . . . 42 B3
Llanbedr Rd CF5 . . . . 31 C3
Llanbleddian Ct
 CF24 . . . . 62 C4
Llanbleddian Gdns
 CF24 . . . . 62 C4
Llanbradach St
 CF11 . . . . 41 B3
Llancaiach Rd **4**
 CF24 . . . . 24 A4
Llandaff Cath ★
 CF5 . . . . 24 A1
Llandaff Chase CF5 . . 23 B1
Llandaff City CW Prim
 Sch CF5 . . . . 32 B4
Llandaff Cl CF64 . . . . 49 C3
Llandaff Ct CF5 . . . . . 32 B4
LLANDAFF /
 LLANDÂF 32 C4
LLANDAFF NORTH . 23 C3
Llandaff Rd CF5 . . . . 33 A2
Llandaff Sq CF3 . . . . 20 A3
LLANDÂF /
 LLANDAFF 32 C4
 Llandaf Sta CF14 . . . 23 B4
Llandegfedd Cl CF14 . 6 A3
Llandennis Ave
 CF23 . . . . 17 C2
Llandennis Ct CF23 . . 17 C2
Llandennis Gn
 CF23 . . . . 17 B2
Llandennis Rd
 CF23 . . . . 17 A2
Llandetty Rd CF5 . . . 31 C3

Llandilo Cl CF64 . . . . 47 C3
Llandinam Cres
 CF14 . . . . 24 A1
Llandinam Rd CF62 . 55 B4
LLANDOCHAU /
 LLANDOUGH 44 A3
Llandogo Rd CF3 . . . 20 C3
Llandough Hill
 CF64 . . . . 44 A3
LLANDOUGH /
 LLANDOCHAU 44 A3
Llandough Prim Sch /
 Ysgol Gynradd
 Llandochau CF64 . . . 44 A3
Llandough St CF24 . . 62 B4
Llandough Trad Est
 CF11 . . . . 44 A4
Llandovery Cl **12**
 CF5 . . . . 38 B3
Llandow Rd CF5 . . . . 31 B1
Llandudno Rd CF3 . . 28 B4
Llandyfrig Cl **9**
 CF64 . . . . 47 C3
LLANEDEYRN 18 B2
LLANE DEYRN 9 A1
Llanedeyrn Cl CF23 . 26 C3
Llanedeyrn Dr
 CF23 . . . . 27 A4
Llanedeyrn High Sch
 CF23 . . . . 27 A4
Llanedeyrn Prim Sch
 CF23 . . . . 27 A4
Llanedeyrn Rd
 CF23 . . . . 27 A3
LLANEURWG / ST
 MELLONS 20 B3
Llanewrwg Way
 CF3 . . . . 20 B3
Llanfair Rd CF11 . . . . 33 A3
LLANFIHANGEL-AR-
 ELAI /
 MICHAELSTON-
 SUPER-ELY 30 B1
Llangattock Rd
 CF5 . . . . 31 C3
Llangefni Pl CF14 . . . 5 C1
Llangorse Rd CF23 . . 17 C3
Llangranog Pl CF14 . . 5 B1
Llangranog Rd CF14 . 5 B1
Llangwm Pl CF3 . . . . 28 B4
Llangybi Cl CF5 . . . . . 37 B3
Llangynidr Rd CF5 . . 31 C3
Llanidloes Rd CF14 . . 24 A2
Llanina Gr CF3 . . . . . 20 B1
LLANISHEN 16 C3
Llanishen Ct CF14 . . . 16 C4
Llanishen Fach Prim
 Sch CF14 . . . . 5 A1
Llanishen High Sch
 CF14 . . . . 6 B1
Llanishen St CF14 . . . 25 B2
Llanishen Sta CF14 . . 16 A1
Llanmaes St CF11 . . . 41 B2
Llanmead Gdns
 CF62 . . . . 60 B1
Llanmorlais Rd
 CF14 . . . . 24 B1
Llanon Rd CF14 . . . . 5 C1
Llanover Rd CF5 . . . . 37 B3
Llanover St **2**
 CF63 . . . . 52 B1
LLANRUMNEY 19 B2
Llanrumney Ave
 CF3 . . . . 19 B1
Llanrumney High Sch
 CF3 . . . . 19 A2
Llansannor Dr
 CF10 . . . . 63 D1
Llanstephan Rd
 CF3 . . . . 28 B3

Llantarnam Dr CF15 . . . . 13 B1
Llantarnam Rd CF14 . . . . 24 C2
Llantrisant Rd CF5 . . . 22 C3
Llantrisant Rise CF5 . . . . 23 B2
Llantrisant St CF24 . . 34 A4
Llantwit Rd
Barry / Y Barri CF63 . . . . 56 A4
Cardiff / Caerdydd CF24 . . . . 62 C4
Llanwern Rd CF5 . . . 31 A1
Llewellyn Ave CF5 . . 30 C2
Llewellyn St CF63 . . . 52 A1
Llewelyn Goch CF5 . . 12 B1
Lloft Deri CF14 . . . . . 15 C3
Lloyd Ave
Barry / Y Barri CF62 . . . . 51 B1
Cardiff / Caerdydd CF5 . . . . 32 A3
Lloyd George Ave / Rhodfa Lloyd George CF10 . . . . 42 A3
Lloyd Pl CF73 . . . . . . 21 C2
Llwyd Coed CF14 . . . . 4 A1
Llwyn Bryn Melyn CF15 . . . . 13 A2
Llwyn Castan CF23 . . 18 B3
Llwyn David CF62 . . . 55 B3
Llwynderw Rd CF14 . . . . 24 C3
Llwyn Drysgol CF15 . . . . 13 A2
Llwynfedw Gdns CF14 . . . . 16 A1
Llwynfedw Rd CF14 . . . . 15 C1
Llwyn Grug CF14 . . . 15 C4
Llwyn Mallt CF15 . . . 14 A4
Llwyn Onn CF14 . . . . 4 B1
Llwyn Passat CF64 . . 45 B2
Llwyn Rhosyn CF14 . . 15 C4
Llwyn-y-Grant Pl CF23 . . . . 26 C2
Llwyn-y-Grant Rd CF23 . . . . 26 C2
Llwyn-y-Grant Terr CF23 . . . . 26 C2
Llwyn Y Pia Rd CF14 . . 6 C3
Llyn CF14 . . . . 17 B1

Llys = court

Llys Caradog CF15 . . 10 A2
Llys Coleg 4 CF14 . . 24 A3
Llys Dewi CF15 . . . . . 10 B2
Llys Dol May 9 CF64 . . . . 45 A1
Llys Dyfodwg CF15 . . 10 B1
Llys Dyfrig CF15 . . . . 10 A1
LLYS FAENLISVANE . . 6 C2
LLYS FAEN / LISVANE 6 C2
Llys-faen / Lisvane & Thornhill Sta CF14 . . 6 A3
Llysfaen Prim Sch CF14 . . . . 6 C3
Llys Gwent CF63 . . . . 52 C3
Llys Gwynno CF15 . . 10 B1
Llys Hafn CF15 . . . . . . 2 B3
Llys Illtyd CF15 . . . . . 10 A2
Llys Pegasus CF14 . . 16 C4
Llys Pum Cyfair CF14 . . . . 24 B2
Llys Tal-y-Bont Rd CF14 . . . . 25 A1
Llys Teilo CF15 . . . . . 10 B1
Llys Iripp CF15 . . . . . 2 B3

Llys Tudful CF15 . . . . 10 B2
Llyswen Rd CF23 . . . . 17 B3
Llys Y Coed CF62 . . . . 54 C3
Llys-yr-Eglwys 10 CF64 . . . . 45 B1
Lochaber St CF24 . . . . 26 B1
Locke Gr 12 CF3 . . . . 21 A2
Lock Keepers Ct CF10 . . . . 34 A4
Locks Rd CF10 . . . . . . 45 C4
Lodge Cl CF14 . . . . . . 6 B4
Lodwick Rise CF3 . . . . 21 A1
Loftus St CF5 . . . . 32 C2
Lombard St CF24 . . . . 55 C4
Lomond Cres CF23 . . . 17 C1
Loncae Porth CF14 . . . 5 A1
Lon Cwrt Ynyston CF11 . . . . 40 B2
Lon Fach CF14 . . . . . . 15 B3
Lon Fferm Felin CF62 . . . . 54 C3
Longacre Cl CF63 . . . 53 A3
Lon Ganol CF14 . . . . . 15 B3
Longcross St CF24 . . . 35 A2
Long House Cl CF14 . . 6 B2
Longleat Cl CF14 . . . . 6 C2
Longmeadow Dr CF64 . . . . 47 B2
Long Meadow Dr CF62 . . . . 52 A2
Longreach Cl CF5 . . . . 37 B4
Longspears Ave CF14 . . . . 25 A3
Longueil Cl CF10 . . . . 42 B3
Longwood Dr CF14 . . 13 C3
Lon Isa CF14 . . . . 15 B3
Lon Madoc CF14 . . . . 24 B4
Lon Owain CF5 . . . . . 38 A3
Lon Penllyn CF14 . . . 15 B2
Lonsdale Rd CF23 . . . . 27 A3
Lon Ty'n-y-Cae CF14 . . . . 15 C2
Lon Ucha CF14 . . . . . 15 B3
Lon-Werdd CF5 . . . . . 30 B1
Lon-Werdd Cl CF5 . . . 30 B1
Lon Y Barics / Barrack La CF10 . . . 63 C2
Lon-y-Castell CF5 . . . 38 B3
Lon-y-Celyn CF14 . . . 14 C2
Lon-y-Dail CF14 . . . . . 15 B3
Lon-y-Dderwen CF14 . . . . 15 B3
Lon-y-Deri CF14 . . . . 15 B3
Lon Y Felin / Mill La CF10 . . . . 63 B2
Lon-y-Ffin CF5 . . . . . . 30 B1
Lon-y-Fro CF15 . . . . . 11 C3
Lon Y Goch CF15 . . . . 11 C1
Lon-y-Groes CF14 . . . . 24 C4
Lon-y-Mynydd CF14 . . . . 16 A3
Lon Y Nant CF14 . . . . 15 C3
Lon-y-Parc CF14 . . . . 15 B1
Lon Y Parc / Park La CF10 . . . . 62 C3
Lon-yr-Efail CF5 . . . . 38 A3
Lon-y-Rhyd CF14 . . . . 15 B3
Lon-Ysgubor CF14 . . . 15 B3
Lon-y-Winci CF14 . . . 15 B3
Lord Pontypridd Ho 6 CF5 . . . . 32 C3
Lord St CF64 . . . . 45 B1
Lothian Cres CF23 . . . 26 C3
Loudoun Sq CF10 . . . . 42 A3
Lougher Cl CF5 . . . . . 31 C3
Louisa Pl CF10 . . . . . . 42 A2
Louise Ct 11 CF14 . . . 23 B3
Lovage Cl CF23 . . . . . 18 B4
Love La CF10 . . . . 63 C2
Lowdon Terr CF62 . . . . 55 B4
Lower Acre CF5 . . . . . 38 A3
Lower Cathedral Rd CF11 . . . . 34 A1

Lower Farm Ct CF62 . . . . 60 C1
Lower Guthrie St CF63 . . . . 56 A4
Lower Holmes St CF63 . . . . 52 C1
Lower Morel St CF63 . . . . 56 A4
LOWER PENARTH . . . 49 A1
LOWER PORTHKERRY 61 C1
Lower Pyke St CF63 . . . . 56 A4
Lowfield Dr CF14 . . . . 5 C2
Lowther Ct CF24 . . . . 62 C4
Lowther Rd CF24 . . . . 62 C4
Lucas Cl CF63 . . . . . . 52 C3
Lucas St CF24 . . . . . . 25 C1
Lucerne Dr CF14 . . . . . 5 B3
Lucknow St CF11 . . . . 41 A3
Ludlow Cl CF11 . . . . . 41 C2
Ludlow La CF64 . . . . . 49 B4
Ludlow St
Cardiff / Caerdydd CF11 . . . . 41 B2
Penarth CF64 . . . . . . 49 A4
Lundy Cl CF14 . . . . . . 16 B4
Luton Ho 3 CF24 . . . . 35 A2
Lydford Cl CF14 . . . . . 15 B2
Lydstep Cres CF14 . . . 24 A2
Lydstep Flats CF14 . . . 24 A2
Lydstep Rd CF62 . . . . . 51 C2
Lynch Blosse Cl CF5 . . . . 23 A2
Lyncroft Cl CF3 . . . . . 20 A4
Lyndhurst St CF11 . . . 33 B1
Lynmouth Cres CF3 . . . . 27 C3
Lynmouth Dr CF64 . . . 58 A1
Lynton Cl
Cardiff / Caerdydd CF3 . . . . 28 A4
Sully CF64 . . . . 58 B2
Lynton Ct CF10 . . . . . 42 A2
Lynton Pl CF3 . . . . . . 28 A4
Lynton Terr CF3 . . . . . 27 C4
Lynwood Ct
4 Cardiff / Caerdydd CF24 . . . . 35 A3
Radyr CF15 . . . . 13 B1
Lyon Cl CF11 . . . . 40 C1
Lyric Way CF14 . . . . . . 5 C2
Lysander Ct CF24 . . . . 36 B3
Lytham Gr 1 CF3 . . . . 21 A4

M

Maberly Ct CF14 . . . . 17 A3
MacAulay Ave CF3 . . . 19 B3
McCale Ave 1 CF5 . . 31 C3
MacDonald Cl CF5 . . . 37 C4
MacDonald Pl CF5 . . . 37 C4
MacDonald Rd CF5 . . 37 C4
Machen Cl CF3 . . . . . 21 A3
Machen Pl CF11 . . . . . 33 C1
Machen St
Cardiff / Caerdydd CF11 . . . . 41 A3
3 Penarth CF64 . . . . . 48 C4
Mackintosh Pl CF24 . . . . 26 A1
McLay Ct 3 CF24 . . . . 31 C3
McQuade Pl CF62 . . . . 55 B1
Madoc Cl CF64 . . . . . 47 C3
Madoc Rd CF24 . . . . . 36 A2
Maelfa CF23 . . . . 27 A4
Maelog Pl CF14 . . . . . 25 A1
Maelog Rd CF14 . . . . 24 B4
Maerdy La CF14 . . . . . 7 A2
Maes Awyr Caerdydd-Cymru / Cardiff International Airport CF62 . . . . 61 A2

Maes Brith Y Garn CF23 . . . . 8 A1
Maes Cadwgan CF15 . . . . 10 B2
Maes Glas
Barry / Y Barri CF62 . . . . 54 C4
Cardiff / Caerdydd CF14 . . . . 24 A4
Maes Magretian / Magretion Pl 6 CF10 . . . . 42 A3
Maes Y Briallu CF15 . . . . 13 A3
Maes Y Bryn CF23 . . . . 19 B4
Maes-y-Bryn CF15 . . 13 B3
Maes-y-Bryn Rd CF14, CF23 . . . . 8 C4
Maes-y-Coed CF62 . . . 54 B1
Maes-y-Coed Rd CF14 . . . . 16 B2
Maes Y Cored CF14 . . 14 B2
Maes-y-Crochan CF3 . . . . 21 B3
Maes Y Crofft CF15 . . 13 A3
Maes-y-Cwm St CF63 . . . . 56 A4
Maes-y-Dderwen CF15 . . . . 10 B1
Maes-y-Deri CF14 . . . . 15 B3
Maes Y Draenog CF15 . . . . 3 B2
Maes-y-Felin CF14 . . 15 B2
Maes-y-Fioled CF15 . . . . 13 A3
Maes Y Gad CF5 . . . . 30 A3
Maes-y-Gollen CF15 . . . . 10 B2
Maes Y Hedydd CF23 . . . . 8 A2
Maes-y-nant CF15 . . . 10 A2
Maes Y Parc CF14 . . . . 15 B2
Maes Yr Annedd CF5 . . . . 32 C3
Maes Yr Awel CF15 . . 13 B2
Maes Yr Haf CF14 . . . 14 C4
Maes-yr-Hafod CF15 . . . . 10 B2
Maes-y-Rhedyn CF15 . . . . 10 B1
Maes Yr Odyn CF15 . . 13 A3
Maes-yr-Onnen CF15 . . . . 10 B1
Maes Yr Orchis CF15 . . . . 13 A3
Maes-Yr-Ysgol CF62 . . . . 55 B4
Maes-y-Sarn CF15 . . . 11 B4
Maes Y Wennol CF23 . . . . 8 A2
Mafeking Rd CF23 . . . 26 C1
Magellan Cl CF62 . . . . 52 A3
Magnolia Cl CF23 . . . 18 A3
Magretion Pl / Maes Magretian 6 CF10 . . . . 42 A3
Maillard's Haven CF64 . . . . 49 B1
Main Ave CF23 . . . . . . 27 A1
MAINDY 25 A1
Maindy Mews CF24 . . 34 B4
Maindy Rd CF24 . . . . 34 A4
Main Rd CF15 . . . . 2 A4
Main St CF63 . . . . 52 B2
Maitland Pl CF11 . . . . 41 A4
Maitland St CF14 . . . . 25 A2
Major Rd CF5 . . . . 33 B1
Maldwyn St CF11 . . . . 33 B3
Malefant St CF24 . . . . 25 C1
Mallard Cl 8 CF3 . . . . 20 C3
Mallard Way CF64 . . . 59 B3
Malmsmead Rd CF3 . . . . 19 C3
Malpas Cl 1 CF3 . . . . 20 C3

Malthouse Ave CF23 . . 8 B2
Maltings The CF23 . . . 8 A1
Maltings The CF3 . . . . 35 C1
Malvern Dr CF14 . . . . . 16 A3
Mandeville Pl 7 CF11 . . . . 33 C1
Mandeville St 8 CF11 . . . . 33 C1
Manitoba Cl CF23 . . . 17 C1
Manod Rd CF14 . . . . . 23 C2
Manorbier Cl 1 CF64 . . . . 47 C3
Manorbier Cres CF3 . . . . 28 B4
Manorbier Ct CF62 . . . 51 C3
Manor Cl CF14 . . . . . . 15 B1
Manor Rise CF14 . . . . . 24 B4
Manor St CF14 . . . . . . 25 B2
Manor Way CF14 . . . . 15 C1
Mansell Ave CF5 . . . . . 37 B4
Mansfield St 12 CF11 . . . . 33 C1
Manston Cl 5 CF5 . . . 23 C1
Maple Cl CF62 . . . . . . 52 A2
Maple Rd
Cardiff / Caerdydd CF5 . . . . 22 A1
Penarth CF64 . . . . . . 48 B3
Maple Tree Cl CF15 . . . . 13 A2
Maplewood Ave 4 CF14 . . . . 23 B3
Maplewood Ct CF14 . . . . 23 C3
Maplewood Flats 3 CF14 . . . . 23 B3
Marchwood Cl CF3 . . 19 C1
Marconi Ave CF14 . . . 44 C2
Marcross Rd CF5 . . . . 37 C4
Mardy Ct CF11 . . . . . . 41 B4
Mardy Rd CF3 . . . . . . 28 B2
Mardy St CF11 . . . . . . 41 B4
Margam Rd CF14 . . . . 24 C2
Margaret Ave CF62 . . 51 C4
Marguerites Way CF5 . . . . 30 B1
Maria Ct CF10 . . . . . . 42 A3
Maria St CF10 . . . . . . 42 A3
Marina Bldgs CF64 . . . 45 B1
Marine Dr CF62 . . . . . . 54 B1
Marine Par CF64 . . . . . 49 B2
Mariner's Hts CF64 . . 45 B1
Marion Ct CF14 . . . . . . 6 B1
Marion St CF24 . . . . . 35 C2
Marionville Gdns CF5 . . . . 31 C4
Market Pl CF5 . . . . . . 33 B2
Market Rd CF5 . . . . . . 33 A2
Market St
Barry / Y Barri CF62 . . . . 55 A2
Tongwynlais CF15 . . . . . 3 A1
Mark St CF11 . . . . 34 A1
Marland Ho CF10 . . . . 63 B1
Marlborough Cl CF63 . . . . 52 C2
Marlborough Ho 2 CF10 . . . . 63 B2
Marlborough Inf Sch CF23 . . . . 35 B4
Marlborough Jun Sch CF23 . . . . 35 B4
Marlborough Rd CF23 . . . . 35 B4
Marlborough Terr CF10 . . . . 33 C4
Marl Ct CF11 . . . . 41 B1
Marle Cl CF23 . . . . . . 18 C4
Marloes Cl CF62 . . . . 51 C2
Marloes Rd CF5 . . . . . 30 C1
Marquis Cl CF62 . . . . . 56 A1
Marshall Cl 2 CF5 . . . 23 A2
Martin Rd CF24 . . . . . . 43 C4

Mary Ann St CF10 ....63 C2
Mary Immaculate High
  Sch CF5 ....38 A2
Maryport Rd CF23 ....26 A2
Mary Price Ct CF24 ..35 C1
Mary St CF14 ....23 B2
Masefield Rd CF64 ...48 C4
Mason Ct CF14 ....15 B2
Mathew Wlk CF5 .....23 A2
Mathias Ct **1** CF23 ..27 A1
Matthew Rd CF62 ....60 A1
Matthewson Cl
  CF14 ....24 B2
Matthew Terr CF14 ..47 C4
Matthysens Way
  CF3 ....21 A1
Maughan La **6**
  CF64 ....45 B1
Maughan Terr **5**
  CF64 ....45 B1
Maureen Ave CF5 ....31 C2
Mavis Gr CF14 ....16 A1
Maxwell Rd CF3 ......28 B4
Mayfair CF5 ....37 C2
Mayfair Dr CF14 ......5 C3
Mayfield Ave CF5 ....32 B2
Mayflower Ave CF14 ..5 B1
Mayflower Way
  CF62 ....60 C1
Mayhill Cl CF14 ......6 A3
Maynard Ct CF5 ......32 B4
May St CF24 ....34 B4
Meadowbank Ct
  CF5 ....22 C2
Meadowbank Specl
  Sch CF14 ....24 A2
Meadow Cl CF23 .....18 A4
Meadow Croft
  CF62 ....61 A1
Meadowgate Cl
  CF14 ....14 C3
Meadow La CF64 .....48 C1
Meadowlane Prim Sch
  CF3 ....20 C1
Meadowlark Cl **6**
  CF3 ....20 B3
Meadowside CF64 ....48 A3
Meadow St CF11 .....33 A3
Meadow Sweet Dr
  CF3 ....21 B2
Meadow Vale CF63 ...52 C3
Meadow View
  CF63 ....53 A3
Meadow View Ct
  CF64 ....58 A2
Meadvale Rd CF3 .....20 A2
Meggitt Rd CF62 .....51 B3
Meirion Cl CF23 ......52 B3
Meirion Pl CF24 ......36 B2
Meirwen Dr CF5 ......37 C2
Melbourne Ct CF14 ..15 B2
Melbourne Rd
  CF14 ....16 C4
Meliden La CF64 .....48 C3
Meliden Rd CF64 .....48 C3
Melingriffith Dr
  CF14 ....14 B1
Melrose Ave CF23 ....26 C1
Melrose Cl CF3 ....20 C4
Melrose Ct
  Cardiff / Caerdydd,
    Canton CF11 ....33 A3
  6 Cardiff / Caerdydd,
    Pen-y-lan CF23 ....26 B2
Melrose Gdns CF23 ..26 C1
Melrose St CF63 .....52 B1
Melville Ave CF3 .....20 C4
Melville Cl CF62 .....51 B4
Melyn Y Gors CF63 ..52 C4
Menai Way CF3 ....20 A2
Mendip Rd CF3 ....19 A1
Mendip View CF63 ...52 C1

Merches Gdns
  CF11 ....63 A1
Merches Pl CF11 .....41 B4
Mercia Rd CF24 ......36 A2
Meredith Rd CF24 ...36 A2
Merganser Ct CF63 ..55 C4
Meridian Ct **1**
  CF14 ....25 A2
Meridian The CF64 ..45 A1
Merioneth Ho **5**
  CF64 ....48 C2
Merioneth Pl CF62 ..51 C2
Merlin Cl
  Cardiff / Caerdydd
    CF14 ....5 C2
  Penarth CF64 ....59 B4
Merlin Pl CF63 ....52 A2
Merret Ct CF24 ......36 B3
MERTHYR DYFAN ...51 B3
Merthyr Dyfan Rd
  Barry / Y Barri
    CF62 ....51 C4
  Barry / Y Barri,
    Gibbonsdown
    CF62 ....51 C2
Merthyr Rd
  Cardiff / Caerdydd,
    Gwaun Treoda
    CF14 ....24 C3
  Cardiff / Caerdydd,
    Whitchurch CF14 ..24 A4
  Tongwynlais CF15 ....3 A1
Merthyr St
  Barry / Y Barri
    CF63 ....55 C4
  Cardiff / Caerdydd
    CF24 ....34 A4
Mervinian Cl CF10 ..63 D1
Mervyn Rd
  Cardiff / Caerdydd,
    Tremorfa CF24 .....36 A2
  Cardiff / Caerdydd,
    Whitchurch CF14 ..24 A4
Messina Ho CF10 ....63 C1
Metal St CF24 ....35 B2
Meteor St CF24 ......35 A2
Mews The **7** CF63 ..55 C4
Meyrick Rd CF5 ......37 C4
Michaelston Cl
  CF63 ....52 B3
Michaelston Com Coll
  CF5 ....37 B4
Michaelston Ct CF5 ..37 B4
Michaelston Rd
  CF5 ....30 A1
MICHAELSTON-SUPER-
  ELY /
  LLANFIHANGEL-AR-
  ELAI 30 B1
Michelston Ct **3**
  CF5 ....38 B4
Miles Ct CF15 ....2 B3
Milestone Cl CF14 ...16 A2
Millbank Prim Sch
  CF5 ....32 A2
Millbrook Cl CF64 ...47 B4
Millbrook Hts CF64 ..47 B4
Millbrook Pk CF64 ...6 B3
Millbrook Rd CF64 ...47 B4
Mill Cl
  Cardiff / Caerdydd
    CF5 ....6 B1
  Dinas Powis / Dinas
    Powys CF64 ....47 A3
Millennium Ct **4**
  CF24 ....35 B3
Millennium Stad ★
  CF10 ....63 A2
Millfield CF14 ....6 B3
Millfield Cl CF3 ......20 B2
Millgate CF14 ....6 B1
Millheath Dr CF14 ...6 B2

Millhill Ct **4** CF5 ....31 C4
Millicent St CF10 ....63 C2
Mill La
  Cardiff / Caerdydd,
    Llandaff / Llandaf
    CF5 ....32 C4
  Cardiff / Caerdydd, Llane
    Deyrn CF3 ....19 C4
Mill La / Lon Y Felin
  CF10 ....63 B2
Mill Pl
  Cardiff / Caerdydd, Ely /
    Tre-lai CF5 ....31 C2
  Cardiff / Caerdydd,
    Lisvane / Llys Faen
    CF14 ....6 C3
Millrace Cl CF14 .....6 B2
Mill Rd
  Cardiff / Caerdydd, Ely /
    Tre-lai CF5 ....31 C2
  Cardiff / Caerdydd,
    Lisvane / Llys Faen
    CF14 ....6 B2
  Dinas Powis / Dinas
    Powys CF64 ....47 A3
Millwood CF14 ....6 B3
Millwood Rise
  CF62 ....54 C3
Milton Pl CF5 ....31 C4
Milton Rd
  Barry / Y Barri
    CF62 ....51 B3
  Penarth CF64 ....48 C4
Milton St CF24 ....62 D4
Milverton Rd CF3 ....19 C3
Milward Rd CF5 ......52 B1
Minafon CF14 ....4 C1
Minavon **1** CF14 ...15 B1
Minehead Ave
  CF64 ....58 A2
Minehead Rd CF3 ....19 C2
Minister St CF24 .....34 B4
Minny St CF24 ....34 B4
Minori Ho CF10 ......42 B2
Minsmere CF3 ....21 B3
Minster Cl CF63 .....52 B3
Minster Rd CF23 .....35 C4
Minton Ct CF24 ......36 B2
Min-y-Coed CF15 ....13 B3
Min-y-Mor CF62 .....54 B1
Min-y-Nant CF14 ....15 B3
Miskin St
  Barry / Y Barri
    CF62 ....55 A2
  Cardiff / Caerdydd
    CF24 ....62 B4
Mitchell Cl CF3 ......21 A1
Miterdale Ct CF23 ...26 A3
Mitre Ct CF5 ....23 C1
Mitre Pl CF5 ....23 C1
Moira Pl CF24 ....62 D3
Moira St CF24 ....35 A2
Moira Terr CF24 .....62 D3
Mona Pl CF24 ....36 A3
Monico The CF14 ....15 C2
Monkstone Cl CF64 ..48 B1
Monkstone Rise
  CF3 ....19 C1
Monkton St CF11 ....31 A3
Monmouth Ho
  Cardiff / Caerdydd
    CF23 ....26 B3
  8 Penarth CF64 ....59 B4
Monmouth St CF11 ..41 B4
Monmouth Way
  CF62 ....51 C1
Montgomery Rd
  CF62 ....55 B3
Montgomery St
  CF24 ....26 B1

Monthermer Rd
  CF24 ....25 C1
Moorby Ct CF10 .....63 D1
Moordale Rd CF11 ...41 C2
Moore Cl CF5 ....31 A1
Moore Rd CF5 ....30 C1
Moorings The CF64 ..45 A1
Moor King Cl CF3 ...21 B2
Moorland Prim Sch
  CF24 ....35 C1
Moorland Rd
  Cardiff / Caerdydd
    CF24 ....36 A1
  Cardiff / Caerdydd,
    Tremorfa CF24 .....35 C2
Moors La CF24 ....35 B1
Morel Ct CF11 ....44 C4
Morel St CF63 ....56 A4
Morfa Cres CF3 ......20 B1
Morfa La CF5 ....46 B2
Morgan Arc CF10 ....63 B2
Morgan St
  Barry / Y Barri
    CF63 ....56 B4
  Cardiff / Caerdydd
    CF24 ....63 C2
MORGANSTOWN /
  TREFORGAN 13 A4
Morlais St
  Barry / Y Barri
    CF63 ....52 C1
  Cardiff / Caerdydd
    CF23 ....26 A1
Morningside Wlk
  CF62 ....51 C4
Mornington Ct CF3 ..27 C3
Morris Ave CF14 .....5 B1
Morris Finer Cl
  CF5 ....31 C1
MORRISTOWN 48 B3
Mortimer Rd CF11 ..33 B3
Morton Ct CF14 .....25 C4
Mostyn Cl CF5 ....37 C4
Mountain Rd CF15 ..11 C4
Mountbatten Cl
  CF23 ....17 A1
Mountbatten Rd
  CF62 ....52 A4
Mountjoy Ave CF64 ..48 C4
Mountjoy Cl **1**
  CF64 ....48 C4
Mountjoy Cres **1**
  CF64 ....48 C3
Mountjoy La **2**
  CF64 ....48 C3
Mountjoy Pl CF64 ...48 C4
Mount Pleasant
  CF63 ....52 B1
Mount Pleasant Ave
  CF3 ....19 C2
Mount Pleasant La
  CF3 ....19 C2
Mount Rd CF64 ......47 A3
Mount St Denys
  CF14 ....6 C4
Mount Stuart Prim
  Sch CF10 ....42 A1
Mount Stuart Sq
  CF10 ....42 A2
Mount The
  Cardiff / Caerdydd
    CF5 ....33 A3
  Dinas Powis / Dinas
    Powys CF64 ....47 A3
Moxon St CF63 ......52 C1
Moy Rd
  Cardiff / Caerdydd
    CF24 ....34 C4
  Taffs Well / Ffynnon Taf
    CF15 ....2 B4
Moy Road Ind Est
  CF15 ....2 B4
Muirton Rd CF24 ....36 A2
Mulberry Ct CF62 ...54 C2

Mulberry Dr CF5 .....8 B3
Mullins Ave CF3 .....20 A1
Mundy Pl CF24 ......34 B4
Munro Pl CF62 ......51 B1
MURCH 47 C3
Murch Cres CF64 ....47 C3
Murch Jun Sch
  CF64 ....47 B3
Murch Rd CF64 ......47 C3
Mur Gwyn CF14 .....15 C4
Murlande Way
  CF62 ....61 B1
Murrayfield Rd
  CF14 ....16 A1
Murray Wlk **13**
  CF11 ....33 B1
Murrel Cl CF5 ....37 C3
Museum Ave CF10 ..62 B4
Museum Pl CF10 ....62 B4
Mylo-Griffiths Cl
  CF5 ....23 A3
MYNACHDY 24 C2
Mynachdy Rd
  Cardiff / Caerdydd
    CF14 ....24 C2
  Cardiff / Caerdydd,
    Gwaun Treoda
    CF14 ....24 B3
Myrtle Cl CF64 ......48 B3
Myrtle Gr CF63 .....52 C2

N

Nailsea Ct CF64 .....58 C2
Nant-Fawr Cl CF23 ..17 B2
Nant-Fawr Cres
  CF23 ....17 B2
Nant-Fawr Rd
  CF23 ....17 B2
Nant Isaf CF5 ....46 B3
Nant Talwg Way
  CF62 ....54 B4
Nant Walla CF14 ....15 C4
Nant Y Dowlais
  CF5 ....37 A4
Nant-y-Drope CF5 ...37 B4
Nant Y Fedw CF14 ..24 C4
Nant Y Garth CF15 ..2 A3
Nant Y Gwladys
  CF5 ....12 B1
Nant Y Pepra CF5 ...37 B4
Nant Y Plac CF5 .....37 B4
Nant Yr Arthur CF5 ..37 B4
Nant-yr-Ely CF5 .....37 A4
Nant Y Rhos CF5 ....37 B4
Nant Y Wedal CF14 ..25 C2
Narberth Rd CF5 ....31 B1
Narberth Ct CF62 ...51 C2
Naseby Cl CF23 .....8 A1
Nasturtium Way
  CF23 ....7 B1
Nat Assembly for
  Wales The /
  Cynulliad
  Cenedlaethol Cymru
  CF10 ....42 B2
National Museum
  Cardiff / Amgueddfa
  Genedlaethol
  Caerdydd ★ CF10 ..62 B4
Neale St CF24 ....51 B1
Neath St CF24 ......35 C1
Neilson Cl CF24 .....35 B1
Nelson Ct CF10 .....63 D1
Nelson Rd CF62 .....52 A3
Nesta Rd CF5 ....33 C2
Nettlefold Rd CF24 ..42 C4
Neville Pl **14** CF11 ..33 C1
Neville St CF11 ......33 C1
Nevin Cres CF3 .....28 B4

Newborough Ave
CF14 . . . . .16 B4
Newby Ct CF10 . . . . . .63 C1
Newent Rd CF11 . . . . . .20 C2
Newfoundland Rd
CF14 . . . . .25 A2
Newgale Cl CF62 . . . . .51 C3
Newgale Ho CF14 . . . .23 C4
Newgale Pl CF5 . . . . . .38 C4
New George St / Stryd George Newydd
CF10 . . . . .42 B1
New House Ct 4
CF63 . . . . .52 B2
Newlands Ct CF14 . . . . .6 B1
Newlands Rd CF3 . . . . .29 B3
Newlands St CF62 . . . .55 C4
Newminster Rd
CF23 . . . . .35 C4
Newport Rd
Cardiff / Caerdydd,
Roath / Y Rhath
CF24 . . . . .35 B3
Cardiff / Caerdydd,
Rumney / Rhymni
CF3 . . . . .19 C1
Newport Road La
CF24 . . . . .62 D3
Newport St CF11 . . . . .41 C2
New Rd CF3 . . . . .28 A2
New Theatre *
CF10 . . . . .62 B3
NEWTON 29 B1
Newton Rd
Cardiff / Caerdydd,
Newton CF3 . . . . .29 B2
Cardiff / Caerdydd,
Saltmead CF11 . . . . . .40 C4
Newton St CF63 . . . . . .52 B1
Newydd Ct CF15 . . . . .13 C4
New Zealand Rd
CF14 . . . . .25 A2
Neyland Ct CF62 . . . . .51 C3
Neyland Pl CF5 . . . . . .38 C4
Nicholas Cl CF15 . . . . .14 A1
Nicholson Webb Cl
CF5 . . . . .22 C3
Nightingale Pl
CF64 . . . . .47 C3
Ninian Park (Cardiff City AFC) CF11 . . . .40 C4
Ninian Park Prim Sch
CF11 . . . . .41 A3
Ninian Park Rd
CF11 . . . . .33 C1
Ninian Park Sta
CF11 . . . . .40 C4
Ninian Rd CF14 . . . . . .24 A4
Nora St CF24 . . . . .35 B2
Norbury Ave CF5 . . . . .31 C3
Norbury Ct 4 CF5 . . .31 C3
Norbury Ho 6 CF5 . . .31 C3
Norbury Rd CF5 . . . . . .31 C3
Nordale Ct CF14 . . . . .17 A4
Nordale Rise CF63 . . . .52 C1
Norfolk Ct 3 CF15 . . .13 B2
Norfolk St CF5 . . . . . . .32 C2
Norman Rd CF14 . . . . .24 A4
Norman St 1 CF24 . . .34 C4
Norrell Cl CF11 . . . . . .32 C1
Norris Cl CF64 . . . . . . .44 A1
Norseman Cl CF62 . . . .60 A1
Northam Ave CF3 . . . . .19 A1
North Church St
CF10 . . . . .63 C1
Northcliffe Dr CF64 . . .45 B1
North Clive St
CF11 . . . . .41 A3

Northcote La CF24 . . . .62 C4
Northcote St CF24 . . . .62 C4
Northcote Terr
CF63 . . . . .52 C1
North Edward St
CF10 . . . . .62 C3
Northern Ave
Cardiff / Caerdydd
CF14 . . . . .15 A2
Cardiff / Caerdydd
CF14 . . . . .15 B1
Northlands CF3 . . . . . .28 A2
North Luton Pl
CF24 . . . . .35 A1
North Morgan St 1
CF11 . . . . .33 C1
North Park Rd
CF24 . . . . .35 C2
North Rd
Barry / Y Barri
CF64 . . . . .53 B1
Cardiff / Caerdydd,
Cathays CF10 . . . . . . .62 A4
North Rise CF14 . . . . . . .6 B1
North St CF11 . . . . .41 B3
Northumberland St
CF5 . . . . .33 A1
North View CF15 . . . . . .2 C4
North Wlk CF62 . . . . . . .51 B1
Norton Ave CF14 . . . . .24 C4
Norwich Rd CF23 . . . . .27 B1
Norwood CF14 . . . . .6 A2
Norwood Cres
CF63 . . . . .52 C2
Norwood Ct 1
CF24 . . . . .35 B3
Nottage Rd CF5 . . . . . .38 A4
Nottingham St CF5 . . .32 C2
NURSTON 60 A2
Nurston Cl CF62 . . . . . .60 A1

O

Oak Ct
8 Cardiff / Caerdydd
CF24 . . . . .35 A3
Penarth CF64 . . . . . . .48 B2
Tongwynlais CF15 . . . . .3 B2
Oakdene Cl CF23 . . . . .26 B4
Oakfield Mews 7
CF24 . . . . .35 B3
Oakfield Prim Sch
CF3 . . . . .20 B3
Oak Field Prim Sch / Ysgol Gwaun-y-Nant
CF62 . . . . .51 C2
Oakfield Rd CF62 . . . . .51 A2
Oakfield St CF24 . . . . .35 B3
Oakford Cl CF23 . . . . . . .7 C1
Oak Ho CF14 . . . . .14 B3
Oaklands Cl CF3 . . . . . .20 B3
Oakleafe Dr CF23 . . . . .18 B4
Oakley Pl CF11 . . . . . . .41 B2
Oakmead Cl CF23 . . . . . .8 A1
Oakmeadow Ct 3
CF3 . . . . .20 C3
Oakmeadow Dr
CF3 . . . . .20 C2
Oakridge CF14 . . . . .6 A2
Oakridge E CF14 . . . . . .6 A3
Oakridge W CF14 . . . . . .6 A2
Oaks The CF14 . . . . .6 C2
Oak Tree Cl CF15 . . . . .13 C4
Oak Tree Ct CF23 . . . . . .8 B3
Oakway CF5 . . . . .31 A4
Oak Wood Ave
CF23 . . . . .27 A3
Oakwood Cl CF64 . . . . .44 B2
Oban St CF63 . . . . .52 B1
Ocean Bldgs CF10 . . . .42 B2
Ocean Ho 17 CF10 . . . .42 A2
Ocean Way CF24 . . . . . .43 A4
Ochr Y Coed CF14 . . . . .6 A3
Odet Ct CF14 . . . . .14 B3

O'donnell Rd CF63 . . . .52 A2
Odyn's Fee CF62 . . . . . .60 A1
Ogmore Pl CF63 . . . . . .52 A3
Ogmore Rd CF5 . . . . . .38 B4
Ogwen Dr CF23 . . . . . .17 C1
Okehampton Ave
CF3 . . . . .19 C4
Old Bakery Ct CF15 . . .11 C4
Old Barry Rd CF64 . . . .44 B2
Old Church Rd
CF14 . . . . .15 B1
Old Clipper Rd
CF10 . . . . .43 B2
Old Farm La CF15 . . . . .10 B2
Old Farm Mews
CF64 . . . . .47 A3
Old Field Rd CF15 . . . .14 B4
Old Garden Ct 7
CF15 . . . . .13 B2
Old Hill CF3 . . . . .20 A2
Old Malt Ho CF64 . . . . .47 A3
Old Market CF5 . . . . . .46 B2
Old Mill Bsns Pk
CF11 . . . . .32 B2
Old Mill Dr CF5 . . . . . . .12 B1
Oldmill Rd CF63 . . . . . .52 C2
Old Mill Rd CF14 . . . . . .6 B2
Old Newport Rd
CF3 . . . . .20 C4
Old Police Sta The
CF3 . . . . .28 A4
Old Port Rd CF5 . . . . . .46 B2
Old Rectory 4 CF5 . . .33 A2
Old School Ct CF15 . . . .3 A1
Old School Rd CF5 . . . .31 C1
Old Vicarage Cl
CF14 . . . . .16 C4
Old Village Rd
CF62 . . . . .54 C2
Oldwell Ct 9 CF23 . . .26 B2
O'Leary Dr CF11 . . . . . .44 C4
Olive Ct 4 CF11 . . . . .33 B2
Ollivant Cl CF5 . . . . . . .22 C3
Ontario Way CF23 . . . . .17 C1
Orange Gr CF5 . . . . . . .22 B1
Orbit St CF24 . . . . .35 A2
Orbit Theatre *
CF10 . . . . .63 B2
Orchard Castle CF14 . . .5 C2
Orchard Cl CF5 . . . . . . .46 B3
Orchard Cres CF64 . . . .47 B3
Orchard Ct CF14 . . . . . . .6 A4
Orchard Dr
Barry / Y Barri
CF62 . . . . .51 C1
Cardiff / Caerdydd
CF14 . . . . .15 A1
Orchard Gr CF15 . . . . . .13 B4
Orchard Park Cl
CF3 . . . . .20 B3
Orchard Pk CF3 . . . . . . .20 B3
Orchard Pl CF11 . . . . . .33 B2
Orchard Rise CF64 . . . .48 B4
Orchid Cl CF3 . . . . .21 B2
Ordell St CF24 . . . . . . .35 B1
Oregano Cl 15 CF3 . . .21 A4
Oriel Ho CF24 . . . . .63 D2
Oriel Rheilffordd Railway Gallery *
CF10 . . . . .42 B2
Orion Ct 4 CF24 . . . . .35 A2
Ormonde CF23 . . . . . . .27 A3
Osborne Sq CF11 . . . . .41 A3
Osprey Cl
Cardiff / Caerdydd
CF3 . . . . .20 C4
Penarth CF64 . . . . . . .59 B3
Osprey Ct 1 CF63 . . . .55 C3
Oswestry Cl CF3 . . . . . .28 B3
Othery Pl CF3 . . . . .19 C4
Oundle Ct 6 CF5 . . . . .31 C2
Overstone Ct CF10 . . . .42 A2
Ovington Terr CF5 . . . .32 C3

Owain Cl
Cardiff / Caerdydd
CF23 . . . . .26 B4
Penarth CF64 . . . . . . .48 B3
Owens Cl CF62 . . . . . . .55 B4
Oxford Arc CF10 . . . . . .63 B2
Oxford La CF24 . . . . . . .35 A2
Oxford St
Barry / Y Barri
CF62 . . . . .54 C2
Cardiff / Caerdydd
CF24 . . . . .62 D4
Oxwich Cl CF5 . . . . . . .32 A3
Oyster Bend CF64 . . . . .58 B1

P

Pace Cl CF5 . . . . .22 C2
Pacific Bsns Pk
CF24 . . . . .43 B4
Pacific Rd CF24 . . . . . . .43 B4
Padarn Cl CF23 . . . . . . .17 B1
Paddock Pl 1
CF63 . . . . .52 B2
Paddocks The CF64 . . .59 B4
Paddock The
Cardiff / Caerdydd,
Lisvane / Llys Faen
CF14 . . . . .6 B3
Cardiff / Caerdydd, Pen-y-lan CF23 . . . . . . .26 B2
Page Dr CF24 . . . . .27 C1
Paget La CF11 . . . . .41 B3
Paget Pl CF64 . . . . .45 B1
Paget Rd
Barry / Y Barri
CF62 . . . . .55 B1
Penarth CF64 . . . . . . .45 B1
Paget St CF11 . . . . .41 B2
Paget Terr CF64 . . . . . .45 B1
Palace Ave CF15 . . . . . .32 C4
Palace Ct CF23 . . . . . . .17 C2
Palace Rd CF5 . . . . .32 C4
Pallot Way CF24 . . . . . .36 A4
Palmers Dr CF5 . . . . . . .31 C1
Palmer St CF63 . . . . . . .53 A2
Palmerston Prim Sch
CF63 . . . . .53 A2
Palmerston Rd
CF63 . . . . .53 A1
Palmerston Workshops CF63 . . . .53 A2
PALMERSTOWN 53 A2
Palmerstown Ho
CF63 . . . . .53 A2
Palmers Vale Bsns Ctr
CF63 . . . . .53 A2
Pantbach Cl CF15 . . . . .11 C3
Pantbach Ave CF14 . . . .24 C4
Pantbach Rd CF14 . . . . .24 C4
Pant-Bach Rd
CF14 . . . . .15 C1
Panteg CF15 . . . . .11 C3
Panteg Cl CF5 . . . . .37 B3
Panteg Mews 3
CF5 . . . . .32 C3
Pantglas CF15 . . . . .11 C3
Pant Glas CF23 . . . . . . .19 A3
Pantgwynlais CF15 . . . .3 B1
PANTMAWR 14 C4
Pantmawr Ct CF14 . . . .14 C4
Pantmawr Rd CF14 . . . .14 C3
Pant Tawel La
CF15 . . . . .12 C2
Pantycelyn Rd
CF64 . . . . .44 A2
Pant-y-Deri Cl 6
CF5 . . . . .38 B4
Pant yr Wyn CF23 . . . . .26 A2
Paper Mill Rd CF11 . . . .32 B2
Parade The
Barry / Y Barri
CF62 . . . . .54 C1

Parade The continued
Cardiff / Caerdydd,
Adamsdown CF24 . . . .62 D3
Cardiff / Caerdydd,
Llandaff North
CF14 . . . . .23 B4
7 Dinas Powis / Dinas Powys CF64 . . . . .47 C3
Parc Castell-y-Mynach CF15 . . . . . . .10 B3
Parc Clwyd 2
CF63 . . . . .52 C3
Parc Hafod CF14 . . . . . .14 C2
Parc Manwerthu Bae Caerdydd / Cardiff Bay Ret Pk
CF11 . . . . .41 B1
Cardiff / Caerdydd
CF11 . . . . .44 C1
Parc St Catwg
CF15 . . . . .11 C3
Parc Ty Glas CF14 . . . . .16 B3
Parc Ty Glas Ind Est
CF14 . . . . .16 B3
Parc-y-Bryn CF15 . . . . .10 A3
Parc-y-Coed CF15 . . . . .10 A2
Parc-y-Felin CF15 . . . . .10 A2
Parc-y-Fro CF15 . . . . . . .10 B3
Pardoe Cres CF62 . . . . .51 B2
Park Ave
Barry / Y Barri
CF62 . . . . .54 C1
Barry / Y Barri
CF62 . . . . .55 A2
Cardiff / Caerdydd
CF14 . . . . .14 C2
Cardiff / Caerdydd,
Culverhouse Cross
CF5 . . . . .37 C2
Park Cres
Barry / Y Barri
CF62 . . . . .54 C3
Cardiff / Caerdydd
CF14 . . . . .14 C2
Park Ct CF62 . . . . .54 C2
Park End Ct CF23 . . . . .17 A2
Park End La CF23 . . . . . .17 A2
Parker Pl CF5 . . . . .38 A4
Parker Rd CF5 . . . . .38 A4
Parkfield Ho CF14 . . . . .25 A1
Parkfield Pl CF14 . . . . . .25 A1
Park Gr CF10 . . . . .62 C4
Park La
Cardiff / Caerdydd
CF14 . . . . .14 C2
Taffs Well / Ffynnon Taf
CF15 . . . . .2 A4
Park La / Lon Y Parc
CF10 . . . . .62 C3
Park Lands CF24 . . . . . .35 A3
Parkland Wlk CF62 . . . .54 C3
Park Pl / Plas Y Parc
CF10 . . . . .62 B4
Park Rd
Barry / Y Barri
CF62 . . . . .54 C2
Cardiff / Caerdydd
CF14 . . . . .14 C2
Dinas Powis / Dinas Powys CF64 . . . . .47 A4
Penarth CF64 . . . . . . .49 B3
Radyr CF15 . . . . .13 B2
Parkside Ct 2 CF5 . . .33 A2
Park St CF10 . . . . .63 B2
Parkstone Ave CF3 . . . .20 B4
Parkview Ct CF64 . . . . .44 C1
Park View Ct
2 Cardiff / Caerdydd
CF11 . . . . .34 A3
11 Cardiff / Caerdydd,
Whitchurch CF14 . . . .15 A2

Parkwall Rd CF14,
   CF23 . . . . 8 B3
Parkway CF3 . . . . .28 C2
Parracombe Ct CF3 . .19 C3
Parracombe Cres
   CF3 . . . . .19 C3
Parry St 5 CF5 . . . . .33 A2
Partridge Ct 5
   CF24 . . . . .35 B3
Partridge La CF24 . . .35 B3
Partridge Rd CF24 . . .35 B3
Pascal Cl CF3 . . . . .21 B4
Pascall Ct CF24 . . . . .62 D4
Pastures The CF62 . . .51 B2
Patchway Cres CF3 . .27 C4
Patmore Cl CF15 . . . . . . 2 A4
Patreane Way CF5 . . .37 B3
Patterdale Cl CF23 . . .26 A2
Pavaland Cl 5 CF3 . .20 C2
Pavin Ct CF5 . . . . . . .23 C1
Peach Pl 2 CF5 . . . .31 B4
Pearce Ct CF3 . . . . . . .21 A1
Pearce Ct CF3 . . . . . . .52 A3
Pearl Ct CF24 . . . . . . .35 C3
Pearl Pl CF24 . . . . . . .35 B2
Pearl St
   Cardiff / Caerdydd,
   Splott CF24 . . . . .35 B2
   Cardiff / Caerdydd,
   Tremorfa CF24 . . . . . . .35 C1
Pearson St CF24 . . . . .62 D4
Peckham Cl CF5 . . . . .22 C3
Pedair Erw Rd
   CF14 . . . . .16 A1
Pellett St CF10 . . . . . .63 C2
Pembridge Dr
   CF64 . . . . .44 C1
Pembroke Cl 4
   CF64 . . . . .47 C3
Pembroke Ct 6
   CF14 . . . . .15 A2
Pembroke Mews
   CF5 . . . . .32 C2
Pembroke Pl CF63 . . .51 C1
Pembroke Rd CF5 . . .33 A2
Pembroke Terr
   CF64 . . . . .45 B1
Penally Rd CF5 . . . . . .39 A4
PENARTH 49 C3
Penarth Head La
   CF64 . . . . .45 B1
Penarth Portway
   CF64 . . . . .45 B1
Penarth Rd CF11 . . . . .44 B3
Penarth Rd / Heol
   Penarth CF11 . . . . . . .41 A2
Penarth Road Ret Pk
   . . . . .44 A3
Pencader Rd CF5 . . . .31 C2
Pencisely Ave CF5 . . .32 B3
Pencisely Cres CF5 . .32 B3
Pencisely Rd CF5 . . . .32 C3
Pencisely Rise CF5 . .32 C3
Pencoedtre Rd
   Barry / Y Barri,
   Cadoxton CF63 . . . . . .52 B3
   Barry / Y Barri CF62,
   CF63 . . . . .52 A4
Pendine Cl CF62 . . . . .51 C3
Pendine Rd CF5 . . . . .31 C2
Pendoylan Cl CF63 . .52 B3
Pendoylan Ct
   11 Cardiff / Caerdydd,
   Caerau CF5 . . . . .38 B4
   Cardiff / Caerdydd, Ely /
   Tre-lai CF5 . . . . .31 C2
Pendragon Cl CF14 . .5 B2
Pendraw Pl CF23 . . . .17 B2
Pendwyallt Rd
   CF14 . . . . .14 B3

Pendyris St CF11 . . . .63 A1
Penedre CF5 . . . . .23 C1
Penffordd CF15 . . . . .11 C3
Penford Ct CF24 . . . . .62 C4
PENGAM GREEN 36 C2
Pengam Rd CF24 . . . .36 A4
Pengwern Rd CF5 . . .31 C2
Penhevad St CF11 . . .41 B2
Penhill Cl CF5 . . . . . . .33 A3
Pen-Hill Rd CF11 . . . .33 A3
Penlan Rd CF64 . . . . . .44 A2
Penlan Rise CF64 . . . .44 A2
Pen Lasgan CF3 . . . . .20 C2
Penlline Ct CF14 . . . . .15 A1
Penlline Rd CF14 . . . .15 A1
Penlline St CF24 . . . . .62 C4
Penllyn Rd CF5 . . . . . .33 B1
Penmaen Wlk CF5 . .37 B3
Penmaes CF15 . . . . . .11 C3
Penmark Gn CF5 . . . .37 C4
Penmark Rd CF5 . . . .37 C4
Pennant Cres CF23 . .17 C2
Pennard Pl CF14 . . . . .24 C3
Pennine Cl CF14 . . . . .16 B3
Pennsylvania CF23 . .18 A1
Pennyroyal Cl CF3 . . .21 A4
Penrhos CF15 . . . . . . .13 A3
Penrhos Cres CF3 . . .28 B4
Penrhyn Ct CF3 . . . . . .20 B1
Pensarn Rd CF3 . . . . .20 B1
Penstone Ct CF10 . . .42 A2
Pentland Cl CF14 . . . .16 A3
Pent-Lee CF23 . . . . . . .18 B3
PENTREBANE 31 A4
Pentrebane Prim Sch
   CF5 . . . . .31 A4
Pentrebane Rd CF5 . .22 A1
Pentrebane St
   CF11 . . . . .41 B2
Pentre Gdns CF11 . . .63 A1
Pentre Pl 3 CF11 . . . .41 B3
Pentre St CF11 . . . . . .41 B3
PENTWYN 18 B3
Pentwyn CF15 . . . . . . .13 A2
Pentwyn Ct CF14 . . . .15 A3
Pentwyn Dr CF23 . . . .18 C3
Pentwyn Link Rd CF3,
   CF23 . . . . .8 C2
Pentwyn Rd CF23 . . .18 B4
PENTYRCH 11 C1
Pentyrch Prim Sch
   CF15 . . . . .11 B3
Pentyrch St CF24 . . . .25 B1
Penuel Rd CF15 . . . . .11 B3
Pen-y-Bryn CF62 . . . .54 B1
Pen-y-Bryn Pl
   CF14 . . . . .25 A2
Pen-y-Bryn Rd
   Cardiff / Caerdydd,
   Cyncoed CF23 . . . . . . .17 C3
   Cardiff / Caerdydd,
   Mynachdy CF14 . . . . . .25 A2
Pen-y-Bryn Way 2
   CF14 . . . . .25 A2
Pen-y-Byrn Prim Sch
   CF3 . . . . .20 A3
Pen-y-Cefn CF14 . . . .5 B2
Pen-y-cwm CF15 . . . .11 C4
Penydarren Dr
   CF14 . . . . .14 B1
Pen-y-Dre CF14 . . . . .15 B2
Penygarn Rd CF5 . . . .31 B2
Penygraig CF14 . . . . . . .4 C1
Pen-y-Groes Ave
   CF14 . . . . .16 A3
Pen-y-Groes Rd
   CF14 . . . . .16 A3
PEN-Y-LAN 26 C1
Pen-y-lan Ct 7 CF23 .26 B1
Penylan Oval CF23 . .26 B3
Pen-y-Lan Pl CF23 . . .26 B1

Pen-y-Lan Rd
   CF24 . . . . .35 A4
Pen-y-Lan Terr
   CF23 . . . . .26 C2
Pen-y-Peel Rd CF5 . .33 A2
Penyturnpike View
   CF64 . . . . .48 A4
Pen-y-Wain La
   CF24 . . . . .26 A1
Pen-y-Wain Pl
   CF24 . . . . .26 A1
Pen-y-Wain Rd
   CF24 . . . . .26 A1
Pen-y-Waun
   Dinas Powis / Dinas
   Powys CF64 . . . . .47 B3
   Pentyrch CF15 . . . . . . .11 C4
Peppermint Dr CF23 . .7 B1
Pepys Cres CF3 . . . . . .19 B2
Percival Cl CF14 . . . . .5 B2
Perclose CF64 . . . . . . .47 B3
Percy St CF10 . . . . . . .63 B1
Perrots Cl CF5 . . . . . . .31 C4
Persondy La CF5 . . . .30 A2
Peter Lea Prim Sch
   CF5 . . . . .22 C1
Peterswell Rd CF62 . .54 C4
Petherton Mews
   CF5 . . . . .23 B1
Petherton Pl 1
   CF3 . . . . .19 C2
Pethybridge Rd
   CF5 . . . . .31 A2
Petrel Cl CF64 . . . . . . .59 B3
Philadelphia Cl
   CF63 . . . . .53 A2
Philip Cl CF14 . . . . . . .16 A2
Philippa Freeth Ct
   CF63 . . . . .56 A3
Philip St CF11 . . . . . . .33 B1
Philog Ct CF14 . . . . . .24 B4
Philog The CF14 . . . . .24 B4
Phoenix Est CF14 . . . .16 A2
Phoenix Ho 3
   CF24 . . . . .35 B2
Phoenix Way CF14 . . .16 A1
Phyllis St CF62 . . . . . .55 C2
Piazza The CF11 . . . . .41 C1
Pickwick Cl CF14 . . . . .6 A2
Picton Pl CF11 . . . . . . .33 B1
Picton Rd CF62 . . . . . .60 C1
Picton Wlk 12 CF11 . .33 B1
Piercefield Pl CF24 . .35 B2
Pierhead St CF10 . . . .42 B2
Pierhead View
   CF64 . . . . .44 C2
Pilgrim Cl CF15 . . . . . .13 B1
Pill St CF64 . . . . .44 C1
Pilton Pl CF14 . . . . . . .24 C2
Pinecrest Dr CF14 . . . .6 A3
Pine Ct CF15 . . . . .3 B1
Pinehurst Rd CF5 . . . .31 A4
Pines The CF14 . . . . . .15 A1
Pine Tree Cl CF15 . . . .13 A3
Pinewood Cl CF64 . . .44 B2
Pine Wood Cres
   CF23 . . . . .27 A3
Piper Cl CF5 . . . . .22 C2
Pipkin Cl 6 CF23 . . . . 8 B1
Pitman La CF11 . . . . . .33 C2
Pitman St CF11 . . . . . .33 C2
Pitmedden Cl 5
   CF3 . . . . .20 C3
Planet St CF24 . . . . . .35 A2
Plantagenet St
   CF11 . . . . .63 A2
Plasbach 5 CF5 . . . . .31 B4
Plas Bute / Bute Pl
   CF10 . . . . .42 B2
Plas Cleddau CF62 . .54 C4
Plas Essyllt CF64 . . . .47 B3
Plas Glen Rosa
   CF64 . . . . .45 A1

Plas Gwernen CF63 . .52 B4
Plas-Mawr Rd CF5 . . .31 B4
Plasmawr Welsh
   Comp Sch / Ysgol
   Gyfun Gymraeg
   Plasmawr CF5 . . . . . . .22 B1
Plas Melin CF14 . . . . .23 B4
Plas Newydd CF14 . . .23 C4
Plasnewydd Pl 3
   . . . . .35 A4
Plasnewydd Rd
   Cardiff / Caerdydd
   CF24 . . . . .34 C4
   Cardiff / Caerdydd
   CF24 . . . . 62 D4
Plasnewydd Sq
   CF24 . . . . .35 A4
Plas Pamir CF64 . . . . .45 A1
Plas St Andresse
   CF64 . . . . .45 B2
Plas St Pol De Leon 2
   CF64 . . . . .45 A1
Plassey Ho 10 CF64 . .45 A1
Plassey Sq CF64 . . . . .45 A1
Plassey St CF64 . . . . .45 A1
Plas Taliesin CF64 . . .45 B2
Plas Treoda CF14 . . . .24 A4
Plasturton Ave
   CF11 . . . . .33 B3
Plasturton Gdns
   CF11 . . . . .33 C2
Plasturton Pl CF11 . .33 C2
Plas Windsor /
   Windsor Pl CF10 . . . .62 C3
Plas Y Biswail CF3 . .20 C2
Plas-y-Coed CF23 . . .26 A3
Plas Y Delyn CF14 . . . .6 C3
Plas-y-Llan CF14 . . . .15 A1
Plas-Y-Mynach
   CF15 . . . . .22 B4
Plas Y Parc / Park Pl
   CF10 . . . . 62 B4
Plas yr Neuadd /
   Guildhall Pl CF10 . . .63 B2
Pleasant View
   CF62 . . . . .51 A3
Plover Way CF64 . . . .59 B4
Plymouth Dr CF15 . . .13 C1
Plymouth Rd
   Barry / Y Barri
   CF62 . . . . .55 C1
   Penarth CF64 . . . . . . .49 B2
Plymouth Road Sta ★ . .55 C1
Plymouth Wood Cl
   CF5 . . . . .31 B2
Plymouth Wood Cres
   CF5 . . . . .31 B2
Plymouth Wood Rd
   CF5 . . . . .31 B2
Poets Field Rd
   CF62 . . . . .51 B3
Pomeroy St CF10 . . . .42 A1
Pommergelli Rd
   CF14 . . . . .23 B4
Pontalun Ct CF63 . . . .52 A3
PONTCANNA 33 B4
Pontcanna Ct CF5 . . .33 A3
Pontcanna Pl CF11 . .33 B3
Pontcanna St CF11 . .33 B3
Pontfaen CF23 . . . . . . .18 A4
PONTPRENNAU 8 B1
Pontrilas Cl CF5 . . . . .37 B3
Pontypridd Rd
   CF62 . . . . .54 C4
Pontypridd St CF63 . .52 B1
Poplar Cl CF5 . . . . . . .22 B1
Poplar Ct CF62 . . . . . .54 B1
Poplar Ho CF14 . . . . .14 B2
Poplar Rd CF5 . . . . . . .31 B4
Poppyfield Cl CF3 . . .20 B2
Porlock Dr CF64 . . . . .58 B2
Porlock Rd CF3 . . . . . .20 A3

Portfield Cres
   CF14 . . . . .16 C3
Porthamal Gdns
   CF14 . . . . .15 C2
Porthamal Rd CF14 . .15 C2
Porthcawl Rd CF5 . . .38 B4
Porthkerry Country Pk
   Nature Trail ★ 54 A2
Porthkerry Pl CF14 . .24 C2
Porthkerry Rd
   Barry / Y Barri
   CF62 . . . . .55 A3
   Rhoose / Y Rhws
   . . . . .61 C1
Porth-y-Castell
   CF62 . . . . .54 B1
Portland Cl CF64 . . . .49 B2
Portland Pl CF14 . . . . .6 C2
Port Madoc Rd CF3 . .20 B1
Portmanmoor Rd
   Cardiff / Caerdydd
   CF24 . . . . .35 C1
   Cardiff / Caerdydd, East
   Moors CF24 . . . . .43 A4
Portmanmoor Road
   Ind Est CF24 . . . . .43 A4
Portmanmoor Road La
   CF24 . . . . .35 C1
Port Mews CF62 . . . . .51 C4
Porto Ho 21 CF10 . . .42 A2
Port Rd
   Barry / Y Barri,
   Merthyr Dyfan
   CF62 . . . . .51 B3
   Cardiff / Caerdydd
   CF5 . . . . .37 B2
   Wenvoe / Gwenfo
   . . . . .46 B1
Port Rd E CF62 . . . . . .51 A3
Port Rd W
   Barry / Y Barri
   CF62 . . . . .50 C1
   Barry / Y Barri, Colcot
   CF62 . . . . .51 A2
Pound La CF5 . . . . . . .46 A2
Powderham Dr
   CF11 . . . . .41 A4
Powell Duffryn Way
   CF62 . . . . .55 B2
Powis View CF63 . . . .52 C2
Powys Cl CF64 . . . . . .47 C4
Powys Gdns CF64 . . .47 C4
Powys Dr CF64 . . . . . .47 B4
Powys Ho 2 CF23 . . .26 B2
Powys Pl CF64 . . . . . .47 C4
Powys Rd 1 CF64 . . .48 C2
Prendergast Pl
   CF5 . . . . .38 C3
Prestatyn Rd CF3 . . . .20 A1
Preswylfa St CF5 . . . .32 C3
Price Ave CF63 . . . . . .52 B2
Priest Rd CF24 . . . . . .35 B3

Prifysgol = university

Prifysgol Caerdydd /
   Cardiff Univ
   (Cathays Park
   Campus) CF10 . . . . . .62 B4
Primrose Cl CF3 . . . . .28 A3
Prince Charles Ct
   CF64 . . . . .45 A1
Prince Edward Ho 3
   CF64 . . . . .45 A1
Prince Leopold St 1
   CF24 . . . . .35 B1
Prince Llewellyn Ho
   2 CF64 . . . . .45 A1

Prince of Wales Dr
CF5 . . . . .12 B1
Prince Rhodry Ho ❶
CF64 . . . . .45 A1
Princes Ave CF24 . . . . .35 B3
Princes Ct CF24 . . . . .62 C3
Princes St
Barry / Y Barri
CF62 . . . . .55 A3
Cardiff / Caerdydd
CF24 . . . . .35 B4
Priority Bsns Pk
CF10 . . . . .41 C3
Priority Ent Pk
CF63 . . . . .53 B2
Priority Workshops
CF63 . . . . .53 B2
Priory Gdns CF63 . . . .52 B3
Pritchard Cl ❶
CF5 . . . . .23 A2
Proctor Cl CF62 . . . . .54 C4
Prospect Dr CF5 . . . . .32 A4
Pum Erw Rd CF14 . . . .16 A1
Purbeck St CF5 . . . . . .33 A2
Purcell Rd
Cardiff / Caerdydd
CF3 . . . . .20 A3
Penarth CF64 . . . . .48 C1
Purdey Cl CF62 . . . . . .50 C2
Pwllheli Ct CF3 . . . . . .28 B4
Pwllhelyg CF15 . . . . . .14 A4
PWLL- MAWR 28 C2
Pwll Mawr Ave CF3 . .28 B3
Pwllmelin La CF5 . . . .32 A4
Pwllmelin Rd CF5 . . . .23 A1
Pyke St CF63 . . . . .56 A4
Pyle Rd CF5 . . . . .38 B4
Pyra Ct CF62 . . . . .54 C2

Q

Quail Ct CF24 . . . . .35 A3
Quarella St CF63 . . . . .52 B1
Quarry Cl CF5 . . . . .31 A4
Quarry Cres CF5 . . . . .31 A3
Quarry Dale CF3 . . . . .28 A2
Quay St / Stryd Y Cei
CF10 . . . . .63 B2
Queen Anne Sq
CF10 . . . . .62 A4
Queen Charlotte Dr
CF15 . . . . .10 C1
Queen St / Heol Y
Frenhines CF10 . . . . .62 C3
Queens Arc ❺
CF10 . . . . .63 B2
Queensbury Rd
CF23 . . . . .27 A3
Queens Dr CF5 . . . . . . .37 C2
Queen's Rd CF64 . . . . .45 B1
Queen St
Barry / Y Barri
CF62 . . . . .55 A3
Tongwynlais CF15 . . . . .3 A1
Queen Street Sta
CF10 . . . . .62 C3
Queens W CF10 . . . . . .62 B3
Queens Way CF63 . . . .56 A2
Queenwood CF23 . . . . .27 A3
Queen Wood Cl
CF23 . . . . .26 B3
Quentin St CF14 . . . . .25 A2

R

Rachel Cl CF5 . . . . .22 C3
Radnor Gn CF62 . . . . . .51 C2
Radnor Ho ❻ CF64 . . .48 C1
Radnor Prim Sch
CF5 . . . . .33 A2
Radnor Rd CF5 . . . . . . .33 A2

RADYR 13 B2
Radyr Comp Sch
CF15 . . . . .22 C4
Radyr Court Cl CF5 . .23 B2
Radyr Court Rd
Cardiff / Caerdydd
CF5 . . . . .23 A3
Cardiff / Caerdydd
CF5 . . . . .23 B2
Radyr Court Rise
CF5 . . . . .23 B2
Radyr Court Sh Prec
CF5 . . . . .23 B2
Radyr Farm Rd
CF15 . . . . .22 B4
Radyr Pl CF14 . . . . . . .24 C2
Radyr Rd CF14 . . . . . . .23 B3
Radyr Sta CF15 . . . . . .13 C1
Raglan Cl
Cardiff / Caerdydd
CF3 . . . . .21 A3
Dinas Powis / Dinas
Powys CF64 . . . . .47 C3
Raglan Ho CF10 . . . . .63 A2
Ragnall Cl CF14 . . . . . . .5 C3
Railway Cres ❽
CF24 . . . . .35 B2
Railway Heritage
Mus* CF62 . . . . .55 C1
Railway St
Cardiff / Caerdydd,
Maindy CF14 . . . . . . .25 A1
Cardiff / Caerdydd,
Splott CF24 . . . . .35 C2
Railway Terr
Cardiff / Caerdydd
CF11 . . . . .33 B1
Dinas Powis / Dinas
Powys CF64 . . . . .47 C4
Penarth CF64 . . . . .49 A4
Tongwynlais CF15 . . . . .3 A1
Raisdale Gdns
CF64 . . . . .49 B2
Raisdale Ho CF64 . . . .49 B2
Raisdale Rd CF64 . . . .49 A2
Raldan Cl CF63 . . . . . . .52 B3
Raleigh Wlk CF10 . . . .63 C1
Rambler Cl CF14 . . . . . .6 A3
Ramsey Rd CF62 . . . . .51 C3
Ramsons Way CF5 . . . .30 B1
Rannoch Dr CF23 . . . . .17 C1
Ravensbrook CF15 . . .13 B4
Ravenscourt CF24 . . . .62 C4
Ravens Court Cl
CF23 . . . . .27 A2
Ravenshoe Rd
CF63 . . . . .53 A2
Ravenswood CF11 . . . .44 C2
Raven Way CF64 . . . . .59 B3
Rawden Mews
CF11 . . . . .33 C1
Rawden Pl CF11 . . . . . .33 C1
Readers La CF62 . . . . .60 C1
Readers Way CF62 . . .60 C1
Reardon Smith Ct
CF5 . . . . .31 B4
Rectory Cl CF5 . . . . . . .46 B2
Rectory Rd
❽ Barry / Y Barri
CF63 . . . . .52 B1
Cardiff / Caerdydd
CF5 . . . . .33 A2
Penarth CF64 . . . . .49 B4
Rectory Road La
CF64 . . . . .49 B4
Redberth Cl CF62 . . . . .51 C2
Redbrink Cres
CF62 . . . . .56 A1
Red Brink Ct CF5 . . . . .31 A2
Redcliffe Ave CF5 . . . .32 B2
Red Dragon Ctr The
CF10 . . . . .42 B2
Red House Cl CF5 . . . .31 B1

Red House Cres
CF5 . . . . .31 B2
Red House Pl CF5 . . . .31 B2
Red House Rd CF5 . . . .31 B2
Redlands Ave CF64 . . .48 B4
Redlands Rd CF64 . . . .48 B4
Redlaver St CF11 . . . . .41 B3
Red Sea Ho ❶
CF10 . . . . .42 A3
Redwell St ❽ CF23 . .26 B2
Redwick Ho CF23 . . . . .17 B1
Redwood Cl ❷ CF3 . .20 B3
Redwood Ct CF14 . . . .16 C4
Regent Ave CF5 . . . . . .37 C2
Regent Gdns CF14 . . . .42 C3
Regents Ct CF24 . . . . .42 C3
Regent St CF62 . . . . . .55 C4
Regina Terr CF5 . . . . . .32 B2
Reigate Cl CF14 . . . . . . .5 C3
Relf Rd CF3 . . . . .28 B4
Rennie St CF11 . . . . . . .33 C1
Reresby Ct CF10 . . . . . .42 A2
Restway Ct CF5 . . . . . .23 A3
Restways Cl CF5 . . . . .22 C2
Retford Ct CF14 . . . . . .24 B4
Retreat The CF23 . . . . .26 C2
Rheidol Ct CF14 . . . . . .17 A4
Rheidol Dr CF62 . . . . . .54 C4
Rhigos Gdns CF24 . . . .25 B1
RHIWBINA 15 B4
Rhiwbina Hill
Cardiff / Caerdydd
CF14 . . . . .4 B1
Tongwynlais CF14,
CF83 . . . . .3 C3
Rhiwbina Prim Sch /
Ysgol Gynradd
Rhiwbeina CF14 . . . .15 B3
Rhiwbina Sta CF14 . . .15 B2
Rhiwddar Ho CF15 . . . .2 B4
Rhiwderyn Cl CF5 . . . .37 B3
Rhiwlas CF14 . . . . .5 A2
Rhodfa Felin CF5 . . . . .54 C3
Rhodfa Lloyd George /
Lloyd George Ave
CF10 . . . . .42 A3
Rhodfa'r Deintyddion /
Dental Dr CF24 . . . . .25 A3
Rhodfa'r Gwagenni
CF63 . . . . .55 C3
Rhodfa'r Orsaf /
Station Terr CF10 . . .62 C3
Rhodfa Sweldon ❷
CF62 . . . . .55 B3
Rhododendron Cl
CF23 . . . . .18 A3
Rhoose Rd CF62 . . . . . .61 A1
Rhos Ddu CF64 . . . . . . .48 B2
Rhos Llan CF14 . . . . . . .15 C4
Rhossily Ave CF3 . . . . .28 B4
Rhossilly Rd CF3 . . . . .28 B4
Rhuddlan Way
CF64 . . . . .47 C4
Rhydhelig Ave
CF14 . . . . .25 A4
RHYDWAEDLYD 15 C3
Rhyd-y-Penau Cl
CF14 . . . . .17 A3
Rhydypenau Prim Sch
CF14 . . . . .17 A3
Rhyd-y-Penau Rd
CF23 . . . . .17 B3
Rhygoes St CF24 . . . . .25 B1
Rhyl Rd CF3 . . . . .28 B4
Rhymney Ct ❷
CF24 . . . . .34 C4
Rhymney River Bridge
Rd CF23 . . . . .27 C1
Rhymney St CF24 . . . . .62 C4
Rhymney Terr CF24 . . .34 B4
RHYMNI /
RUMNEY 28 A3
Rialto Ct CF14 . . . . . 15 B1

Richard Lewis Cl
CF5 . . . . .23 A2
Richards Pl CF24 . . . . .35 B3
Richards St CF24 . . . . .34 B4
Richard St CF62 . . . . . .55 C4
Richards Terr CF24 . . .35 B3
Richmond
Appartments
CF24 . . . . .62 C4
Richmond Cres
CF24 . . . . .62 C4
Richmond Ct CF24 . . . .62 C4
Richmond Rd CF24 . . .62 C4
Richs Rd CF14 . . . . .24 C4
Ridgeway CF14 . . . . . . .6 A3
Ridgeway Rd
Barry / Y Barri
CF62 . . . . .51 A3
Cardiff / Caerdydd
CF3 . . . . .27 C4
Ridgeway The CF3 . . . .27 C4
Rimini Ho CF10 . . . . . . .42 B3
Rinaston Ct CF5 . . . . . .32 A4
Ringside Bsns Ctr
CF3 . . . . .28 C2
Risca Cl CF3 . . . . .20 C3
Rise The
Barry / Y Barri
CF63 . . . . .51 C1
Cardiff / Caerdydd
CF14 . . . . .6 B1
Riverbank Sch CF5 . .31 C1
River Dale 31 B2
River Glade CF15 . . . . .2 B3
Riversdale CF5 . . . . . . .23 B2
RIVERSIDE 33 C1
Riverside Ct CF15 . . . . .2 C2
Riverside Pl CF63 . . . . .53 A1
Riverside Terr CF5 . . . .32 A2
River View
Cardiff / Caerdydd
CF14 . . . . .23 C2
Cardiff / Caerdydd,
Gabalfa CF14 . . . . . . .24 B1
River View Ct CF5 . . . .23 B2
Roath Court Pl
CF24 . . . . .35 B4
Roath Court Rd
CF24 . . . . .35 B4
Roath Dock Rd
CF10 . . . . .43 A3
ROATH PARK 26 A3
Roath Park Prim Sch
CF24 . . . . .26 A1
ROATH / Y
RHATH 35 A4
Robert St
Barry / Y Barri
CF63 . . . . .56 B4
Cardiff / Caerdydd,
Cathays CF24 . . . . . . .25 C1
Cardiff / Caerdydd, Ely /
Tre-lai CF5 . . . . .32 A2
Roberts Villas CF14 . . .23 B4
Robin Cl CF23 . . . . .18 A3
Robin Hill CF64 . . . . . . .47 B2
Robins La CF63 . . . . . . .52 B2
Robinswood Cl
CF64 . . . . .49 A2
Robinswood Cres
CF64 . . . . .49 A2
Roche Cres CF5 . . . . . .22 B1
Rochester Mans ❹
CF14 . . . . .14 C2
Rockrose Way
CF64 . . . . .44 B1
Rockwood Rd CF15 . . .2 C4
Roden Ct ❷ CF24 . . . . .35 A3
Roehampton Ct
CF3 . . . . .27 C3
Rogersmoor Cl
CF64 . . . . .49 A2
Rogerstonc Cl CF3 . . .20 C3
Roland St CF10 . . . . . . .63 C1

Rolls St CF11 . . . . .33 B1
Roma Ho CF10 . . . . . . .63 C1
Roman Cl CF5 . . . . .38 C3
Romilly Ave CF62 . . . . .54 C2
Romilly Bldgs
Barry / Y Barri, Barry
Dock CF63 . . . . .56 B3
Barry / Y Barri
CF62 . . . . .55 A2
Romilly Cres CF11 . . . .33 B2
Romilly Ct CF62 . . . . . .55 A2
Romilly Inf & Jun Schs
CF62 . . . . .55 A3
Romilly Park Rd
CF62 . . . . .54 C1
Romilly Pl ❸ CF5 . . . .33 A2
Romilly Rd
Barry / Y Barri
CF62 . . . . .55 A2
Cardiff / Caerdydd
CF5 . . . . .33 A2
Romilly Rd W CF5 . . . .32 C3
Romney Wlk ❺
CF64 . . . . .44 C1
Ronald Pl CF5 . . . . .31 B2
Rookery Cl CF64 . . . . . .58 A2
Rookery Wood
CF64 . . . . .58 A2
Rookwood Ave CF5 . .23 B1
Rookwood Cl CF5 . . . . .23 B1
Rookwood Hospl
CF5 . . . . .23 C1
Rookwood St CF11 . . . .41 A3
Roper Ct CF5 . . . . .22 C2
Rosebery Pl CF64 . . . . .49 A3
Rosedale Cl CF5 . . . . . .31 A4
Rosemary St CF10 . . . .63 C2
Rosemount Pl
CF14 . . . . .24 C3
Rose St CF24 . . . . .62 C4
Rosewood Cl CF14 . . . .6 B3
Rosset Cl CF3 . . . . .20 B2
Rossetti Cl CF5 . . . . . . .23 A3
Roundel Ct CF14 . . . . . .6 A4
Round Wood CF23 . . . .18 B1
Round Wood Cl
CF23 . . . . .27 A3
Rover Way
Cardiff / Caerdydd
CF24 . . . . .36 B4
Cardiff / Caerdydd,
Pengam Green
CF24 . . . . .36 C2
Rover Way Cvn Site
CF24 . . . . .36 C2
Rowan Cl CF64 . . . . . . .49 A1
Rowan Ct
Barry / Y Barri
CF62 . . . . .54 C2
Cardiff / Caerdydd
CF5 . . . . .32 B4
Rowan Ho ❸ CF64 . . . .44 C1
Rowan Way CF14 . . . . . .6 C3
Rowena Ct CF5 . . . . . . .31 A4
Roxburgh Garden Ct
CF64 . . . . .49 B3
Roxby Ct CF10 . . . . .63 C1
Royal Arc CF10 . . . . . . .63 B2
Royal Bldgs
Cardiff / Caerdydd
CF10 . . . . .62 C3
Penarth CF64 . . . . .49 A3
Royal Cl CF64 . . . . .45 A1
Royal Hamadryad
Hospl CF10 . . . . .42 A1
Royal Stuart La
CF10 . . . . .42 A2
Royal The CF64 . . . . . . .45 A1
Royde Cl CF5 . . . . .37 A4
Ruby St CF24 . . . . .35 B2
Rudry St
Cardiff / Caerdydd
CF11 . . . . .41 A3

Rudry St continued
Penarth CF64 . . . . . . .48 C4
Rugby Cl CF5 . . . . .31 C2
Rumney High Sch
CF3 . . . . .19 C1
Rumney Inf Sch
CF3 . . . . .28 A3
Rumney Jun Sch
CF3 . . . . .28 A3
Rumney Pottery *
CF3 . . . . .27 C2
**RUMNEY /
RHYMNI** 28 A3
Runcorn Cl
Barry / Y Barri
CF63 . . . . .53 A2
Cardiff / Caerdydd
CF3 . . . . .20 A4
Runway Rd CF24 . . . . .36 B3
Ruperra Cl CF3 . . . . . .20 A4
Rushbrook Cl CF14 . .23 A4
Ruskin Cl CF3 . . . . . . .19 B3
Russell St CF24 . . . . .62 C4
Ruthen Terr CF62 . . . .55 A4
Ruthin Gdns CF24 . . .62 B4
Rutland Cl CF3 . . . . . .20 A4
Rutland St CF11 . . . . .41 A4
Ryder St CF11 . . . . . . .33 C2

S

Sable Cl CF14 . . . . 6 B4
Sachville Ave CF14 . . .25 A3
Saffron Dr CF3 . . . . . .21 A4
Sain Ffagan
Amgueddfa Werin
Cymru / St Fagans
National History
Mus * CF5 . . . . .30 A3
**SAIN FFAGAN / ST
FAGANS** 30 B3
St Agatha Rd CF14 . . .25 A4
St Agnes Ct CF24 . . . .35 C3
St Agnes Rd CF14 . . . .24 C4
St Aidan Cres CF14 . .24 C4
St Aiden's Rise
CF63 . . . . .52 C1
St Alban Ave CF14 . . .24 C4
**St Albans RC Prim Sch
/ Ysgol Gynradd
Sain Alban** CF24 . . .36 A3
St Ambrose Cl CF64 . . . . .47 A2
St Ambrose Rd
CF14 . . . . .25 A4
St Andrew's Cres
CF10 . . . . .62 C3
St Andrews Ho CF5 . .49 B4
St Andrew's La
CF10 . . . . .62 C3
St Andrew's Pl
CF10 . . . . .62 C3
St Andrew's Rd
CF62 . . . . .51 B1
St Angela Rd CF14 . . .25 A3
St Anne's Ave CF64 . .48 C2
St Anne's CW Inf Sch
CF24 . . . . .35 A3
St Ann's Ct CF62 . . . . .52 A3
St Anthony Rd
CF14 . . . . .25 A4
St Arvans Cres CF3 . .20 C3
St Asaph Cl CF14 . . . .16 B2
St Augustine Rd
CF14 . . . . .25 A4
St Augustine's Cres CF64 . . . . .45 B1
St Augustine's Path CF64 . . . . .45 B1
St Augustine's Pl CF64 . . . . .45 B1
St Augustine's Rd
CF64 . . . . .45 B1

St Baruch Cl CF64 . . . . .47 A2
St Baruchs Ct CF62 . .55 C1
St Benedict Cres
CF14 . . . . .25 A4
**St Bernadettes RC
Prim Sch** CF23 . . . .18 C4
St Brannocks Cl
CF62 . . . . .54 C4
St Brides Ct CF5 . . . .38 B4
St Brides Ho CF64 . . . . .49 B4
St Bride's Way
CF63 . . . . .52 A3
St Brigid Rd CF14 . . . .16 B2
St Brioc Rd CF14 . . . .16 B2
St Cadoc Rd CF14 . . . .16 B1
St Cadoc's Ave
CF64 . . . . .47 A2
St Cadoc's Prim Sch
CF3 . . . . .19 B3
St Cadoc's Rise
CF63 . . . . .53 A3
St Canna Cl CF5 . . . . .33 A2
St Catherine's Ct
CF62 . . . . .51 C3
St Catherines Mews CF11 . . . . .33 B3
St Cenydd Rd CF14 . .16 C2
St Clair Ct CF10 . . . . .42 B2
St Cuthbert's Ct CF10 . . . . .42 A2
**St Cuthberts RC Prim
Sch / Ysgol Gynradd
Sant Cuthbert**
CF10 . . . . .42 B3
St Cyres Cl CF64 . . . . .48 B4
St Cyres Comp Sch
CF64 . . . . .48 B4
St Cyres Lower Sch
CF64 . . . . .47 C2
St Cyres Rd CF64 . . . .48 B4
St David Ave CF64 . . .47 B4
St Davids Cres CF5 . .31 B1
St David's Cres
CF64 . . . . .48 A3
St David's Ct CF11 . . .33 C2
St David's Ctr CF10 . .63 B2
**St David's CW Prim
Sch** CF23 . . . . .18 C2
St David's Hall *
CF10 . . . . .63 B2
St David's Ho CF10 . . . . .63 B2
St Davids Hosp
CF11 . . . . .33 C2
St Davids Mansion CF11 . . . . .33 C1
**St David's
Metropolitan
Cathedral Church**
CF10 . . . . .63 C2
St David's Mkt
CF10 . . . . .63 C2
St David's RC Coll
CF23 . . . . .26 B2
St David's Rd CF14 . . .24 A4
St David's Way
CF10 . . . . .63 B2
St Denis Rd CF14 . . . .16 C1
St Dogmael's Ave
CF14 . . . . .16 C3
St Donats Cl CF64 . . . .47 C3
St Donats Ct CF5 . . . . .38 B4
St Donats Ho CF64 . . . . .49 B4
St Donats Rd CF11 . . .40 C4
St Dyfrig Cl CF64 . . . . .47 B2
St Dyfrig Rd CF64 . . . .48 B2
St Dyfrig's Ct CF3 . . . . .19 C2
St Edeyrns Ct CF23 . . .18 A2

St Edeyrn's Rd
CF23 . . . . .17 C2
St Edwen Gdns
CF14 . . . . .16 B1
St Fagans Ave
CF62 . . . . .51 B1
St Fagans Cl CF5 . . . .31 C3
St Fagans Ct CF5 . . . .37 B4
**St Fagan's CW Prim
Sch** CF5 . . . . .37 B4
St Fagans Dr CF5 . . . .30 B3
St Fagans Ho CF64 . . . . .49 B4
St Fagans National
History Mus / Sain
Ffagan Amgueddfa
Werin Cymru *
CF5 . . . . .30 A3
St Fagans Rd CF5 . . . .31 B3
St Fagans Rise CF5 . .31 A4
**ST FAGANS / SAIN
FFAGAN** 30 B3
St Fagan's St CF11 . . .41 B2
St Francis Ct
Cardiff / Caerdydd,
East Moors CF24 . . . .36 A1
Cardiff / Caerdydd,
Whitchurch CF14 . . . .15 A1
**St Francis RC Prim
Sch** CF5 . . . . .30 C1
St Francis Rd CF14 . . .15 A1
St Garmon Rd CF64 . .48 B2
St Georges Rd
CF14 . . . . .24 C3
St Germans Ct CF24 . . . . .35 B2
St Germans Mews CF24 . . . . .35 B2
St Gildas Rd CF14 . . . .16 C1
St Govan's Cl CF62 . . .51 C3
St Gowan Ave CF14 . .16 B1
St Gwynnos Cl
CF64 . . . . .47 B3
St Helens RC Inf Sch
CF63 . . . . .56 A4
**St Helens RC Jun Sch /
Ysgol Iau Sant Helen**
CF62 . . . . .51 C1
St Helen's Rd CF14 . .24 C4
St Hilary Ct CF5 . . . . .38 C4
St Illtyd Cl CF64 . . . . .47 B2
St Illtyds RC High Sch
CF3 . . . . .20 A1
St Ina Rd CF14 . . . . . . .16 B2
St Isan Rd CF14 . . . . . .16 B1
St James Cres
CF62 . . . . .54 B4
St James Ct CF64 . . . .48 B2
St James Mans CF10 . . . . .42 A2
St James Mews CF11 . . . . .33 B3
**St John Lloyd RC Prim
Sch** CF3 . . . . .20 B4
St John's Coll CF3 . . . .20 B4
St John's Cres
Cardiff / Caerdydd,
Canton CF5 . . . . .33 B1
Cardiff / Caerdydd,
Coryton CF14 . . . . . .15 A2
St John's Ct CF11 . . . .33 B1
St John's Pl
Cardiff / Caerdydd
CF14 . . . . .15 A2
Rhoose / Y Rhws
CF62 . . . . .60 A1
St John St CF10 . . . . . .63 B2
St Joseph's Ct
CF14 . . . . .25 B2

**St Joseph's RC Prim
Sch**
Cardiff / Caerdydd
CF14 . . . . .25 A2
Penarth CF64 . . . . . . .48 A3
St Joseph's School Ho CF64 . . . . .45 A1
St Julian Cl CF63 . . . .52 C2
St Luke's Ave CF64 . .48 B2
St Lythan Cl CF64 . . . . .47 A2
St Lythan Ct CF5 . . . . .38 A2
St Lythan's Rd
CF62 . . . . .54 C4
St Malo Rd CF14 . . . . .16 B2
St Margaret's Cl CF14 . . . . .15 A2
St Margaret's Cres CF23 . . . . .35 B4
St Margaret's Pk
CF5 . . . . .31 C2
St Margaret's Pl CF14 . . . . .15 A2
St Margaret's Rd
CF14 . . . . .15 A3
St Mark's Ave CF14 . .25 A3
St Mark's Gdns
CF14 . . . . .25 A3
St Mark's Rd CF64 . . .48 C2
St Martin's Cl CF64 . .48 C2
St Martins Cres
CF14 . . . . .16 C3
St Martins Row CF24 . . . . .34 C4
**St Mary St / Heol
Eglwys Fair** CF10 . .63 B2
St Mary's Ave CF63 . .56 A3
St Marys Cl CF5 . . . . .38 C3
St Marys Ct
Cardiff / Caerdydd
CF5 . . . . .38 B2
Cardiff / Caerdydd
CF14 . . . . .15 A1
St Mary's RC Prim Sch
CF11 . . . . .33 B2
St Mary's Rd CF14 . . .15 A2
**St Mary the Virgin CW
Prim Sch** CF10 . . . .63 C1
St Mellons Bsns Pk
CF3 . . . . .21 B4
**St Mellons CW Prim
Sch** CF3 . . . . .20 A3
**St Mellons Enterprise
Workshops** CF3 . . . .20 C3
**ST MELLONS /
LLANEURWG** 20 B3
St Mellons Rd CF14 . . .7 C2
St Michael's Cl CF15 . .3 A1
St Michael's Coll
CF5 . . . . .32 B4
St Michaels Ct
Cardiff / Caerdydd,
Llandaff / Llandaf
CF5 . . . . .32 C4
Cardiff / Caerdydd,
Maindy CF24 . . . . . . .25 B1
St Michaels Gdns
CF62 . . . . .51 B3
St Michael's Rd
CF5 . . . . .32 B3
**St Monica's CW Prim
Sch** CF24 . . . . .34 A4
St Nicholas Cl CF64 . . . . .47 A2
St Nicholas Ct
Barry / Y Barri
CF62 . . . . .54 C2
Cardiff / Caerdydd
CF5 . . . . .38 B4
St Nicholas Ho CF64 . . . . .49 B4

St Nicholas' Rd
CF62 . . . . .54 C2
St Nicolas Ct CF23 . . .18 B4
St Oswald's Rd
CF63 . . . . .52 C2
St Osyth Ct CF62 . . . .54 C1
**St Patrick's RC Prim
Sch** CF11 . . . . .41 B3
St Paul's Ave
Barry / Y Barri
CF62 . . . . .55 B3
Penarth CF64 . . . . . . .48 C2
St Pauls Cl CF64 . . . . .47 A2
St Paul's Ct CF5 . . . . .23 C1
St Paul's CW Prim Sch
CF11 . . . . .41 B2
St Peter's RC Prim Sch
CF24 . . . . .35 A3
St Peter's Rd CF64 . . .48 B2
St Peter's St CF24 . . .62 C4
**St Phillip Evans RC
Prim Sch** CF23 . . . .18 B1
St Pierre Cl CF23 . . . .21 A4
**St Richard Gwyn RC
High Sch** CF63 . . . .53 A3
St Siors Meade
CF62 . . . . .60 B1
St Stephens Mans CF10 . . . . .42 A2
St Tanwg Rd CF14 . . . .16 B1
St Teilo Ave CF62 . . . .51 B1
St Teilo Cl CF64 . . . . .47 B2
St Teilo's CW High Sch
CF23 . . . . .26 C3
St Telio's Ct CF23 . . . . .35 B4
St Thomas Cl CF14 . . .15 C1
St Thomas' Ct CF63 . .52 C1
St Winifreds Ct
CF64 . . . . .47 A2
Salisbury Ave CF64 . .48 C3
Salisbury Cl CF64 . . . . .48 C2
Salisbury Ct CF64 . . .48 C2
Salisbury Rd
Barry / Y Barri
CF62 . . . . .54 C3
Cardiff / Caerdydd
CF24 . . . . .62 C4
Salmon Cl CF23 . . . . .27 A1
Salop Ho CF64 . . . . . .45 A1
Salop Pl CF64 . . . . . . .45 B1
Salop St CF64 . . . . . . .49 A4
SALTMEAD 41 A4
Saltmead Ct CF11 . . . .41 A4
Salvia Cl CF3 . . . . .21 A3
Sanatorium Rd
CF11 . . . . .32 C1
Sanctuary Ct CF5 . . . .37 C2
Sanctuary The CF5 . . .37 C2
Sandbrook Rd CF3 . . .21 B2
Sanderling Dr CF3 . . .20 C4
Sandon St CF24 . . . . . .63 C2
Sandown Ct CF5 . . . . .31 C1
Sandpiper Cl CF3 . . . .20 C4
Sandringham Cl
CF62 . . . . .50 C3
Sandringham Rd
CF23 . . . . .26 B1
Sand Wharf The
CF11 . . . . .41 C1
Sandwick Ct CF23 . . .17 C3
Sanquahar St CF24 . .35 B1
Sapele Dr CF24 . . . . . .35 B1
Sapphire St CF24 . . . .35 B3
Saundersfoot Cl
CF5 . . . . .38 C3
Saunders Rd CF10 . . .63 B1
Sawyer Ct CF5 . . . . . . .33 A2
School La CF15 . . . . . . .2 A4
School St CF10 . . . . . .63 C1

Schooner Way
CF10 . . . . .63 D1
Scotney Way CF23 . . . . 8 B1
Scott Ct CF23 . . . . .26 A3
Scott Rd CF10 . . . . .63 B2
Seager Dr CF11 . . . . . . .44 C4
Seaview Ct **6** CF64 . .49 B4
Seaview Ind Est
CF24 . . . . .35 C1
Sea View Terr
Barry / Y Barri
CF63 . . . . .52 C2
Wenvoe / Gwenfo
CF5 . . . . 46 A4
Seawall Rd CF24 . . . . . .36 B2
Second Ave CF23 . . . . . .27 A1
Sedgemoor Rd CF3 . .19 C3
Sefton Cl **6** CF15 . . . .13 B2
Selwyn Morris Ct
CF24 . . . . .35 C1
Senghennydd Pl
CF24 . . . . .62 C4
Senghennydd Rd
CF24 . . . . .62 B4
Senlan Ind Est
CF23 . . . . .27 C1
Senni Cl CF62 . . . . .50 C1
Sevenoaks Rd CF5 . . .30 C1
Sevenoaks St CF11 . . .41 B2
Severn Ave CF62 . . . . . .50 C1
Severn Ct CF11 . . . . . . .33 B2
Severn Gr CF11 . . . . . . .33 B3
Severn Inf Sch
CF11 . . . . .33 B2
Severn Jun Sch
CF11 . . . . .33 B2
Severn Rd CF11 . . . . . . .33 B2
Severn Sq **3** CF11 . .33 B2
Seymour St CF24 . . . . .35 C2
Sgwar Callaghan /
Callaghan Sq
CF10 . . . . .63 C1
Shaftesbury Ct CF14 . .5 C3
Shakespeare Ave
CF64 . . . . .48 B4
Shakespeare Ct
CF24 . . . . .62 D4
Shakespeare Rd
CF62 . . . . .51 C3
Shakespeare St
CF24 . . . . .62 D4
Shamrock Rd CF5 . . . .31 A4
Sharpe Cl **3** CF23 . .27 A1
Shaw Cl CF3 . . . . .19 B3
Shearman Pl CF11 . . . .45 A4
Shears Rd CF5 . . . . .32 A3
Shearwater Cl
CF64 . . . . .59 B3
Sheerwater Cl **3**
CF3 . . . . .20 B3
Shelburn Cl CF11 . . . .41 A4
Shelley Cres
Barry / Y Barri
CF62 . . . . .51 B3
Penarth CF64 . . . . . .48 C4
Shelley Wlk CF24 . . . .62 D4
Sherborne Ave
CF23 . . . . .17 C3
Sherbourne Cl
CF62 . . . . .50 B3
Sheridan Cl CF3 . . . . . .19 B3
Sherman Theatre ★
CF24 . . . . .62 B4
Sherwood Ct CF5 . . . .22 C1
Shields Cl CF23 . . . . . . .8 C1
Ship La CF10 . . . . .42 B2
Shirley Cl CF63 . . . . . . .53 A2
Shirley Rd CF23 . . . . . .25 C2
Showle Acre CF62 . . . .60 B1
Sidney Ames Ct **9**
CF24 . . . . .35 B2

Sienna Ho CF10 . . . . . .63 C1
Silurian Pl CF10 . . . . . .42 A3
Silver Birch Cl
CF14 . . . . .24 B3
Silver Jubilee Cotts
CF5 . . . . .31 B1
Silver St CF24 . . . . .35 B1
Silverstone Cl **5**
CF3 . . . . .20 A4
Sinclair Dr CF23 . . . . . .27 A1
Sindercombe Cl
CF23 . . . . .8 A1
Singleton Rd CF24 . . . .35 C1
Sir Ivor Pl CF64 . . . . . . .47 C2
Skaithmuir Rd
CF24 . . . . .36 A3
Skelmuir Rd CF24 . . . .36 A3
Skibereen Cl CF23 . . . . .8 B1
Skomer Ct **2** CF11 . .41 B3
Skomer Rd CF62,
CF63 . . . . .52 A3
Slade Cl CF64 . . . . .58 B2
Slade Rd CF62 . . . . .51 C3
Slade Wood Ho
CF62 . . . . .51 C3
Slipway The CF64 . . . .45 A1
Slocombe Trust Cotts
1 CF5 . . . . .32 C3
Sloper Rd CF11 . . . . . . .40 C3
Smeaton St CF11 . . . . .33 C1
Smithies Ave CF64 . . . .58 B1
Sneyd St CF11 . . . . .33 B3
Snipe St CF24 . . . . .35 A3
Snowden Rd CF5 . . . . .30 C1
Soarel Cl CF3 . . . . .20 C2
Soberton Ave CF14 . . .25 C1
Solent Rd CF63 . . . . . . .52 C3
Solva Ave CF14 . . . . . . .17 A4
Solva Cl CF62 . . . . .51 C2
Somerset Ct CF3 . . . . .19 C3
Somerset Rd CF62 . . . .51 C1
Somerset Rd E
CF63 . . . . .51 C1
Somerset St CF11 . . . .41 A4
Somerset View
CF64 . . . . .58 B1
Sophia Cl CF11 . . . . . . .33 C2
Sophia Gdns
Glamorgan CCC /
Canolfan Criced
Genedlaethol
CF11 . . . . .33 C3
Sophia Wlk CF11 . . . . .33 C2
Sorrento Ho CF10 . . . .63 C1
Soudrey Way CF10 . . .42 A2
Southbourne Cl
CF62 . . . . .55 C1
South Clive St
CF11 . . . . .41 B1
Southcourt Rd
CF23 . . . . .26 C1
Southern Way
CF23 . . . . .27 B2
Southesk Pl CF62 . . . . .54 C1
Southey St
Barry / Y Barri
CF62 . . . . .55 C4
3 Cardiff / Caerdydd
CF24 . . . . .35 A3
Southglade CF15 . . . . . .2 B3
South Loudoun Pl **7**
CF10 . . . . .42 A3
South Luton Pl
CF24 . . . . .35 A1
South Mews **5**
CF10 . . . . .42 A3
Southminster Rd
CF23 . . . . .35 C4
South Morgan Pl **6**
CF11 . . . . .33 C1
South Park Rd
CF24 . . . . .36 A1
South Point CF10 . . . .43 B2
Southra CF64 . . . . .47 A2

South Rd CF64 . . . . . . .58 B2
South Rise CF14 . . . . . .17 A4
South View CF15 . . . . . .2 C4
South View Dr CF3 . . .19 C1
South Wales Baptist
Coll CF24 . . . . .62 C4
South Wlk CF62 . . . . . .51 B1
Speedwell Dr CF62 . .60 B1
Spencer David Way
CF3 . . . . .20 C1
Spencer Dr CF64 . . . . .44 A3
Spencer's Row CF5 . .23 C1
Spencer St
6 Barry / Y Barri
CF62 . . . . .55 C4
Cardiff / Caerdydd
CF24 . . . . .25 C1
Spillers & Bakers
CF10 . . . . .63 D1
Spinney Cl CF5 . . . . . . .31 A2
Spinney The CF14 . . . . .6 C2
Spires Wlk CF63 . . . . . .52 B3
SPLOTT 35 C2
Splott Ind Est CF24 . .35 C1
Splott Rd CF24 . . . . . . .35 C2
Springfield Cl CF5 . . .46 B2
Springfield Gdns
CF15 . . . . .13 B4
Springfield Pl CF11 . .33 B2
Springfield Rise
CF63 . . . . .52 A2
Spring Gardens Pl
CF24 . . . . .35 C3
Spring Gardens Terr
CF24 . . . . .35 C3
Spring Gr CF14 . . . . .6 A2
Springhurst Cl
CF14 . . . . .14 C3
Spring Meadow Bsns
Pk CF3 . . . . .28 B2
Spring Meadow Rd
CF3 . . . . .28 C2
Spring Meadow Trad
Est CF3 . . . . .28 B2
Spring St CF63 . . . . .53 A1
Springwood CF23 . . . .18 A1
Springwood Prim Sch
CF23 . . . . .18 A1
Spruce Cl CF24 . . . . . . .35 B1
Square The CF64 . . . . .47 A3
Stacey Ct **6** CF24 . .35 B4
Stacey Prim Sch
CF24 . . . . .35 B3
Stacey Rd
Cardiff / Caerdydd
CF24 . . . . .35 B3
Dinas Powis / Dinas
Powys CF64 . . . . . . .47 A3
Stadium Cl CF11 . . . . . .41 A1
Stafford Mews
CF11 . . . . .41 B4
Stafford Rd CF11 . . . . .41 B4
Staines St CF5 . . . . .32 C3
Stallcourt Ave
CF23 . . . . .27 A1
Stallcourt Cl CF23 . . . .27 A1
Stangate Ho **1**
CF64 . . . . .49 B4
Stanier Ct **7** CF24 . .35 B2
Stanton Way CF64 . . . .59 C4
Stanway Pl CF5 . . . . . . .30 C2
Stanway Rd CF5 . . . . . .31 A1
Stanwell Cres CF64 . .45 B1
Stanwell Rd
Penarth CF64 . . . . . .48 C3
Penarth CF64 . . . . . .49 A3
Stanwell Sch CF64 . . .48 C3
Star St CF24 . . . . .35 B2
Station App CF64 . . . .49 A3
Station Approach Ind
Est CF64 . . . . .49 A3
Station Approach Rd
CF62 . . . . .55 C1
Station Hos CF15 . . . .10 B2

Station Rd
Cardiff / Caerdydd
CF14 . . . . .6 A1
Cardiff / Caerdydd,
Landaff North
CF14 . . . . .23 B3
Creigiau CF15 . . . . . .10 B2
Dinas Powis / Dinas
Powys CF64 . . . . . . .47 A3
Penarth CF64 . . . . . .49 A3
Radyr CF15 . . . . .13 C1
Station Rd E CF5 . . . . .46 C3
Station Rd W CF5 . . . .46 B2
Station St CF63 . . . . . . .56 A3
Station Terr
Cardiff / Caerdydd
CF5 . . . . .32 A2
Penarth CF64 . . . . . .49 A3
Station Terr /
Rhodfa'r Orsaf
CF10 . . . . .62 C3
Steep St **4** CF64 . . .45 A1
Steffani Ct CF10 . . . . . .42 A3
Stella Cl CF14 . . . . .6 A3
Stella Maris Cl
CF15 . . . . .13 B1
Stenhousemuir Pl
CF24 . . . . .36 A3
Stephenson Ct **2**
CF24 . . . . .35 A2
Stephenson St
CF11 . . . . .33 C1
Sterling Cl CF24 . . . . . .36 C3
Stirling Rd
Barry / Y Barri
CF62 . . . . .50 C2
Cardiff / Caerdydd
CF5 . . . . .37 C4
Stockland St CF11 . . . .41 B3
Stonechat Cl **2**
CF3 . . . . .21 A2
Stoneleigh Ct **4**
CF11 . . . . .33 B3
Stonewell Ct **7**
CF23 . . . . .26 B2
Storrar Pl CF24 . . . . . . .36 B4
Storrar Rd CF24 . . . . . .36 B4
Stradling Cl
Barry / Y Barri
CF62 . . . . .50 B1
Sully CF64 . . . . .58 B2
Stratford Gn **5**
CF63 . . . . .52 C3
Strathnairn St
CF24 . . . . .34 C4
Strathy Rd CF3 . . . . . . .21 A3
Stryd Adelaide /
Adelaide St CF10 . . .42 A1
Stryd Bute / Bute St
CF10 . . . . .63 C1
Stryd Caroline /
Caroline St CF10 . . .63 B2
Stryd George Newydd /
New George St
CF10 . . . . .42 B1
Stryd Herbert /
Herbert St CF10 . . . .63 C1
Stryd Hope / Hope St
CF10 . . . . .63 C1
Stryd John / John St
CF10 . . . . .63 C1
Stryd Stuart / Stuart
St CF10 . . . . .42 A1
Stryd Womanby /
Womanby St
CF10 . . . . .63 B2
Stryd Y Cei / Quay St
CF10 . . . . .63 B2
Stryd yr Eglwys /
Church St CF10 . . . .63 B2
Stuart Cl CF11 . . . . .40 C1
Stuart Pl CF10 . . . . .42 B1
Stuart St / Stryd
Stuart CF10 . . . . .42 A1

Sturminster Rd
CF23 . . . . .35 C4
Stuttgarter Strasse
CF10 . . . . .62 C3
Subway Rd CF63 . . . . .56 A3
Sudcroft St CF11 . . . . .40 B4
Sullivan Cl
Cardiff / Caerdydd
CF3 . . . . .20 A3
Penarth CF64 . . . . . .48 C1
SULLY 58 B2
Sully Moors Rd
CF64 . . . . .53 C1
Sully Pl CF64 . . . . .49 B3
Sully Prim Sch
CF64 . . . . .58 A1
Sully Rd CF64 . . . . .48 A1
Sully Terr CF64 . . . . . . .49 A2
Sully Terrace La
CF64 . . . . .49 A2
Sully View CF63 . . . . . .53 B2
Summerau CF5 . . . . . . .33 A3
Summerfield Ave
CF14 . . . . .25 B2
Summerfield Pl
CF14 . . . . .16 A1
Summerhill Cl CF3 . . .21 A3
Summerland Cl
CF64 . . . . .44 A2
Summerland Cres
CF64 . . . . .44 A2
Summerwood Cl
CF5 . . . . .30 C4
Sumner Cl CF5 . . . . . . .23 A2
Sundew Cl
Cardiff / Caerdydd
CF5 . . . . .22 C2
Penarth CF64 . . . . . .44 B1
Sunningdale Cl
CF23 . . . . .26 A4
Sunnybank CF64 . . . . .47 C4
Sunnybank Cl CF14 . .24 C3
Sunnybrook Cl CF5 . .22 C1
Sunnycroft Cl CF64 . .47 B3
Sunnycroft La CF64 . .47 B2
Sunnycroft Rise **4**
CF64 . . . . .47 B2
Sun St CF24 . . . . .35 B2
Suran-y-Gog CF63 . .52 B4
Surrey St CF11 . . . . .33 C2
Sussex St CF11 . . . . . . .41 B4
Sutherland Mans **8**
CF14 . . . . .14 C2
Sutton Gr CF23 . . . . .7 B1
Swallowhurst Cl
CF5 . . . . .37 B4
Swanage Cl CF3 . . . . . .21 A3
Swanbridge Gr
CF64 . . . . .58 C1
Swanbridge Rd
CF64 . . . . .58 C2
Swansea St CF24 . . . .35 C1
Sweldon Cl CF5 . . . . . .38 A3
Swift Bsns Ctr The
CF24 . . . . .35 B1
Swift Cl CF3 . . . . .19 B3
Swinton St CF24 . . . . .35 C2
Swn-Y-Mor CF62 . . . .54 A2
Sycamore Cl
Dinas Powis / Dinas
Powys CF64 . . . . . . .47 B2
Llandough / Llandochau
CF64 . . . . .44 B2
Sycamore Cres
CF62 . . . . .52 A2
Sycamore Ho CF14. .14 B2
Sycamore Pl **1**
CF5 . . . . .31 B4
Sycamore St CF15 . . . .2 B4
Sycamore Tree Cl
CF15 . . . . .13 A2
Sylvan Cl CF5 . . . . .23 A1
Syon Park Cl CF3 . . . .21 A3

Syr David's Ave
CF5 . . . . 32 C3
Syr David's Ct CF5 . . 32 C3
System St CF24 . . . . . . 35 B2

T

Tabor St CF15 . . . . 2 B4
Tacoma Sq CF10 . . . . . 42 B1
Taf Cl CF62 . . . . 50 C1
Taff Emb CF11 . . . . . . 41 C2
*Taff Gorge
Countryside Ctr*★
CF15 . . . . 3 B2
Taffs Mead Emb
CF11 . . . . 63 A1
Taff St
Cardiff / Caerdydd
CF24 . . . . 63 C2
Tongwynlais CF15 . . . . 3 A1
Taffs Well Sta CF15 . . 2 B3
Taff Terr
Cardiff / Caerdydd
CF11 . . . . 41 C2
Radyr CF15 . . . . 13 C1
Taff Workshops
CF10 . . . . 63 B1
Taibah Sch CF24 . . . . 35 A3
Tair Erw Rd CF14 . . . 16 A1
Talbot St CF11 . . . . . 33 C2
Taliesin Ct CF10 . . . . 42 A2
Talworth St CF24 . . . 62 D4
Talybont Ct CF14 . . . 33 C4
Talybont Rd CF5 . . . 31 B1
Tal-y-bryn CF14 . . . . 48 B2
Talygarn St CF14 . . . 25 B2
Tanglewood Cl CF14 . . 6 B2
Tangmere Dr CF5 . . . 22 C2
Tank Farm Way
CF64 . . . . 53 B1
Tansy Cl CF14 . . . . 5 B3
Tan-y-Fron CF62 . . . 54 B2
Tapley Cl CF5 . . . . 38 B3
Tarragon Way CF23 . . 7 C1
Tarrws Cl CF5 . . . . . . 46 B3
Tasker Sq CF14 . . . . . 16 A3
Tatem Dr CF5 . . . . . . 31 A3
Tath Gwaun CF64 . . . 48 B1
Taunton Ave CF3 . . . 19 C1
Taunton Cres CF3 . . 19 C1
Tavistock St CF24 . . 62 C4
Taymuir Green Ind Pk
CF24 . . . . 36 A4
Taymuir Rd CF24 . . . 36 A3
Tealham Dr CF3 . . . . 21 B3
Teal St CF24 . . . . 35 A3
Teamans Row CF15 . 13 B4
Teasel Ave CF64 . . . . 44 B1
Techniquest★
CF10 . . . . 42 A1
**Techno Ctr / Canolfan
Technoleg** CF24 . . . . 42 C4
Tedder Cl CF14 . . . . . 16 C3
Tegfan CF11 . . . . 33 B2
Tegfan Cl CF14 . . . . . 16 B4
Teifi Dr CF62 . . . . 54 C4
Teifi Pl CF5 . . . . 31 B1
Teilo St CF11 . . . . . . 33 B3
Telford St CF11 . . . . 33 C1
Temperance Ct
CF15 . . . . 11 B4
Templar Parc CF24 . . 42 B4
Templeton Ave CF14 . 5 C1
Templeton Cl CF14 . . 5 C1
Tenby Cl CF64 . . . . . . 47 C3
Tennyson Rd
Barry / Y Barri
CF62 . . . . 51 B3
Penarth CF64 . . . . . . 48 C4
Tensing Cl CF14 . . . . . 6 A1
Tensing Terr 11
CF63 . . . . 52 B1
Tern Cl CF3 . . . . 20 C4

Terrace The CF15 . . . 10 B3
Terra Nova Way
CF64 . . . . 44 C1
Tewkesbury Pl
CF24 . . . . 25 C2
Tewkesbury St
CF24 . . . . 25 C1
Thackeray Cres
CF3 . . . . 19 B3
Tharsis Cl CF24 . . . . 63 D2
Theobald Rd CF5 . . . 33 A1
Theodora St CF24 . . 35 C3
Thesiger Ct 7
CF24 . . . . 34 B4
Thesiger St CF24 . . . 34 B4
Thistle Cl CF62 . . . . . 51 A1
Thistle Way CF5 . . . . 32 B4
Thomas Davies Ct 8
CF3 . . . . 28 A3
Thomas St CF11 . . . . 41 B3
Thompson Ave CF5 . . 32 B3
Thompson Ct 1
CF5 . . . . 33 A2
Thompson Pl CF5 . . . 32 B3
Thompson St CF63 . . 55 C3
Thorley Cl CF23 . . . . 26 A4
Thornaby Ct CF10 . . 63 C1
Thornbury Cl CF14 . . 15 C1
Thorne Way CF5 . . . . 38 A3
Thorn Gr CF64 . . . . . 59 B4
THORNHILL 5 C2
Thornhill Ct CF14 . . 16 A4
Thornhill Prim Sch
CF14 . . . . 5 C3
Thornhill Rd CF14 . . . 5 C3
Thornhill St CF5 . . . 33 A2
Thornwood Cl CF5 . . . 5 C3
Three Arches Ave
CF14 . . . . 17 A2
Threipland Dr CF14 . 16 A1
Thrush Cl 1 CF3 . . . . 21 A2
Thurston St 7 CF5 . . 33 B1
Tidal Sidings CF24 . . 36 A1
Tide Fields Rd
CF24 . . . . 36 B1
Tidenham Ct CF5 . . . 38 C4
Tidenham Rd CF5 . . . 38 C4
Timbers Sq CF24 . . . 35 B4
Timber Yd The
CF24 . . . . 42 C4
Timothy Rees Cl
CF5 . . . . 22 C3
Tin St CF24 . . . . 35 B2
Tintagel Ct CF14 . . . . 5 B2
Tintern Ct 13 CF5 . . 33 A2
Tintern St CF5 . . . . . 33 A2
Titan Rd CF24 . . . . . . 42 C4
Tiverton Dr CF3 . . . . 27 C4
Toftingall Ave
CF14 . . . . 16 A1
Toghill Dr CF15 . . . . . . 2 C3
Tollgate Cl CF11 . . . 40 C1
TONGWYNLAIS 3 B2
Tongwynlais Prim Sch
CF15 . . . . 13 C4
Ton The CF3 . . . . 20 A3
Ton-Yr-Ywen Ave
CF14 . . . . 16 B1
Ton-yr-ywen Prim
Sch CF14 . . . . 16 B2
Topaz St CF24 . . . . . 35 B2
Tordoff Way CF62 . . 51 B1
Torrens Dr CF23 . . . 26 A4
Torrington Rd CF3 . . 19 C3
Tower Hill CF64 . . . . 49 B3
Tower Hill Ave
CF64 . . . . 49 B3
Tower Way CF64 . . . 53 B1
Towyn Rd CF3 . . . . . . 28 B4
Towy Rd CF14 . . . . . . 17 A3
Trade La CF10 . . . . . . 41 C3
Trade St CF10 . . . . . . 63 B1
Trafalgar Ct 1
CF24 . . . . 26 B1

Trafalgar Rd CF23 . . . 35 B4
Traherne Dr CF5 . . . 37 B4
Tramore Way CF23 . . . 8 B1
Trebanog Cl CF3 . . . 20 B3
Trebanog Cres CF3 . 20 B3
Treborth Rd CF3 . . . 20 B1
Trecastle Ave CF14 . . 5 C1
Trecinon Rd CF3 . . . 20 C1
Tredegar St CF14 . . . 14 C1
Tredegar St CF10 . . 63 C2
**Tredegarville CW Prim
Sch** CF24 . . . . 62 D3
Tredelerch Rd CF3 . . 27 C2
TREDOGAN 61 B3
Tredogan Rd CF62 . . 61 A3
Treetops CF15 . . . . . . 22 A1
Trefaser Cres CF3 . . 20 B2
**TREFORGAN /
MORGANSTOWN** . . . 13 A4
Tregaron Rd CF5 . . . 30 C1
Tregarth Cl CF15 . . . 10 A3
Tregarth St CF15 . . . 10 A3
Treharne Rd CF63 . . 52 A2
Treharris St CF24 . . 62 D4
Treherbert St CF24 . 34 A4
Trelai Ct CF5 . . . . . . 38 B3
TRE-LAI / ELY 31 B2
Trelai Prim Sch
CF5 . . . . 31 C1
Trelawney Ave 1
CF3 . . . . 28 A3
Trelawney Cres 2
CF3 . . . . 28 A3
Trem Mapgoll CF63 . 52 B4
TREMORFA 43 B4
Tremorfa Ind Est
CF24 . . . . 43 B4
Trem Powys CF63 . . 52 C3
Trem Y Coed CF63 . . 52 B4
Trem-y-Don CF62 . . 54 B1
Trenchard Dr CF14 . 16 C2
Treoda Ct 3 CF14 . . 61 A1
Treorky St 4 CF24 . . 34 B4
Treseder Way CF5 . . 31 C1
Tresigin Rd CF3 . . . . 20 B2
Tressillian Terr
CF10 . . . . 63 B1
**Tressillian Way / Fford
Tresillian** CF10 . . . . 63 B1
Tressillian Way Ind Est
CF10 . . . . 63 B1
Trevethick St CF11 . 33 C1
Trewartha Ct 7
CF14 . . . . 15 B1
Triangle CF62 . . . . . . 55 C1
Trident Ct CF24 . . . . 42 B4
Trinity Ct CF24 . . . . 62 D3
Trinity St
Barry / Y Barri
CF62 . . . . 55 A3
Cardiff / Caerdydd
CF10 . . . . 63 B2
Triscombe Dr CF5 . . 23 A1
Tristram Cl CF14 . . . . 5 B3
Troed-y-Garth
CF15 . . . . 11 B4
Troed Y Rhiw CF14 . . 4 B1
Trotman Dickenson Pl
CF14 . . . . 25 A1
TROWBRIDGE 20 C1
Trowbridge Gn CF3 . 20 B2
Trowbridge Inf Sch
CF3 . . . . 20 B1
Trowbridge Jun Sch
CF3 . . . . 20 B1
Trowbridge Rd
CF3 . . . . 28 C4
Tudor Cl
Cardiff / Caerdydd
CF5 . . . . 31 B3
Penarth CF64 . . . . . . 49 A1
Tudor Ct CF14 . . . . . 16 A1
Tudor La CF11 . . . . . 63 A1
Tudor St CF11 . . . . . 41 B4

Tudors The CF23 . . . 26 C1
Tulloch St 4 CF24 . . 26 B1
Tummel Cl CF23 . . . . 17 C1
Turberville Pl CF11 . 33 B2
*Turner House
Gallery*★
CF64 . . . . 49 B3
Turner Rd CF5 . . . . . 32 C2
Turnham Gn CF23 . . 27 B2
Turnpike Cl CF64 . . . 47 B4
Tuscan Cl CF64 . . . . 44 A3
Tweedsmuir Rd
CF24 . . . . 36 A3
Twin-y-Fedwen
CF14 . . . . 24 C3
TWYN-YR-ODYN . . . 46 B3

Ty = house

Ty Bryncoch CF15 . . . 2 B4
Ty Camlas 3 CF63 . . 55 C3
Ty-capel CF15 . . . . 2 B3
Ty-Cefn Rd CF5 . . . . 31 B2
Ty Celyn Mews
CF14 . . . . 14 C3
Ty Cerrig
5 Barry / Y Barri
CF63 . . . . 52 B2
Cardiff / Caerdydd
CF23 . . . . 18 B4
Ty Charlotte CF64 . . 45 A2
Ty-Coch Rd CF5 . . . . 31 A1
Ty Cwmpas 8
CF63 . . . . 55 C3
Ty Devonia CF64 . . . 44 C2
Tydfil Pl CF23 . . . . . . 26 A2
Tydfil St CF63 . . . . . . 52 B1
Ty-Draw Pl CF23 . . . 26 B1
Ty-Draw Rd
Cardiff / Caerdydd,
Pentwyn CF23 . . . . 7 C1
Cardiff / Caerdydd, Pen-y-
lan CF23 . . . . 26 A2
Ty Ffynnon CF62 . . . 51 C3
Ty-Fry Ave CF3 . . . . 28 A3
Ty-Fry Cl CF3 . . . . . . 28 A3
Ty-Fry Gdns CF3 . . . 28 A3
Ty-Fry Rd CF3 . . . . . 28 A4
Ty-Glas Ave CF14 . . 16 B4
Ty-Glas Rd CF14 . . . 16 B4
Ty Glas Sta CF14 . . . 16 B4
Ty Gwalia CF64 . . . . 44 C2
Ty Gwendollen
CF64 . . . . 45 A2
Ty Gwenfo CF63 . . . . 52 C1
Ty-Gwyn Ave CF23 . . 26 B2
Ty-Gwyn Cres CF23 . 26 B3
Ty-Gwyn Rd
Cardiff / Caerdydd,
Pen-y-lan CF23 . . . . . 26 B2
Cardiff / Caerdydd,
Rhydwaedlyd
CF14 . . . . 15 C3
Ty Gwyn Specl Sch
CF23 . . . . 26 B3
Tyla Teg CF14 . . . . . . 14 C4
Tyler St CF24 . . . . . . 35 C3
Ty Levant 7 CF63 . . 55 C3
Ty-Mawr Ave CF3 . . 27 C2
Tymawr Cl CF3 . . . . . 27 C2
Ty-Mawr Rd
Cardiff / Caerdydd,
Rumney / Rhymni
CF3 . . . . 27 C2
Cardiff / Caerdydd,
Whitchurch / Yr Eglwys
Newydd CF14 . . . . . . 23 B3
Tymynydd Cl CF15 . . 13 B3
Tynant CF14 . . . . 24 A4
Ty Nant Cl CF15 . . . . . 2 C1

Tynant Rd CF15 . . . . 10 A2
Ty-Nant Rd CF15 . . . 13 B3
Ty-Nant St CF11 . . . 41 A3
Tyndall St CF10 . . . . 63 D1
Tyndall Street Ind Est
CF10 . . . . 63 C1
Tyneside Rd CF10 . . 42 C2
Tynewydd CF14 . . . . 24 A4
Ty Newydd CF14 . . . 23 C4
Ty-Newydd Rd
CF62 . . . . 51 C1
Ty'n-y-Cae Gr
CF14 . . . . 15 C2
Ty'n-y-Coed La
CF24 . . . . 26 A1
Ty'n-y-Coed Pl
CF24 . . . . 26 A1
Tyn-y-Coed Rd
CF15 . . . . 11 B4
Ty'n-y-parc Rd
2 Cardiff / Caerdydd
CF14 . . . . 15 B1
Cardiff / Caerdydd
CF14 . . . . 15 B2
Ty'n-y-Pwll Rd
CF14 . . . . 15 A1
Ty Parc CF15 . . . . . . 22 C3
Ty-Pica Dr CF5 . . . . 46 B3
TY-RHIW 3 A4
Ty Rhiw CF15 . . . . 2 C4
Ty'r Holl Saint 5
CF24 . . . . 35 A1
Ty'r Sianel 4 CF63 . 55 C3
Tyrwhitt Cres CF23 . 17 A1
Tyr Winch Rd CF3 . . 20 A4
Tyr-y-Sarn Rd CF3 . 28 A2
Ty'r Ysgol 4 CF24 . . 35 A1
Tytherley CF64 . . . . . 47 A2
Ty-To-Maen Cl
CF3 . . . . 20 B4
Ty Uchaf CF14 . . . . . 48 B2
Ty-Verlon Ind Est
CF63 . . . . 53 B2
Ty-Wern Ave CF14 . . 15 C2
Ty-Wern Rd CF14 . . 15 C2
Ty Westonia CF64 . . 44 C2
Ty Windsor CF64 . . . 45 A2

U

Ullswater Ave CF23 . 25 C3
Underhill Mans 3
CF14 . . . . 14 C2
Universal St CF11 . . 63 A1
University Pl CF24 . . 35 C2
**Univ Hospl of Wales /
Ysbyty Athrofaol
Cymru** CF14 . . . . . . 25 B3
**Univ of Wales Coll of
Medicine** CF14 . . . . 25 B3
**Univ of Wales Dental
Sch** CF14 . . . . 25 A3
**Univ of Wales Inst
Cardiff**
Cardiff / Caerdydd,
Adamsdown CF24 . . . 62 D3
Cardiff / Caerdydd
CF23 . . . . 26 C4
**Univ of Wales Inst
Cardiff (Colchester
Ave Campus)**
CF23 . . . . 27 A1
**Univ of Wales Inst,
Cardiff (Llandaff
Campus)** CF5 . . . . . 24 A1
Uphill Cl CF64 . . . . . 58 B3
Uphill Rd CF3 . . . . . . 19 B1
Uplands Cres CF64 . 44 B2

Uplands Rd CF5 . . . . . .27 C2
Uplands The CF15. . . . . .13 C2
Uppercliff Cl CF64 . . . . .45 C1
Uppercliff Dr CF64 . . . . .45 C1
Upper Clifton St **3**
CF24 . . . . .35 B3
Upper Cosmeston
Farm CF64. . . . . .59 B3
Upper Kincraig St
CF24 . . . . .35 A4
Upper Mdw CF5 . . . . . .38 A3
Upper Ty' n-y-parc
Terr CF14. . . . . .15 B2
Uppingham Ct **3**
CF5 . . . . .31 C2
Usk Ct **8** CF14. . . . . .15 C1
Uskley Ct CF3 . . . . . . .20 B2
Usk Rd CF14 . . . . .17 A4
Usk Way CF62 . . . . . . .50 C1

V

Vachell Rd CF5 . . . . . .31 B1
Vaendre Ct CF3 . . . . . .20 C4
Vaendre La
Cardiff / Caerdydd
CF3. . . . . .20 C4
Cardiff / Caerdydd
CF3. . . . . .21 A4
Vaindre Cl **5** CF3 . . .21 A4
Vaindre Dr **6** CF3 . . .21 A4
Valarian Cl CF3 . . . . . .21 B2
Vale Ct CF64. . . . . .47 B3
Vale Ent Ctr CF64. . . .57 C4
Valegate Ret Pk
CF5 . . . . .37 B2
Vale Rd CF24 . . . . .35 C3
Vale St CF62. . . . . .54 C2
Vale View 51 A3
Vale View Cl CF64 . . . .44 C2
Vale View Cres
CF64 . . . . .44 A2
Valley View CF3 . . . . . .29 A4
Vanguard Way
CF24 . . . . .43 A4
Van St CF13 . . . . .41 A3
Vaughan Ave CF5 . . . .32 B4
Velindre Ct CF14 . . . . .14 C1
Velindre Hospl /
Ysbyty Felindre
CF14 . . . . .14 C1
Velindre Pl CF14 . . . . .14 C1
Velindre Rd CF14 . . . .14 C1
Vellacott Cl / Clos
Vellacott CF10 . . . . . .63 C1
Vennwood Cl CF5 . . . .46 B2
Ventnor Pl CF14 . . . . . .24 C2
Verallo Dr CF11 . . . . . .32 C1
Verbena Cl CF3 . . . . . .21 A4
Vere St
Barry / Y Barri
CF63 . . . . .52 C1
Cardiff / Caerdydd
CF24 . . . . 62 D4
Verland Cl CF5 . . . . . .32 B4
Verlon Cl CF63. . . . . . .53 B2
Verona Ho CF10 . . . . . .63 C1
Verona Pl CF63 . . . . . .52 C2
Vervain Cl CF5. . . . . . .30 B1
Viaduct Rd
Barry / Y Barri
CF63 . . . . .56 B3
Taffs Well / Ffynnon Taf
CF15 . . . . .2 B2
Viceroy Ct **14** CF10 . .42 A2
Viceroy Mans **13**
CF10 . . . . .42 A2
Victoria Ave
Cardiff / Caerdydd
CF5 . . . . .32 C2
Penarth CF64 . . . . . . .49 A3

Victoria Bridge
CF64 . . . . .49 A4
Victoria Ct **7** CF5 . . .32 C3
Victoria Hall CF10 . . . .34 A4
Victoria Mews **3**
CF14 . . . . .25 A2
VICTORIA PARK. 32 B2
Victoria Park Rd
CF63 . . . . .52 C2
Victoria Park Rd E
CF5 . . . . .32 C2
Victoria Park Rd W
CF5 . . . . .32 B2
Victoria Prim Sch
CF64 . . . . .48 C4
Victoria Rd
Barry / Y Barri
CF62 . . . . .54 C2
Cardiff / Caerdydd
CF14 . . . . .15 A1
Penarth CF64 . . . . . . .49 A3
Victoria Sq CF64. . . . . .49 A3
Vienna Ho **19** CF10. . .42 A2
Viking Pl CF10. . . . . . . .43 B2
Village Way CF15 . . . .14 B4
Vincent Cl CF63. . . . . .52 C2
Vincent Ct CF5 . . . . . .31 C1
Vincent Rd CF5 . . . . . .31 C1
Violet Pl CF14 . . . . . . .24 C4
Violet Row CF24 . . . . .34 C4
Virgil Ct CF11. . . . . . . .41 A3
Virgil St CF11. . . . . . . .41 A3
Vishwell Rd
Cardiff / Caerdydd
CF5 . . . . .32 C3
Wenvoe / Gwenfo
CF5 . . . . .46 B1
Vista Ct **3** CF64 . . . . .45 B1
Vista Rise CF5 . . . . . . .22 C2
Voysey Pl CF5 . . . . . . .31 A3

W

Wain Cl CF23 . . . . .8 C1
Wakehurst Pl CF3. . . . .20 C3
Wales Millennium Ctr /
Canolfan Mileniwm
Cymru CF10 . . . . .42 B2
Walford Pl CF11 . . . . . .33 B1
Walker Rd
Barry / Y Barri
CF62 . . . . .55 B4
Cardiff / Caerdydd
CF24 . . . . .35 C1
Walk The
Cardiff / Caerdydd,
Cathays CF24 . . . . . . .62 C3
Cardiff / Caerdydd,
Rumney / Rhymni
CF3 . . . . .27 C3
WALLSTON 46 A3
Walnut Tree Cl
CF15 . . . . .13 A3
Walpole Cl CF3 . . . . . .19 C4
Walston Cl CF5 . . . . . .46 B3
Walston Rd CF5 . . . . . .46 A3
Walton Pl CF11 . . . . . .40 C3
Walwyn Pl CF3 . . . . . . .21 A1
Wanderers Cres
CF5 . . . . .37 C4
Warren Evans Ct **1**
CF14 . . . . .24 A4
Warwick Ho CF10. . . .63 A2
Warwick Pl **1**
CF11 . . . . .41 B3
Warwick St CF11 . . . .41 B3
Warwick Way CF62 . .51 C1
Wasdale Cl CF23. . . . .26 A2
Washford Ave CF3 . . .19 C3
Washington Bldgs **8**
CF64 . . . . .49 A4
Washington Flats **7**
CF64 . . . . .49 A4

Washington Shops
CF64 . . . . .49 B4
Watchet Cl CF3. . . . . .19 B1
Water Avens Cl
CF3 . . . . .21 B2
Waterford Cl CF11 . . .41 A4
Waterhall Rd CF5 . . . .22 C2
Waterhouse Dr
CF11 . . . . .41 A3
Waterloo Cl **6**
CF23 . . . . .27 A1
Waterloo Gdns
CF23 . . . . .35 B4
Waterloo Rd CF23 . . .26 C1
Waterston Rd CF14 . .24 A2
Watford Rd CF24. . . . .36 A4
Watkins Sq CF14. . . . .16 A3
Watson Rd CF14 . . . . .23 C2
Watson Rd CF3. . . . . .56 A4
Watton Cl CF14. . . . . .16 B4
Waun Ddyfal CF14 . . .16 A2
Waun Fach CF23. . . . .18 B3
Waun-Fawr Rd
CF14 . . . . .16 A2
Waun Ganol CF64. . . .48 B1
Waun-gron Park Halt
CF5 . . . . .32 A3
Waun-Gron Rd CF5. . .32 B3
Waun Lee Ct CF23 . . .18 B4
Wauntreoda Rd
CF14 . . . . .24 B4
Waun-y-Groes Ave
CF14 . . . . .16 A3
Waun-y-Groes Rd
CF14 . . . . .16 A3
Wavell Cl CF14 . . . . . .16 C2
Waverley Cl CF64 . . . .44 B2
Waverley Ct CF63 . . . .56 A3
Waverley Sq CF10. . . .42 A1
Waycock Cross
CF62 . . . . .50 B1
Waycock Rd CF62. . . .50 A1
Wayside Cotts
CF64 . . . . .47 C4
Wedal Rd CF14 . . . . . .25 C2
Wedmore Rd CF11. . .41 A4
Weekes Cl CF3. . . . . .20 A3
Welby La **5** CF5 . . . .33 B1
Welby Rd **4** CF5 . . . .33 B1
Welch Regiment
Mus★ CF10. . . . . .62 B3
Welford St CF62 . . . . .55 A2
Wellfield Ct CF63 . . . .52 B4
Wellfield Pl **2**
CF24 . . . . .35 A4
Wellfield Rd CF24. . . .26 B1
Wellington Ct **3**
CF11 . . . . .33 C1
Wellington Mews **4**
CF11 . . . . .33 C1
Wellington St
Cardiff / Caerdydd
CF11 . . . . .33 C1
Tongwynlais CF15. . . . . .3 A1
Wells St CF11. . . . . . . .33 C1
Wells Street La **15**
CF11 . . . . .33 C1
Well Wlk CF62. . . . . . .54 C1
Wellwood CF23. . . . . .27 A3
Well Wood Cl CF23. . .27 A2
Wellwood Dr CF64 . . . 47 A2
Wellwright Rd CF5. . .31 B3
Welsh Assembly
Government
CF10 . . . . .62 A4
Welsh Coll of Music &
Drama / Coleg
Cerdd a Drama
Cymru CF10 . . . . .62 A3
Welsh Comp Sch
Glantaf The / Ysgol
Gyfun Gymraeg
Glantaf CF14 . . . . . . .23 B2

Welsh Hawking Ctr★
CF62. . . . . .50 A2
Welsh Inst of Sport /
Athrofa Chwaraeon
Cymru CF11 . . . . .33 C3
Welsh National Tennis
Ctr CF24. . . . . .42 C4
Welwyn Rd CF14. . . . .15 C1
Wembley Rd CF5 . . . .33 A1
Wenallt Ct CF14 . . . . .15 B4
Wenallt Rd CF14,
CF83 . . . . .4 B3
Wentloog Rd CF3 . . . .28 B3
Wentloog Ave CF3 . . .28 B2
Wentloog Ct CF3. . . . .28 A3
Wentloog Corporate
Ind Pk CF3 . . . . .29 B4
Wentloog Ct CF3. . . . .28 A3
Wentloog Rd CF3 . . . .28 A3
Wentworth Cl **4**
CF3 . . . . .21 A4
Wentworth La CF3. . . .21 A4
Wenvoe Cl CF5 . . . . . .46 B2
Wenvoe Ct **13** CF5 . . .38 B4
WENVOE /
GWENFO 46 B2
Wenvoe Terr CF62. . . .55 A3
Werfa St CF23 . . . . . . .26 A1
Wern Fawr La CF3 . . .20 B4
Wern Gethin La
CF3 . . . . .20 C2
Wern Goch E CF23. . .18 B2
Werngoch Rd CF23 . .17 C2
Wern Goch W CF23 . .18 A2
Wern Migna CF5. . . . .12 B1
Wesley Ct
Cardiff / Caerdydd
CF3 . . . . .19 C1
Dinas Powis / Dinas
Powys CF64 . . . . .47 A3
Wesley La CF10. . . . . .63 C2
Wessex Pl CF62. . . . . .54 C1
Wessex St CF5. . . . . . .32 C2
Westbourne Cres
CF14 . . . . .23 B4
Westbourne Ct
Cardiff / Caerdydd
CF3 . . . . .28 B2
Penarth CF64 . . . . . . .49 A1
Westbourne Prim Sch
CF64 . . . . .49 A3
Westbourne Rd
Cardiff / Caerdydd
CF14 . . . . .23 B4
Penarth CF64 . . . . . . .49 A2
Westbourne Sch
CF64 . . . . .49 A4
Westbury Cl CF63. . . .52 B2
Westbury Terr CF5 . . .32 C3
West Bute St CF10 . . .42 B2
West Canal Wharf /
Glanfa Gorllewin Y
Gamlas CF10 . . . . . . .63 B1
West Cl / Clos Y
Gorllewin **10**
CF10 . . . . .42 A2
West Ct **2** CF64 . . . .49 A4
Western Ave CF24 . . .24 B1
Western Ave N
CF14 . . . . .24 B2
Western Bsns Ctr
CF5 . . . . .32 A2
Western Ct
10 Barry / Y Barri
CF63 . . . . .52 B1
1 Cardiff / Caerdydd
CF11 . . . . .33 B3
Western Dr CF14. . . . .24 B2
Westfield Ave CF14 . .15 C1
Westfield Dr CF64 . . .48 B2
Westfield Rd CF14 . . .24 B4
Westgate St / Hcol Y
Porth CF10 . . . . .63 B2

West Gr
Cardiff / Caerdydd,
Cathays CF24 . . . . . . .62 C3
Cardiff / Caerdydd,
Culverhouse Cross
CF5 . . . . .37 B2
West Grove Ct
CF24 . . . . .62 C3
Westland Cl CF24 . . . .36 B3
West Lee CF11. . . . . . .33 C2
West Luton Pl **2**
CF24 . . . . .35 A1
Westminster Cres
CF23 . . . . .17 C3
Westminster Dr
Cardiff / Caerdydd
CF23 . . . . .17 C4
Sully CF64. . . . . .58 B2
Westmoreland St
CF5 . . . . .33 A1
Weston Ave CF64 . . . .58 B1
Westonbirt Cl CF3 . . .20 C2
Weston Rd CF3 . . . . . .19 B1
Weston Sq CF63 . . . . .52 C1
Weston St **7** CF63 . . .52 B1
West Orchard Cres
CF5 . . . . .32 B3
West Point Ind Est
CF11 . . . . .44 A4
Westra Ct **2** CF5 . . . .32 C3
West Rd CF14. . . . . . . .23 B3
West Rise CF14 . . . . . .17 A4
West Terr CF64 . . . . . .49 A4
West View CF15. . . . . . .2 C4
Westville Rd CF23 . . .26 C1
Westville Wlk CF23 . .26 B1
Westward Rise
CF62 . . . . .54 B2
West Wlk CF62 . . . . . .51 A1
Westwood Ct **9**
CF64 . . . . .49 A4
Wexford Ct CF23. . . . . .8 B2
Wharfedale Rd
CF23 . . . . .18 C4
Wharton St / Heol y
Cawl CF10. . . . . .63 B2
Wheate Cl The
CF62 . . . . .60 C1
Wheatley Rd CF5 . . . .31 A1
Wheeler Ct CF24. . . . .35 C2
Whinberry Way
CF5 . . . . .30 B1
Whinchat Cl **8**
CF3 . . . . .21 A4
Whitaker Rd CF24 . . .36 B4
WHITCHURCH 23 C4
Whitchurch High Sch
(Lower) CF14. . . . . . .15 B1
Whitchurch High Sch /
Ysgol Uwchradd Yr
Eglwys Newydd
CF14 . . . . .15 A1
Whitchurch Hospl /
Ysbyty Eglwys
Newydd CF14. . . . . . .14 C2
Whitchurch Pl **1**
CF24 . . . . .25 C1
Whitchurch Rd
CF14 . . . . .25 B2
Whitchurch Sta
CF14 . . . . .15 A2
WHITCHURCH / YR
EGLWYS
NEWYDD 14 B1
Whitcliffe Dr CF64 . . .59 C4
Whiteacre Cl CF14 . . . .6 A2
White Barn Rd
CF14 . . . . .16 A4
Whitefield Rd CF14 . .23 C2
Whitehall Ave CF3 . . .28 A3
Whitehall Cl CF5. . . . .46 A3
Whitehall Par CF3 . . .28 A3
Whitehall Pl CF3. . . . .27 C3

Whitehall Rd CF5 ....23 B1
White Oaks Dr CF3...20 B4
Whitesands Rd CF14...5 B1
Whitewell Rd CF62 ..51 B2
Whitland Cl CF5 .....22 C1
Whitland Cres CF5...23 A1
Whitland Ho CF14 ...23 C4
Whitmore Park Dr
CF62 ....50 C2
Whitmuir Rd CF24 ..36 A3
Whittle Rd CF11 .....40 C3
Whitworth Cl CF11..41 B4
Whitworth Sq CF14 ..14 B3
Wholesale Fruit Ctr
CF11...............40 C2
Wicken Cl CF3......21 A3
Wicklow Cl CF23...8 B1
Widecombe Dr CF3 ..27 C3
Wigmore Cl CF14 ....22 C4
Wilde Cl CF15 ....22 C4
Wild Gardens Rd
CF23 ....17 B1
Wilfred Brook Ho
CF11 ....41 B2
Wilfred St CF63.....56 B4
Wilkinson Cl CF24 ..35 B1
William Belcher Dr
CF3 ....21 A1
William Nicholls Dr
CF3 ....20 B4
Williams Cres CF62 ..55 B4
William St CF11.....33 B3
Williams Way CF10 ..41 C3
Willie Seager Cotts
CF23 ....26 C1
Williton Rd CF3.....19 C3
Willowbrook Dr
CF3 ....20 B2
Willowbrook Gdns
CF3 ....20 B3
Willowbrook Prim Sch
CF3 ....21 A2
Willow Cl CF64 .....48 B3
Willow Cl CF24 .....35 A3
Willowdale Cl CF5 ..31 A4
Willowdale Rd CF5 ..31 A4
Willowdene Way
CF3 ....21 A4
Willowfield Ct
CF23 ....17 C2
Willow Gr CF3 ......21 A4
Willow Herb Cl CF3..21 B2
Willowmere CF44 ...44 A3
Willows Ave CF24 ...36 A2
Willows Cres CF63 ..52 A2
Willows High Sch
CF24 ....36 B2
Willow Tree Cl
CF15 ....12 C2
Wilson Pl CF5 ......38 B4
Wilson Rd CF5 ......30 C1
Wilson St CF24 .....35 C3
Wimborne Bldgs
CF63 ....56 C3
Wimborne Cres
CF64 ....58 B2
Wimborne Rd CF63 ..56 C4
Winchester Ave
CF23 ....26 C2
Winchester Cl
CF62 ....55 A4
Windermere Ave
CF23 ....25 C3
Windflower Cl 7
CF3 ....21 A3
Windhover Cl 3
CF3 ....21 A2
Windlass Ct CF10...42 B3
Windmill Cl CF14 ...5 C2
Windmill Ind Area
CF64 ....57 A3
Windrush Pl 6
CF5 ....31 B4

Windsor Arc 3
CF64 ....49 B4
Windsor Ave CF15 ..13 B2
Windsor Cl CF15....13 B2
Windsor Clive Dr
CF5 ....12 B1
Windsor Clive Inf Sch
CF5 ....31 A1
Windsor Clive Jun Sch
/ Ysgol Iau Windsor
Clive CF5...........31 A1
Windsor Cres CF15 ..13 C1
Windsor Ct
Cardiff / Caerdydd
CF24 ....62 D3
Penarth CF64 ....49 B3
2 Radyr CF15 ......13 B2
Windsor Espl CF10...42 A1
Windsor Gdns 2
CF5 ....31 C2
Windsor Gn CF5 ....31 C2
Windsor Gr CF15 ...13 B2
Windsor Ho CF10 ...63 A2
Windsor La
Cardiff / Caerdydd
CF10 ....62 C3
Penarth CF64 ....45 A1
Windsor Mews 3
CF24 ....35 A1
Windsor Pl 1 CF64 ..49 A4
Windsor Pl / Plas
Windsor CF10 ......62 C3
Windsor Rd
Barry / Y Barri
CF62 ....55 A2
Cardiff / Caerdydd
CF24 ....35 A1
Penarth CF64 ....44 C1
Radyr CF15 ....13 C1
Windsor Terr
Cardiff / Caerdydd
CF10 ....42 A1
Penarth CF64 ....49 B4
Windsor Terrace La
CF64 ....49 B4
Windway Ave CF5...32 B3
Windway Rd CF5 ....32 B3
Windyridge CF64 ....47 C2
Wingate Dr CF14 ...16 C2
Wingfield Rd CF14 ..23 C4
Winifred Ave CF62 ..51 B3
Winnipeg Dr CF23 ..17 C1
Winsford Rd CF14...58 C1
Winston Ave CF5 ...37 C2
Winston Rd CF62 ...51 B3
Wisley Pl CF23......7 C1
Withycombe Rd
CF3 ....19 C3
Witla Court Rd CF3 ..19 C1
Wolfe Cl CF63 ......52 C2
Wolfs Castle Ave
CF14 ....5 C1
Womanby St / Stryd
Womanby CF10......63 B2
Wood Cl CF14 ......6 C1
Woodcock St CF24 ..35 A3
Woodfield Ave
CF15 ....22 B4
Woodford Cl CF5 ...23 A1
Woodham Cl CF62 ..51 A1
Woodham Halt *
CF62 ....55 B3
Woodham Pk CF62 ..51 A1
Woodham Rd CF63 ..56 A3
Woodland Cres
Cardiff / Caerdydd
CF23 ....26 B4
Creigiau CF15 ......10 B3
Woodland Dr CF64 ..49 A4
Woodland Pl
1 Cardiff / Caerdydd
CF24 ....35 A3
Penarth CF64 ....49 A4
Woodland Rd CF14 ..23 B4

Woodlands Ct 4
CF62 ....55 C4
Woodlands High Sch /
Ysgol Uwchradd
Woodlands CF5......31 C1
Woodlands Park Dr
CF5 ....38 B3
Woodlands Rd
CF62 ....55 C4
Woodlands The
CF14 ....6 C2
Woodlawn Way
CF14 ....5 C2
Woodley Ct CF5 ....22 C2
Woodruff Way CF14..5 B3
Woodside Ct CF14 ..6 B1
Wood St
Cardiff / Caerdydd
CF10 ....63 B1
Penarth CF64 ....49 A4
Woodstock Cl CF62 ..55 A4
Woodsy Cl CF23 ....8 B2
Woodvale Ave
CF23 ....18 A3
Woodville Ct 6
CF24 ....34 B4
Woodville Rd
3 Cardiff / Caerdydd
CF24 ....25 C1
Cardiff / Caerdydd
CF24 ....34 B4
Woolacombe Ave
CF3 ....19 C2
Woolaston Ave
CF23 ....17 C1
Woolmer Cl CF5 ....22 C2
Woosnham Cl CF23 ..27 A1
Worcester Cl CF11..41 B2
Worcester Ct CF11...41 B1
Worcester Ho CF23 ..26 B3
Worcester St CF11...41 B2
Wordsworth Ave
Cardiff / Caerdydd
CF24 ....35 A3
Penarth CF64 ....48 C4
Working St CF10.....63 B2
Worle Ave CF3.......19 B1
Worle Pl CF3 ....19 B1
Worrells Pl CF5.....38 A2
Wren Cl CF3 ....21 A2
Wrexham Ct CF3....20 B1
Wroughton Pl CF5...31 C2
Wye Cl CF62.........50 C1
Wyeverne Rd CF24 ..34 B4
Wyfan Pl CF14......24 C2
Wyncliffe Rd CF23 ..19 A4
Wyndham Arc CF10 ..63 B2
Wyndham Cres
CF11 ....33 B2
Wyndham Pl CF11...33 C1
Wyndham Rd CF11...33 B2
Wyndham St
Barry / Y Barri
CF63 ....56 A4
Cardiff / Caerdydd
CF11 ....33 C1
Tongwynlais CF15....3 A1
Wyndham Terr
CF14 ....17 A4
Wynd St CF63.......52 B1
Wynnstay Cl CF11...41 A3
Wyon Cl CF5........22 C3

Y

Yarrow Cl CF5 ......30 B1
Y BARRI / BARRY ...55 B2
Yew St CF15 ....2 B4
Yewtree Cl CF5 .....31 A4
Yew Tree Ct
Barry / Y Barri
CF62 ....54 C2
Cardiff / Caerdydd
CF23 ....26 B2

Y Goedwig CF14 .....15 A4
Y Groes CF14........15 B3
Y Gwter / Golate
CF10 ....63 B2
YMCA Bldgs 10
CF62 ....55 C4
YMCA Wales Com Coll
CF14 ....16 C3
Ynys Bridge CF15 ..2 C2
Ynys Y Coed CF5....32 B4
Yorath Rd CF14 .....15 B1
York Ct
Cardiff / Caerdydd
CF10 ....63 D1
5 Radyr CF15 ......13 B2
York Mans 7 CF14...14 C2
York Pl
Barry / Y Barri
CF62 ....55 A2
Cardiff / Caerdydd
CF11 ....41 B1
York St CF5.........33 A1
Youghal Cl CF23 ....8 B2
Youldon Ho CF64 ...47 B3
Y Porth / Gateway
The CF14 ....25 A3
Yr Aes / The Hayes
CF10 ....63 B2
YR EGLWYS NEWYDD /
WHITCHURCH 14 B1
Y RHATH /
ROATH 35 A4
Yr Hen Dy CF5.......23 C1
Y Rhodfa CF62,
CF63 ....55 C3

Ysbyty = hospital

Ysbyty Athrofaol
Cymru / Univ Hospl
of Wales CF14 ......25 B3
Ysbyty Eglwys Newydd
/ Whitchurch Hospl
CF14 ....14 C2
Ysbyty Felindre /
Velindre Hospl
CF14 ....14 C1

Ysgol = school

Ysgol Bro Eirwg
CF3 ....27 C4
Ysgol Bro Morgannwg
CF62 ....51 A2
Ysgol Erw'r Delyn
CF64 ....48 A3
Ysgol Gwaun-y-Nant /
Oak Field Prim Sch
CF62 ....51 C2
Ysgol Gyfun Gymraeg
Glantaf / The Welsh
Comp Sch Glantaf
CF14 ....23 B2
Ysgol Gyfun Gymraeg
Plasmawr /
Plasmawr Welsh
Comp Sch CF5......22 B1
Ysgol Gyfun Uchaf
Bryn Hafren / Bryn
Hafren Comp Sch
CF62 ....51 C4
Ysgol Gymraeg Coed-
y-gof CF5 ....22 C2
Ysgol Gymraeg Melin
Gruffydd Sch
CF14 ....23 C4
Ysgol Gymraeg Pwll
Coch CF11..........40 B4
Ysgol Gynradd
Creigiau / Creigiau
Prim Sch CF15......10 A3
Ysgol Gynradd Glan-yr-
Afon / Glan-yr-Afon
Prim Sch CF3.......19 B3

Ysgol Gynradd
Gwaelod-y-garth
CF15 ....2 A4
Ysgol Gynradd
Llandochau /
Llandough Prim Sch
CF64 ....44 A3
Ysgol Gynradd RC
Crist y Brenin /
Christ The King RC
Prim Sch CF14......6 B1
Ysgol Gynradd
Rhiwbeina /
Rhiwbina Prim Sch
CF14 ....15 B3
Ysgol Gynradd Sain
Alban / St Albans
RC Prim Sch
CF24 ....36 A3
Ysgol Gynradd Sant
Cuthbert / St
Cuthberts RC Prim
Sch CF10............42 B3
Ysgol Iau Sant Helen /
St Helens RC Jun
Sch CF62 ....51 C1
Ysgol Iau Windsor
Clive / Windsor
Clive Jun Sch
CF5 ....31 A1
Ysgol Maes Dyfan
CF63 ....52 A2
Ysgol Mynydd Bychan
CF14 ....25 B2
Ysgol Pencae CF5 ..23 B2
Ysgol Pen-y-Garth
CF64 ....44 A1
Ysgol Sant Curig
CF62 ....55 B4
Ysgol Uwchradd Glyn
Derw / Glyn Derw
High Sch CF5.......39 A4
Ysgol Uwchradd
Woodlands /
Woodlands High Sch
CF5 ....31 C1
Ysgol Uwchradd Yr
Eglwys Newydd /
Whitchurch High
Sch CF14 ....15 A1
Ysgol y Berllan Deg
CF23 ....27 A4
Ysgol-y-llys / The
Court Specl Sch
CF14 ....6 B1
Ysgol-Y-Wern CF14...5 C1

Ystad = estate

Ystrad Cl CF3.......21 A3
Ystrad St CF11......41 C2

Z

Zinc St CF24........35 B2

List of numbered locations

In some busy areas of the maps it is not always possible to show the name of every place.

Where not all names will fit, some smaller places are shown by a number. If you wish to find out the name associated with a number, use this listing.

The places in this list are also listed normally in the Index.

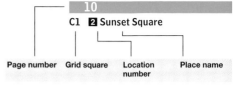

Page number   Grid square   Location number   Place name

PHILIP'S MAPS

the Gold Standard for drivers

◆ **Philip's street atlases cover every county in England, Wales, Northern Ireland and much of Scotland**

◆ Every named street is shown, including alleys, lanes and walkways

◆ Thousands of additional features marked: stations, public buildings, car parks, places of interest

◆ Route-planning maps to get you close to your destination

◆ Postcodes on the maps and in the index

◆ Widely used by the emergency services, transport companies and local authorities

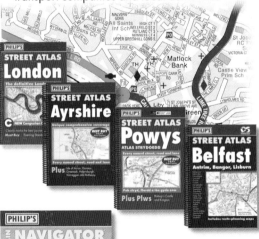

For national mapping, choose
Philip's Navigator Britain
the most detailed road atlas available of England, Wales and Scotland. Hailed by Auto Express as 'the ultimate road atlas', the atlas shows every road and lane in Britain.

Street atlases currently available

England
Bedfordshire and Luton
Berkshire
Birmingham and West Midlands
Bristol and Bath
Buckinghamshire and Milton Keynes
Cambridgeshire and Peterborough
Cheshire
Cornwall
Cumbria
Derbyshire
Devon
Dorset
County Durham and Teesside
Essex
North Essex
South Essex
Gloucestershire and Bristol
Hampshire
North Hampshire
South Hampshire
Herefordshire Monmouthshire
Hertfordshire
Isle of Wight
Kent
East Kent
West Kent
Lancashire
Leicestershire and Rutland
Lincolnshire
Liverpool and Merseyside
London
Greater Manchester
Norfolk
Northamptonshire
Northumberland
Nottinghamshire
Oxfordshire
Shropshire
Somerset
Staffordshire
Suffolk

Surrey
East Sussex
West Sussex
Tyne and Wear
Warwickshire and Coventry
Wiltshire and Swindon
Worcestershire
East Yorkshire Northern Lincolnshire
North Yorkshire
South Yorkshire
West Yorkshire

Wales
Anglesey, Conwy and Gwynedd
Cardiff, Swansea and The Valleys
Carmarthenshire, Pembrokeshire and Swansea
Ceredigion and South Gwynedd
Denbighshire, Flintshire, Wrexham
Herefordshire Monmouthshire
Powys

Scotland
Aberdeenshire
Ayrshire
Dumfries and Galloway
Edinburgh and East Central Scotland
Fife and Tayside
Glasgow and West Central Scotland
Inverness and Moray
Lanarkshire
Scottish Borders

Northern Ireland
County Antrim and County Londonderry
County Armagh and County Down
Belfast
County Tyrone and County Fermanagh

How to order
Philip's maps and atlases are available from bookshops, motorway services and petrol stations. You can order direct from the publisher by phoning **0207 531 8473** or online at **www.philips-maps.co.uk**
For bulk orders only, e-mail philips@philips-maps.co.uk

STREET ATLAS London
STREET ATLAS Ayrshire
STREET ATLAS Powys ATLAS STRYDOEDD
STREET ATLAS Belfast Antrim, Bangor, Lisburn

NAVIGATOR Britain

'The ultimate in UK mapping'
The Sunday Times